HOPE IN TROUBLED TIMES
A NEW VISION FOR CONFRONTING GLOBAL CRISES

BOB GOUDZWAARD, MARK VANDER VENNEN,
AND DAVID VAN HEEMST

Foreword by **Archbishop Emeritus Desmond M. Tutu**
Nobel Peace Prize Laureate

BakerAcademic
Grand Rapids, Michigan

Published by Baker Academic
a division of Baker Publishing Group
P.O. Box 6287, Grand Rapids, MI 49516-6287
www.bakeracademic.com

Printed in the United States of America

Library of Congress Cataloging-in-Publication Data

Goudzwaard, B.
    Hope in troubled times : a new vision for confronting global crises / Bob Goudzwaard, Mark Vander Vennen, and David Van Heemst ; foreword by Desmond M. Tutu.
        p.   cm.
    Includes bibliographical references and index.
    ISBN 10: 0-8010-3248-2 (pbk.)
    ISBN: 978-0-8010-3248-6 (pbk.)
    1. Globalization—Religious aspects—Christianity. 2. Ideology—Religious aspects—Christianity. 3. Christian sociology. I. Vennen, Mark Vander. II. Van Heemst, David, 1966– III. Title.
    BR115.G59G87 2007
    261.8—dc22   2006038840

Unless otherwise indicated, Scripture quotations are from the HOLY BIBLE, NEW INTERNATIONAL VERSION®. NIV®. Copyright © 1973, 1978, 1984 by International Bible Society. Used by permission of Zondervan. All rights reserved.

Scripture quotations marked KJV are from the King James Version of the Bible.

Scripture quotations marked NEB are from *The New English Bible*. Copyright © 1961, 1970, 1989 by The Delegates of Oxford University Press and The Syndics of the Cambridge University Press. Reprinted by permission.

Scripture quotations marked NRSV are from the New Revised Standard Version of the Bible, copyright 1989, by the Division of Christian Education of the National Council of the Churches of Christ in the United States of America. Used by permission. All rights reserved.

Scripture quotations marked RSV are from the Revised Standard Version of the Bible, copyright 1952 [2nd edition, 1971] by the Division of Christian Education of the National Council of the Churches of Christ in the United States of America. Used by permission. All rights reserved.

Portions of this book have appeared, in altered form, in *Capitalism and Progress* (Wm. B. Eerdmans, 1979), *Idols of Our Time* (InterVarsity Press, 1984; repr. Dordt Press, 1989), *Beyond Poverty and Affluence* (University of Toronto Press, 1994), and "Globalization and Christian Hope" (Citizens for Public Justice, 2003).

"These authors are spot on. Their words should be read widely!"

The Most Reverend Njongonkulu W. H. Ndungane,
Anglican Archbishop, Cape Town, South Africa

"We have needed what this book provides—a balanced, intelligent, and biblically sound interpretation of the current events we read about in our newspapers. The authors also give us cogent Christian alternatives to political policies that are having disastrous consequences for millions of oppressed people in our global village."

Tony Campolo, professor emeritus, Eastern University

"This truly is a book of hope—one that combines vision with expert analysis of the major threats to humanity. It should be read by all who care for our future."

Edy Korthals Altes, former ambassador of the Netherlands;
honorary president, World Conference of Religions for Peace

"Without an in-depth struggle with the realities that render us paralyzed, numbed out, and fated, hope is mere sentimentality—a cheap wishfulness. *Hope in Troubled Times* grasps the nature of our troubles and the complex interrelatedness of the issues with a stunning and sometimes devastating clarity. . . . In the tradition of the Hebrew prophets, Goudzwaard, Vander Vennen, and Van Heemst deconstruct the ideologically loaded idolatries that plague us. And then, in a move of breathtaking audacity, they propose that paths of justice, love, and truth can be unshackled from their idolatrous chains and embraced as principles and directives embedded in nothing less than the very landscape of reality itself."

Brian J. Walsh, campus minister, University of Toronto;
coauthor of *Colossians Remixed: Subverting the Empire*

"The authors bear no trace of rancor toward Islam and Muslims, only understanding and empathy. The book draws a line between Islam—the religion of peace—and the terrorists who have hijacked Islam. In a desperate post-9/11 world, it searches for answers by analyzing the actions and the psyche of the two warring sides, echoing the views of both."

Javed Akbar, director of outreach, Pickering Islamic Centre, Ontario

"This is actually the book everybody should read, so that the West can stop and take stock before calamities come."

Elaine Storkey, senior fellow, Wycliffe Hall;
Alan Storkey, author of *Jesus and Politics*

"If one form of insanity is doing the same things over and over while expecting different results, our world has gone hopelessly mad. More development, more progress, more sound economics, and more political will has not and cannot transform spiraling violence, terminal poverty, ballooning wealth, indifferent market forces, and technologies and systems with wills of their own. Goudzwaard, Vander Vennen, and Van Heemst see all this with 'epiphany eyes.' Their account of reality and the concrete hope they see is an awakening for those of us too long and too comfortable in the asylum we call the status quo."

Peter Vander Meulen, co-chair, Micah Challenge USA; coordinator,
Office of Social Justice and Hunger Action of the
Christian Reformed Church in North America

"*Hope in Troubled Times* is a must read for our bewildering era, when accepted political and economic solutions no longer work. In naming ideology as the real culprit, the authors provide a deeper and more compelling analysis than Samuel Huntington does in his *Clash of Civilizations*. Ideology points beyond paradigms and civilizations to the no-alternative absolutes that threaten humanity's very existence today."

> **William F. Ryan, SJ,** founding director, Center of Concern, Washington, DC; former General Secretary of the Canadian Conference of Catholic Bishops

"Fired by a stirring biblical vision of shalom, the authors deploy their ample social science expertise to diagnose the idolatrous obsessions driving our global social, economic, and political crises and blocking their resolution. And they invite all of us—people of faith as well as those who open the book supposing they have none—to take the healing steps that already lie at hand. This book certainly afflicts the comfortable, but only so that the afflicted may indeed be comforted."

> **Jonathan Chaplin,** director of the Kirby Laing Institute for Christian Ethics, Tyndale House, Cambridge

"A profound analysis of root causes of—and root solutions to—the problems that plague the modern world. A provocative compass for taking us, step by small step, out of the woods. This book offers powerful understanding to thinkers and doers alike."

> **Armine Yalnizyan,** research associate, Canadian Centre for Policy Alternatives

"I agree with this book's learned analysis of the devastating effects on humanity and its natural environment produced by the globalization of the unregulated market, the political aspirations of American empire, and the ethical void mediated by the dominant culture, even if my own philosophical and theological categories are somewhat different. In the grave present situation, this book offers hope in the name of Jesus Christ, who has embraced the entire human family and summons people to testify to his truth in counter-movements stemming the tide of the dominant current."

> **Gregory Baum,** professor emeritus, McGill University

"*Hope in Troubled Times* analyzes the profound seriousness of the planet's present crises and the pathetic inadequacies of the ideologies we have to address the situation. It concludes with an appeal for a complete change in values and behaviors. This compelling volume is a moving piece of writing that deserves the attention of every person who cares about the world they are leaving their children and grandchildren."

> **Walter Pitman, OC,** former member of Parliament, Canada; past president, Ryerson University

To

Gerald Vandezande, C.M.
tireless advocate for public justice for all

and

Ellie and Maggie Van Heemst
two of God's precious children

CONTENTS

FOREWORD

During the darkest days of apartheid, when so many of God's precious children in South Africa were being brutally dehumanized, tortured, and murdered simply because of a biological irrelevance (their skin color), I used to say to white South Africans that they should join the winning side. I used to tell them that we had already won, that victory over the injustice of apartheid was assured.

At the time you would have been forgiven if you had thought me more than a little nuts or even that I had lost my mind altogether! So little seemed to support the view that apartheid's days were numbered. Legally sanctioned separation of married couples and families, crippling restrictions on education for black children, enforced deep poverty, tear-gassing, bombing, arrest, banning, detention, imprisonment, torture, and murder were rampant and getting worse. Apartheid's cruel reach extended even beyond South Africa: later we were to learn that from 1980 to 1988 the South African Defense Force, in pursuit of so-called terrorist bases outside of our territory, caused the deaths of 1.5 million people and created four million refugees in neighboring countries. South Africa was then in the grip of a deadly racist ideology, one that controlled virtually every institution and every aspect of life. The apartheid ideology was an all-pervasive set of values, judgments, and perceptions of reality, and it was pressing its crushing reign of terror on so many of God's vulnerable people.

So you might have called me crazy for saying that we had already won, when all the evidence said that apartheid was winning. Yet I was expressing my real conviction that God has created a *moral* universe, that God cares deeply about justice and injustice. Unjust regimes ultimately always fall because they seek to deny something that cannot be denied.

In God's precious world, there is no way that injustice, oppression, racism, hatred, and dehumanization can have the final word! At the end of the day, "in the fullness of time" (to use the apostle Paul's marvelous phrase), God's higher laws would prevail. To top it off, the prayers of so many people around the world upheld us. How could we fail?

Even at that dark moment God was already transfiguring the darkest evil into a shining good. Nelson Mandela was released on February 11, 1990, a man who after twenty-seven years of harsh imprisonment emerged without bitterness but full of compassion and forgiveness. Then came the historic election of April 27, 1994, the first democratic election in South Africa, when at age 63 I voted for the first time. Though powerful forces had aligned with the intent to disrupt that event violently, astonishingly, to the surprise of so many, especially the cynics, none of the predicted violence happened. And on May 10, 1994, a day of national celebration, Nelson Mandela was inaugurated as the first democratically elected president of South Africa. Apartheid had been defeated!

Many people, not just in South Africa but throughout the world, anticipated an orgy of violent reprisal and retribution in postapartheid South Africa. The world held its breath, waiting for the almost certain bloodbath. Miraculously, it didn't happen. The Truth and Reconciliation Commission was established, and a wrenching but exhilarating national reconciliation process began. Confounding the skeptics, South Africa found a third way, rejecting the options of retributive justice and general amnesty. Amnesty was offered for politically motivated human rights abuses under the strict condition that perpetrators reveal the whole truth of their actions. Dark secrets that otherwise would probably never have been told were disclosed, making possible sometimes astounding moments of repentance, forgiveness, and restoration. Critics called our process the "Kleenex commission," but this was not "namby-pamby social work," as some would have it; this was the stuff of hardcore realpolitik. We learned that peace is not a goal to be achieved but a way of life to be lived.

As the work of the Truth and Reconciliation Commission moved ahead, I wondered if the downfall of apartheid and South Africa's subsequent process of national reconciliation could serve as a message, a lesson for the world.

As I have traveled since to some of the most conflict-ridden areas of the world, including Northern Ireland, the Middle East, Haiti, and various parts of Africa, I have met intense interest in South Africa's story, and I have come to see, amazingly, that the answer is yes.

Hope in Troubled Times affirms a resounding yes again, and I am delighted to commend this book to you.

In our troubled world, apartheid is not the only ideology that has programmed the thinking and the behavior of people. Ideologies of identity, materialism, and security undermine development and progress in so many parts of the world. Yet at the center of this book is a message of hope. The authors are inviting us to join the winning side. Contrary to all the evidence, *Hope in Troubled Times* makes the audacious claim that ideologies of identity, limitless materialism, and absolute security have already been defeated. Bob Goudzwaard, Mark Vander Vennen, and David Van Heemst are not optimists but realists. Their specific proposals are the stuff of political realism. In God's world, where each of us is God's precious child and where the risen Jesus is reconciling all things, the last word does not belong to vicious ideologies but rather to the One who tenderly holds our history in his hands. God's justice, forgiveness, truth, mercy, and love—they shall overcome.

That is South Africa's message to the world, one that affirms the claim of this book. South Africa's victory over apartheid is living evidence that deadly ideologies do not in the end carry the day. Remarkably, humorously, through us (of all weak, wounded people) God is saying to the world, "See, they had a nightmare called apartheid. They had what many thought was an intractable problem. They were not exceptionally smart, they lacked power and expertise, and they were more of a hopeless case. But because of them, no longer can anyone say, 'We have an intractable problem.' If apartheid can fall in South Africa, then ideologies of identity, materialism, and security can end too." God is dreaming of a world where all people, black and white, rich and poor, clever and not so clever, are drawn into one family, a world where all of us participate as agents in God's inexorable transfiguration of evil into good. How can we lose?

I accept the invitation offered by the authors to join the winning side, and I wholeheartedly invite you to do the same.

Desmond M. Tutu
Archbishop Emeritus
Nobel Peace Prize Laureate

PART 1

// SETTING THE STAGE //

/ 1 /

IN THE SHADOWS OF PROGRESS

A Parable

Our world seems to live under the curse of scrambling for solutions but not finding them.

The disturbing upshot is that most in-depth international reports now express the resounding conviction that today's most pressing, implacable problems—dilemmas like global poverty, environmental devastation, and global violence—really can deteriorate no further without catastrophic consequences.

A story from an unlikely time and place may shed some light on our own situation. In the eighteenth century, a European explorer happened upon an island in the South Pacific almost completely denuded of vegetation, trees, fresh water, and animal life. The island, named Rapa Nui by its inhabitants and Easter Island by the explorer, was populated by only a few unwell people and by hundreds of gigantic, spectacular stone-sculpture idols. Even now the best engineering minds have scarcely grasped how the islanders could have sculpted and positioned the colossal statues. According to the few survivors, though the island had been fertile and had supported thousands of inhabitants, the chiefs and priests had promised that stone gods would deliver prosperity the likes of which had not been seen before. "The people had been seduced by a kind of progress that becomes a mania, an 'ideological pathology,' as some anthropologists call it."[1] Caught up in that mania, the islanders gradually off-loaded their practice

15

of caring for each other and the island to their stunning stone creations, the perceived source of their prosperity. But the stone idols, spectacular marvels of human engineering, exacted a punishing revenge instead. Chillingly, their insatiable demands for resources consumed their makers and the island's once abundant life.

This book argues that, in a vastly different environment, contemporary "ideological pathologies" not unlike the one that ravaged Easter Island lie at the foundation of some of today's seemingly most irresolvable global problems. We suggest that many of the spectacular forces of Western progress today—unprecedented marvels of human achievement such as contemporary market forces, technological development, scientific progress, the state, and power unleashed—have become elevated to a status not unlike the position of privilege occupied by the stunning stone idols on Easter Island. Most basically, against this backdrop we seek to help build the capacity of all of us, from all walks of life, to participate in implementing actual solutions. But we do so inspired by a deep hope, for it is our unwavering, enduring conviction that there is real hope for our troubled, mired world—genuine, concrete hope that deeply engages global poverty, environmental destruction, and widespread violence.

This chapter introduces the approach that then serves as the foundation for the remainder of the book.

Missing Solutions

The opening statement, "Our world seems to live under the curse of scrambling for solutions but not finding them," would sound overly dramatic, not to mention tinged with fatalism, if it were not for the fact that over the last three years a number of researchers have sounded new alarm bells. Strikingly, however, the solutions proposed in almost all their reports do not sound convincing. The medicines prescribed do not correspond with the depth of the ailments. Consider three examples.

The Environment

In 2005 the United Nations published a compelling report entitled "Millennium Ecosystem Assessment."[2] More than 1,300 scientists from 95 countries collaborated over a period of four years to produce this study. Its primary conclusion, supported by numerous investigations in various disciplines and by reams of empirical data, is that the collapse of a number of natural systems is imminent. The belching of greenhouse gases into the atmosphere is accelerating climate change, while the overuse of natural resources is causing irreversible damage to the environment.

Never before, argues the report, has the destruction wreaked by people on the environment been as pronounced as it is today.

The report makes an invaluable contribution by thoroughly documenting these realities. However, if its readers are looking in it for concrete ways of slackening the pressure on the environment, they leave disappointed. The report merely comes to the "overriding conclusion that it lies within the power of human society to ease the strains we are putting on the natural resources of the planet."[3] Beyond that it makes only the all-too general observations that "acquiring this will require radical changes in the way nature is treated at every level of decision-making" and that nature's value "[should] be taken into account for all economic decisions."[4]

Terror and Technology

Our second witness is the internationally esteemed astronomer Sir Martin Rees of Cambridge, England. In 2004 Rees published a fascinating book entitled *Our Final Century: Will Civilization Survive the Twenty-first Century?*[5] In Rees's estimation, the odds of humanity surviving this century are not high. The nature of technological development causes him grave concern:

> Science is advancing faster than ever, and on a broader front: bio-, cyber-, and nanotechnology all offer exhilarating prospects; so does the exploration of space. But there is a dark side: new science can have unintended consequences; it empowers individuals to perpetuate acts of megaterror; even innocent errors could be catastrophic. The "downside" of twenty-first century technology could be graver and more intractable than the threat of a nuclear devastation that we have faced for decades. . . . The theme of this book is that humanity is more at risk than at any earlier phase in history.[6]

Rees raises alarm, for example, about the prospect that some of the remaining stockpiles of Russian long-range nuclear missiles, still capable of destroying the world many times over, could fall into the hands of criminal states. Yet he does not go beyond issuing incisive warnings. In his view we cannot stop technological development as such; only here and there, at the most, have people successfully been able to alter its course or slow it down.

Global Poverty

A third example is *The End of Poverty*, an outstanding study done by Jeffrey Sachs, the tireless director of the United Nations' well-known

Millennium Project.[7] The Millennium Project originated in official agreements made in 2000 by government leaders from 189 countries. By 2015, among other commitments, leaders agreed to provide at least basic education for all children, reduce the number of people who live in extreme poverty by at least half, substantially cut child and maternal mortality rates, and reverse the spread of HIV/AIDS and malaria. Achieving these objectives is desperately needed, particularly in Africa. However, meeting them is not going well.[8] By 2005, the United Nations Development Program (UNDP) had already expressed doubts that the goals would be met. The concern explains the passionate appeal issued by Sachs and by "One: The Campaign to Make Poverty History": the project can work and must work, but it will not work without large sums of money. "The big money is what the year 2005 is about," Sachs declared in the March 14, 2005, issue of *Time*. In as short a period as possible, the wealthy countries need to increase their development assistance to 0.7 percent of their gross domestic product.

Sachs's impassioned appeal is well-intentioned and essential, and it represents only one of numerous recommendations. But consider two observations. First, this is not the first time that experts have proposed to combat world poverty by dramatically increasing development assistance. That very proposal launched the United Nations' so-called Development Decade in 1970. The initiative failed (partly because of the oil crisis of 1973).[9] Moreover, at that time the approach included an appeal to renew the distribution of labor around the world, an issue we hear nothing about today; now money alone will do the job. The second observation involves the length of the time frames adopted. The deadline for achieving many current environmental objectives (the Kyoto Protocol) is 2012; the date for the Millennium Goals is 2015. Why do decision-makers not adopt at least a few more limited objectives in the short term? It is difficult to suppress the suspicion that government leaders have wanted to make a good impression; perhaps in the background lurks the thought that by 2012 or 2015 they personally will not have to bear responsibility for meeting the objectives. Making promises is easier than keeping them.

Political Will

These examples illustrate that the concern is genuine. Further, never have experts voiced the concern more articulately and forcefully than today. But the solutions are either stereotypical or even simply missing.

Critics often claim that today's impasses do not become resolved because of a lack of political will. They argue that politicians in the wealthy countries have their hands tied because the majority of their constituents now belong to the content majority, voters who do not want anything to interfere with their economic interests. No doubt this plays a role. But in our view lack of political will does not sufficiently explain why we do not put real solutions into practice, especially now, when so much is at stake not only for the world's poor but also for the inhabitants of the wealthy countries—even their very survival. Is the answer then that most politicians today simply give in, capitulate to the current problems? That seems hard to believe. On the contrary, today's world seems more and more gripped by the urgency of finding new ways out, because the existing remedies hardly work. But we have not yet found new ways.

Why then has the ability to find new solutions, and to build the capacity to implement them, proved to be so elusive?

Endings

Perhaps a first clue to an answer lies in a striking new development, one that may discourage people from becoming engaged in redirecting the current crises. More and more commentators use the word "end" to describe our time. Book titles such as *The End of History*, *The End of Ideology*, *The End of Faith*, *The End of Nature*, and *The End of Science* point to a gathering awareness that the world is deeply changing.[10] So profound are the changes that people can make out something like a fissure or a break in time. Taken together, titles like these seem to suggest that as a society we do not know what lies ahead, but we do know that the future will not unfold according to the patterns and certainties of the past. Though the predictions of experts have reached new levels of sophistication, what the future holds may be less clear than ever because the future lies on the other side of the divide. It is therefore not surprising that the standard approaches have begun to fail and that, as a result, the public at large is now grappling with heightening anxiety about the future.

The advent of globalization and the rising complexity of our postmodern society do not adequately explain that anxiety. Mingled with it are elements of loss of perspective, helplessness, and even despair. Indeed, many people in today's society feel they no longer have a significant impact on the events that most influence their lives. Sometimes people even admit to a baffling sense that the future does not belong to them as much as it once did, as if the future itself decided to embark upon its own self-determined course. But that is a most disquieting, even paralyzing feeling, one that could cause people to enter zones of distraction (such as with iPods and other amenities of modern technology) and dissociate themselves from the grave crises of our time. If the future to a certain extent seems to be setting off on its own, dislodging itself from our influence, then where will it bring us? And what might it do to us?

The Solution Paradox

Add to this a second, possibly related clue. Remarkably, not only have terrorism, global poverty, and environmental destruction become unresponsive to current approaches, but also the solutions themselves often either intensify the problems they were intended to solve or create new and even more serious problems. Too often the cure is worse than the disease. Four examples serve to illustrate this "solution paradox."

The Distribution of Global Wealth and Poverty

In today's world, deepening impoverishment and increasing enrichment appear to go hand in hand. In 1969 the incomes of the wealthiest 20 percent of the world's population were 30 times higher than those of the poorest 20 percent of the earth's people. By 1990 that gap had doubled: the incomes of the wealthiest 20 percent were 60 times higher than those of the poorest 20 percent. The difference factor is now 83.[11] Jeffrey Sachs reports that not only does half of Africa's population live in extreme poverty, but also "this proportion has actually grown worse over the past two decades as the rest of the world has grown more prosperous."[12] How could this grim reality have come about precisely on the heels of the 1970s, the decade designated by world leaders to "end world poverty"?

The solutions implemented during the "Development Decade" centered on transferring more money and technology to the South. Strikingly, however, that solution triggered a powerful boomerang effect, one that has operated since the beginning of the 1980s. Capital still flows from the North to the South in the form of development aid and so-called direct foreign investments. But each year since 1982, the total combined amount of official capital flows to the South, both multilateral and bilateral, has been substantially lower than the amount of capital the South has had to send back to the North in the form of interest payments and amortization on debts.[13] In 2000, debt payments made by the so-called developing countries to the rich nations and their banks equaled 6.3 percent of their gross domestic product (GDP); in that same year direct foreign investments totaled 2.5 percent of their GDP, while official development assistance (ODA) accounted for no more than 0.6 percent.[14] Margaret Thatcher, the former prime minister of Great Britain, once accurately described this "negative net transfer"—the net outflow of capital from the poor countries of the South to the rich countries of the North—as the exact opposite of development aid.[15] And it is partly this reality—the fact that the reverse net transfer of capital carries on unimpeded—that causes a number of experts to voice skepticism that the Millennium Goals will be achieved. Regrettably, the hard-won debt cancellation agreement arrived at in June 2005 by the G8 finance ministers does not alter the boomerang effect: the debt canceled represents only 2 percent of the total external debt owed by the developing countries, and the initiative leaves altogether untouched the conditions that create indebtedness among the poor countries.[16]

Security

Global poverty is not the only area plagued by the solution paradox. Tragically, mounting evidence—including the violent deterioration of civil society in Iraq and the terrorist bombings in Bali, Madrid, and London—shows that terror and homeland security have also worsened in the face of the current remedies. Clearly, preemptive war, curtailing civil liberties for the purpose of preventing further attacks, increasing armament levels through the application of more advanced technology and increased expenditures, and enhancing the destructive capacity of the military for strategic purposes—these have not solved terrorism. Even as world government military expenditures exceeded US$1 trillion in 2004, the number of serious international terrorist attacks, according to official US government figures, more than tripled (from 175 to 655) from 2003 to 2004.[17] The wealthy countries try to guarantee their security by vigorously expanding their arsenals of destruction, yet it is largely this escalation that threatens peace. Even a child understands that if countries all around the world, particularly neighboring ones, adopt arms escalation as the primary prescription for security, then global insecurity increases rather than decreases. Moreover, the alarming pressure that arms escalation is now putting on the world's increasingly scarce resources, especially oil, causes further destabilization. The winning of wars now occupies such prominence that the winning of peace seems less and less conceivable.

An almost unlimited faith in the power of increasingly advanced arms technology is thriving today. That faith animates the US Space Command's report *Vision for 2020*, which proposes to "dominate the space dimension of military operations" by deploying advanced space-based laser weapons technology, technology that can, in principle, link with nuclear, biological, and chemical weapons. It was therefore not an accident that the United States, without whose efforts the long-standing treaty banning space-based weapons would not have come into effect, recently withdrew from its provisions.

The Environment

News media reports today portray increasing disruption in the environment. Stories document melting ice caps and glaciers, a rise in the number and severity of tornados and hurricanes, serious flooding, rapid desertification, greater temperature extremes in the summer and winter, possible rerouting of ocean currents, and an accelerating decline in animal and plant species.

But the solutions proposed sound one-dimensional. They rely largely on either market forces—such as the trade in emission or pollution quotas, which in fact amounts to the East and the South "selling" their environment for use by others—or developing and deploying new environmental technologies. Of course, efforts to put a price tag on current environmentally destructive activities and to apply technologies to lighten the human footprint on the earth are most welcome. But far too few decision-makers recognize that, at best, solutions like these help only temporarily. They merely postpone rather than resolve the dilemma. Deploying market forces and more advanced environmental technologies do not help if, at the same time, the volume of mass consumption expands relentlessly. Mass consumption, which is increasingly highly energy- and environment-intensive, is rising sharply not only in the wealthy North but also in countries whose economies are rapidly expanding, such as India and China. Again and again this cumulative effect cancels out the conservation effect of the accepted solutions. Conserving the environment is then like trying to drain a flood without first shutting off the tap, as the global conferences on environmental issues in Rio de Janeiro, Kyoto, and Johannesburg only partially admitted.

Casting market forces and future technological development as the ultimate solution to present-day global environmental problems therefore creates a contradictory effect because it allows us to sidestep almost every painful measure needed now. And insistently hammering away only on solutions such as these, in the context of decision-makers' ongoing, renewed faith in what technology and the market can do, merely aggravates rather than eases the predicament. Sooner or later, solutions portrayed as panaceas turn against their users.

The consumption effect means that well-intentioned measures to curb the decline of plant and animal species around the globe are rarely effective. In 1989 one species disappeared each day; by 2002, despite widespread adoption of the Treaty on Biodiversity, that rate had reached one species each hour.[18]

Financial Markets

Finally, perhaps the most intriguing solution paradox involves the unpredictability and volatility of today's so-called financial markets. Traditionally, decision-makers have viewed money and finance as means that enable the "real" economy of goods and services to function properly. But indications suggest that the world of finance now enjoys an unprecedented degree of independence or autonomy, to the point where its relationship with the real economy is more that of master than of servant. Financial markets, with their products and derivatives, have expanded far faster than real markets. They have largely become global markets (currency markets, share markets, option markets, and so forth) through which financiers channel immense flows of capital. As a startling sign of how much these markets have assumed center stage in our international financial system, consider that every day and a half the amount of capital that circulates around the globe in the so-called pure financial circuit roughly equals the total debt of the developing countries. Every six hours more money is exchanged in this circuit than has been disbursed by the World Bank in its entire fifty-year history.[19]

The order of dependency has actually been reversed. To a large extent, the world's real economies have become dependent on the financial markets, not the other way around. These markets decide whether the currency of a country rises or falls, and they determine which companies and countries receive capital assistance and which do not. For most such markets, the decisive factor is maximum short-term profitability. A number of countries today are therefore deeply plagued by real concern, if not outright fear, over what global speculative capital and the financial markets will do to their economies. Global capital can leave a country almost overnight, and fear over possible rapid losses of huge sums of capital might be called the new Big Brother syndrome.

What explains this transfer or reversal of power? Why do nations and the world as a whole make themselves so dependent on the so-called autonomy of modern global financial markets, so much so that even today governments lower their taxes on capital and burden their economies with huge expenditure cuts just to remain acceptable in the eyes of this new, ever-watchful Big Brother?

The answer aside, one commentator observes: "Financial capital enjoys a privileged position, . . . [but] financial markets are inherently instable."[20] The instruments that have assumed the captain's seat and now largely steer the real economy are by nature unstable and unreliable pilots, contributing to the reality that the world's future course is becoming harder and harder to discern.

The Shadow Sides of Progress

Let us now draw together these two clues—the emerging dividing line in time and today's solution paradox. Clearly, they converge. Unexpectedly, more money, technology, science, and market forces—solutions that until recently seemed self-evident—often cause global poverty, global insecurity, environmental ruin, and the tyranny of financial markets to deteriorate even further. The solutions themselves lead to stalemates or deadlocks, to a number of specific, discernible end points in our time. The presence of such end points suggests that, to some extent, the means people use have begun to take control, with the result that the end of history, science, and nature as we now know them is approaching.

Perhaps then the current sense of a threatening future has surfaced not just in response to external events, such as the shocking, hideous attacks on the Twin Towers and the Pentagon on September 11, 2001. It has also arisen internally within Western society as a result of the failing forces of progress, failures intimately related to the four illustrations just sketched. In one way or another each example centers around what the forces of progress—such as economic growth, capital, and technology—are capable of doing, not just for us but also *to* us and *against* us.

In short, the arrival of a better society by means of ongoing economic and technological progress has not lived up to expectations. As members of Western society, we do still value any number of important technological breakthroughs, and we embrace the positives of economic growth. But economic growth and technological development have not solved the gnawing problem of rising poverty, despite the fact that we live in an age of unprecedented wealth. Never before has society witnessed such high numbers of addicted and overfed people living next door to millions of underfed people, even as people on both sides fear losing everything. Technological development and economic growth have even cast frightening shadows over us by increasing our power to destroy the earth and to manipulate people's minds and tastes, not to mention genes. Indeed, though we usually see ourselves as the movers and shakers of science, economy, and technology, in the end we too often find ourselves in the vulnerable position of feeling like objects that are themselves in the process of being moved.

Of course, advanced technologies still do improve health, enhance crops, clean the environment, increase modes of communication, and develop faster means of transportation. But the problems they often leave in their wake—genetic risks, an overabundance of information, rising addiction, more stress and burnout in the workplace, the poor without access to agricultural production, and enormous growth in the means of mass destruction—are often more serious and more obstinate than the problems they solve.

Yet despite the fact that the processes of progress exhibit such damaging shadow sides, leaders today insist that their further implementation is simply inevitable. They rule out resistance or protest in advance. Subscribing to the dictum "There is no alternative" (TINA), they recommend them to us as the inescapable consequences of our changing world.[21] Apparently, then, sometimes forces of growth and progress can become more powerful than the groups or institutions that set them into motion. Ironically, that seems to be the case especially where such groups or institutions fully embrace them.

Stated differently, on one hand a number of problems today are becoming increasingly immune to the tools and instruments of progress. And on the other hand those same tools and instruments weigh more and more heavily on us because we view them as inevitable manifestations of the very progress we simply cannot miss out on.

Perhaps, then, progress itself has become our problem.[22] Is the issue, as Karl Löwith once lamented, that "progress itself goes on progressing; we can no longer stop it or turn it around"?[23] Or is it that we, to a greater or lesser extent, pay homage to the forces of progress, and they in turn, to varying degrees, paralyze us, freezing us into inaction?

Engaging the Crises of Our Time

Against this backdrop, this book attempts in a somewhat new way to engage entrenched global poverty, worsening environmental destruction, and rising insecurity—the grievous, stubborn dilemmas that now plague our world. Its goal is to help all of us, concerned citizens and decision-makers from various walks of life, retrieve the capacity to participate in turning these major predicaments around.

How do we go about doing that? Having highlighted the shadow sides of progress, we propose a thesis: perhaps, as decision-makers and citizens, we have become more or less trapped inside the cocoon of an extremely narrow, reduced view or perspective that considers acceptable only the solutions that fall in line with the way Western society defines its further "progress." Indeed, key actors in Western society expect to overcome virtually all the stubborn, intractable obstacles thrown up by global poverty, environmental ruin, and violence by further deploying the means of progress (such as money, economic growth, and technological development) and the mechanistic institutions of progress (such as the market mechanism, the plan mechanism, and even the democratic mechanism). Moreover, the means and mechanisms of progress have become elevated to such a prominent place that they now, to some degree, chart their own course, as if independent of us. They therefore display aspects of autonomy, of a relative immunity from our influence, and thereby gradually shut down or in key respects foreclose our future.

No doubt this is a formidable thesis. But if it has some validity, then it confirms our feeling that almost every current diagnosis of the crisis of our time lacks something fundamental. Many observers neglect how deep desires can coalesce into a modernist perspective, orientation, or worldview that, despite its claims to the contrary, is capable of contributing to, sustaining, and even entrenching global poverty, environmental devastation, and widespread violence. They forget or ignore the roles played by people's deepest longings, dreams, and commitments and how those profound aspirations become inscribed in the dynamic forces, interactional patterns, and institutions of contemporary Western society. Assessments usually miss altogether what goes on at the deepest level in people's hearts and minds, what engages and moves them, what captures their imaginations, fills their hearts, and satisfies their expectations. We call this the "spiritual" or "religious" dimension, understood in its broadest sense, of contemporary events.[24] In a moment, using the issue of structural unemployment, we offer a concrete illustration of this dimension in action. In our view, neglecting this dimension deeply hampers the ability to break through the solution deadlock and find responsible solutions to the world's most complex, pressing problems.

This book seeks to add this missing element to the debate. In no way do we pretend to possess a simple way out, as if we could produce a magic key that would put an end to insecurity and open the door to a better future for all. But searching for approaches from outside a rigid, compulsive fixation on further implementing the instruments of progress may open doors to alternative, perhaps unforeseen solutions, genuine solutions that could actually help turn around rising insecurity, global poverty, and environmental degradation.

Have the Gods Betrayed Us?

How has the expanding autonomy of technology, science, economy, and finance come about? It is highly improbable that it has occurred on its own or that somehow a fate called progress brought it upon us. We therefore dare to think the almost unthinkable, that a pattern similar to the "obsession" or "possession" that often structures the social order of so-called primitive societies actually operates today in our so-called modern civilization.

What do we mean by that? In brief strokes we sketch the possibility explored in subsequent chapters. As persons and societies, it is entirely legitimate to set our hearts on ends like prosperity, health, cultural or group identity, and protection. But a point of desperation may arrive where we slip into reaching for these goals regardless of the cost. Then we become obsessed by our ends (goals). We conscript every available object or force into a tool or means for reaching the all-encompassing objective. From that moment forward, the means to our ends function as idols or gods; we enthrone them as the developmental powers that will deliver us the promised end. As cultural anthropologists have found in various cultures, when obsessed by health, identity, prosperity, and/or security, both persons and societies tend to put their faith or trust in things or forces that their own hands have made. And in a kind of trade-off or exchange, they then become dependent on their own creations.

But we also know from many practices around the world, both current and past, that gods never leave their makers alone. As soon as people put themselves in a position of dependence on their gods, invariably the moment comes when those things or forces gain the upper hand, when they begin to mold the lives and thoughts of their adherents. Humanly made things or forces begin to control their makers even to the point where they become powers of domination. Against them the human will weakens or even vanishes, while the initial goals tend to become bleak, obscured, or forgotten, building to the moment when the gods' betrayal becomes transparent. But by then it could be too late.

In our view this old cultural and religious insight deserves more exploration in our time. We may not simply dismiss the possibility that the means of progress that our own hands have made have become forces that increasingly display autonomy and domination in Western society today, dynamically moving toward the point at which their betrayal becomes evident, much like the activity of the gods on Easter Island.

Of course, comparing Westerners to the inhabitants of Easter Island might seem far-fetched. Surely modern and postmodern people have roundly rejected all forms of superstition! Yet it would be irresponsible simply to reject out of hand the prospect that a similar devotion and betrayal surround the means and institutions of Western progress today.

Consider an example. If we examine an issue like structural unemployment, we quickly realize that the problem of unemployment today is tied to the pattern and rate of economic growth. For years in Western society we have seen unhampered, maximum economic growth as *the* prescription for achieving greater material prosperity. This pursuit has made us wealthier but also more vulnerable. The unquestioned necessity of economic growth means that our production factors—land, labor, capital, organizational processes—must be of maximum efficiency and must lead to the highest possible productivity. Intensive global competition now almost compels industrialized societies to pursue the vigorous, uninterrupted growth of their gross domestic product.[25] Consider the analogy of the cyclist: as long as the cyclist maintains her speed, she remains balanced on her seat, but if she tries to stop, she loses her balance. The same can be said of Western economies: they remain in balance only as long as economic growth persists.[26] But that implies that if technological innovations can make the workplace more efficient, then we eliminate jobs. If unbridled competition obliges us to pursue the cheapest possible production costs regardless of the consequences, then we shift production overseas to places of cheap labor and inadequate standards for employees and the environment. Structural unemployment and further environmental damage are then the inevitable price, or sacrifice, that economic expansion exacts of us. As citizens we pay this price in the name of what once became and still is, to some extent, our ultimate goal or end: greater material prosperity. Obsessed by an end (rising material prosperity), we have off-loaded our responsibility and allowed various forces, means, and powers in our society (such as untrammeled economic expansion) to become gods who dictate their wills to us.

Setting the Stage

In the following chapters we explore the possibility that similar goal obsessions or ideological pathologies continue to lie at the foundation of at least some of our society's most urgent problems. We test the hypothesis that, driven by such ideological pathologies, our own age is familiar with the pattern of following idols that human hands have made, a pattern that hampers our ability to find structural solutions.

But supporting this argument requires more than providing a few concrete examples for empirical verification. We first need to understand how ideological obsessions and the idolatry they set in motion might arise in a thoroughly secular, irreligious society, perhaps even as a fruit of Western secular thought itself. In that vein, the remainder of part 1 (chaps. 2–3) addresses the interrelationship between myth, classical ideology, and the birth of modern idolatry. In chapter 3 some of the great ideologies of the recent past, such as Communism and Fascism, serve to illustrate the developmental phases of modern ideologies. Then in part 2 (chaps. 4–6) we explore contemporary ideologies of identity, material progress, and guaranteed security in action, keeping our eyes focused on the risks they may pose, which can be global in scale. And part 3 (chaps. 7–8) explores the ominous, deadly spirals created by the collisions of various overpowering ideologies today.

Ways of Love and Justice for All

We write this book for all who are concerned about the crises of our time. As authors we approach the issues from our deep commitment to the way of Christ. Yet our aim throughout is to stimulate and contribute to the broadest dialogue possible, a dialogue that invites and includes many different perspectives. At most points, therefore, we address all concerned citizens. At others, we engage members of various faith communities in dialogue. At still others, we speak specifically to members of our own Christian faith community. You as a reader are invited to listen in and contribute to the discussion at any of these junctures from your own vantage point and perspective. All of us are searching together for new ways, new approaches. And all of us—most decidedly we ourselves—bring only a partial view. Under no circumstances may Christians claim at the outset that they possess better insights than others, nor do they have the right to equate their own partial insights with the unique message of the gospel itself.

What then is the value of adopting a specific vantage point or perspective? Let us describe two ways in which the Christian faith is inscribed in the reflections we make in this book. First, when it comes to analyzing the concrete problems of society, contrary to the Western rationalism of the Enlightenment, biblical faith suggests that ways of justice, solidarity, love of one's neighbor, reconciliation, peace, and care for the earth are not human constructs. Rather, their origin lies in a loving Creator and in the Creator's design for life in all its fullness. They are life-affirming, inclusive ways, paths for people to walk down, liberating ways that broaden and widen.[27] Because they have a "reality" value, merely casting them aside is simply imprudent.

Second, biblical revelation suggests that, especially in a climate of fear and uncertainty, individual persons, groups of people, and even societies as a whole can fall prey to a self-made world of illusions, a world that gradually loses its hold on reality. Both persons and societies can become spiritually enchanted; they can fall under the powerful spell of self-spun illusions. They can become entrapped in a world of illusion, in a disengaged universe of unreal infatuation, and the resulting narrowing of consciousness can make it extremely difficult to discover possible ways out. We must therefore be open to the possibility that all people—whether they profess a faith or not, or whether they are Christians or members of other faith communities—are susceptible to this religious or spiritual seduction in the public life of society.

Slinging the Suitable Stone

Finally, let us introduce the issue we take up in part 4: hope. In the face of seemingly autonomous forces, or powers of domination, we can feel helpless and our hope can easily disappear. Where then is hope to be found today?

In our view, hope does not lie in overthrowing technology, the economy, science, the market, the state, or even the corporation as such. The real enemy has deeper roots. The enemy's deepest power, as we try to demonstrate, lies in the stubbornness of the human heart. It is a power vested in people like us, people who are tempted again and again to elevate human-made powers or institutions, enthroning them as forces of liberation and deliverance, and thereby paving the way for their gradual development into tyrannical idols. Campaigns that seek to eradicate the structures of society therefore almost always miss the mark. They can even pull people into the very force field they wish to oppose. The enthusiasm of a new revolution easily disappears in a new iconoclasm. Full-scale, radical revolution often amounts to a prostration before perpetual violence, an idol even more tyrannical and merciless than the forces of progress.

Some in our society have lost all hope. Deathly afraid of possible escalations of violence or falling back into poverty, or feeling helpless in relation to the ongoing ruin of the environment, they have become pessimists or fatalists. Such calamities may indeed come, but they will strike only if we continue to sustain the forces threatening to make them realities.

When tyrannical powers, with their absolute claims and powerful temptations, come into focus, our courage may sink down to our toes. But let us remember the lesson of the stone. Centuries ago a young, unarmed shepherd boy named David found a way to conquer a seemingly unbeatable giant, Goliath, by accurately throwing a small stone. Like Goliath, today's awful powers and belief systems also have points of vulnerability. Let us never underestimate what ordinary people can do today when confronting oppressive powers, as David did against the vicious warrior Goliath. But that means we must first discern the weaknesses and vulnerabilities of the giants taunting us before we sling the suitable stone. And let us always be mindful that, to some extent, the real enemy resides within ourselves: within our own thoughts, hearts, imaginations, and lifestyles.

Times that deserve the label "a world possessed" are not times without hope. Helplessness, expertise, and mass revolution threaten to extinguish hope. But genuine hope is deeper than these threats. It flares up just when the night is at its darkest.

/ 2 /

MYTH, IDEOLOGY, AND IDOLATRY

In chapter 1 we made an urgent plea to explore what lies underneath the many practical dilemmas afflicting today's society. The plea is prompted by a new, puzzling irony. Remarkably, many of today's problems seem to have developed immunity to our well-intended solutions. They have become like viruses that resist medicine or like pests that have developed a defense against pesticide. All too frequently the remedies applied—more money, improved scientific research, better technologies, or more robust economic growth—seem to exacerbate the difficulties we intended them to solve or to create new and even more serious problems.

Consider this alarming turn of events for a moment. In our sophisticated, advanced age, the inability of all of us, politicians included, to influence today's stubborn problems must have a deeper cause than simply a failure to apply the right mix of standard remedies. Perhaps the answer does not lie in tinkering with the accepted solutions. We need to look deeper instead and ask a more fundamental question: in the face of today's intractable problems, and in an age of unprecedented power, where does our overwhelming sense of helplessness, ineffectiveness, and powerlessness come from?

Postmodern thinkers often answer this question by claiming that the world of things itself has become independent. The things themselves—the results of technology and the economy—now follow their own autonomous courses. They have set themselves up against our ability to control them. In his book *Fatal Strategies*, the well-known French postmodernist philosopher Jean Baudrillard writes that the primary issue today is not the misguided strategies of people, but the strategy of the things themselves, to which we as people, for better or for worse, have been handed. *Fatal Strategies* begins with this sentence: "Things have found a way of avoiding the dialectics of meaning [that is, questions of good and evil, or of the rightness or wrongness of certain developments] that was beginning to bore them: by proliferating indefinitely, increasing their potential, outbidding themselves in an ascension to the limit."[1]

Baudrillard's claim is impressive but not satisfying. He has not answered a prior question: how have the results of technology and the economy acquired such enormous power and influence over us? Did they do it on their own? That hardly seems likely. Perhaps we ought then to explore the possibility that, before the things themselves began at least partially to determine their own course, we as people in various ways, possibly even unconsciously, engaged in a process of relinquishing our ability to influence them. But if that is the case, then what would have brought us to the point of handing over our power and influence? Was it fear? Or perhaps the prospect of increased prosperity?

Both of these possibilities occupy us in this book. And they launch us into an examination of the nature and activity of ideology in today's society.

The Explosive Origin of Ideology

Generally, sociologists (along the lines of Karl Mannheim) define "ideology" as the entire set of conceptions and beliefs subscribed to by a specific group of people. According to this definition, everyone has an ideology of one sort or another. But if we explore the origin of the word "ideology," we find that the original definition is far more loaded, even explosive. The fiery passion and deep conviction expressed through ideology can, in certain circumstances, even bring people to delegate their own power and influence to particular forces or institutions.

The person who coined the term "ideology" was a French education reformer named Destutt de Tracy.[2] De Tracy was a fervent revolutionist. As an educator he concerned himself with how education could lead children to embrace the ideals of the French Revolution—freedom, equality, and brotherhood—as self-evident truths. John Locke had persuasively argued that there is nothing in the mind that does not first exist in the senses. Locke therefore saw the original human mind as a blank slate, a tabula rasa. Now if Locke is correct, de Tracy surmised, this means that one can develop a discipline or science whose task is to study the origin and development of human ideas.

He called that science "ideology." Ideology was therefore born as a science, and according to de Tracy, because ideology focused entirely on ideas, it was the purest form of science possible. At the same time, however, he saw ideology as uniquely suited to practical application. Indeed, people could easily apply such a science to the task of changing human ideas for the purpose of achieving certain predetermined social ends. Thus for him ideology was "the greatest of all arts, . . . that of regulating society in such a way that man finds there the most help, and the least possible annoyance of his own kind."[3] For de Tracy, religion had no place in that endeavor. Quite the contrary: "All religion can be defined as an obstacle to sound logic and to sane morality," he once pontificated.[4]

Notice what is happening here. This is not just a charter document drafted by an educator about how to develop the thought world of children in a nonreligious manner, using certain values and norms. No, here for the first time we encounter a deliberate political attempt to systematically regulate or manipulate people's currently held ideas in order to achieve certain societal ends.

Naturally, de Tracy chose ends that he felt would genuinely "help" people. Nurturing a sufficiently revolutionist fervor was key. Reigning ideas, values, and norms had to be filled in and rebuilt in education to such an extent that a new kind of people would emerge. By way of their ideas, these new citizens would implement in the most effective manner the all-controlling aim of a society of freedom, equality, and brotherhood. For de Tracy, that absolute end legitimated re-forming the human mind from square one, using the educational process as an essential means or instrument.

From de Tracy's work we can extrapolate three elements that, combined, define the classical concept of ideology. First, ideology consists of an *absolutized* political or societal *end* (goal). Second, ideology requires a *redefinition of currently held values, norms, and ideas* to such an extent that they legitimize in advance the practical pursuit of the predetermined end.[5] Finally, ideology involves establishing a standard by which to *select the means* or instruments necessary for effectively achieving the all-important goal.

In this classical definition of ideology, we detect nothing less than traces of the French Revolution itself. Only by means of the power of such a strong ideology is it possible to comprehend how the French Revolution, carried out with both such romanticism and such business-like precision, could execute hundreds of citizens day after day in the middle of Paris, using a brand-new, efficient technology: the guillotine. In no sense was this slaughter an accidental, highly charged emotional event about which people felt remorse later. No, a new kind

of rationality came to reign in this modern society. It was a rationality that inspired people to believe that, for the purpose of achieving
the overarching revolutionist end—the prosperity and freedom of all
citizens—efficient executions were unquestionably "good" and "just."
This was a critical reinterpretation of values.[6] Even today we hear
echoes of the ideology in the French national anthem, which urges all
children of the fatherland to march on to glory as the blood-stained
flag is raised high.

After the ideology of the French Revolution burst into the open, a
tidal wave of ideologies rolled successively over Europe, as if a barrier of
principle had been removed once and for all. In chapter 3 we explore that
development in more detail. But at this point let us observe that the two
major Western ideologies of the twentieth century that also spearheaded
radical societal change—Nazism and Communism—displayed the three
trademarks of ideology we described earlier. In each of them the *end* or
objective was absolute (the arrival of the Third Reich; the victory of the
working class). Ideas and moral concepts were then *reoriented* entirely
to the goal (the Nazis insisted that "the Party is always right"; Lenin
claimed that "truth" is whatever advances the arrival of the Communist
utopia). Finally, on the basis of such ideological reinterpretations, the
ideology's adherents justified the most horrific intimidation and violence
as *means* for achieving the end (such as concentration camps and gulag
archipelagos).

This observation teaches us an unmistakable lesson. Let us not underestimate the profound impact that a living ideology's reinterpretation of
the prevailing norms and values has on society. Making an end absolute
involves ascribing evil to whatever gets in the way of achieving the end.
Evil, untruth, and immorality are concentrated on the opponents of the
objective; they are made into the scapegoats of everything that is wrong.
The Jews were forced into this position under the Nazi ideology, resulting
in the justification of their complete annihilation (the so-called Final Solution to the Jewish Question). With ideology the decisive moment is not
that the opponents must be destroyed because they represent evil. Quite
the opposite: because they oppose the overarching end, they are declared
to be evil itself; they become the very definition of evil. In contrast, those
who fully pursue the all-encompassing end are by definition good, even
if their actions result in other people suffering under cruel treatment.

How close, in our view, this lies to the demonic! Ideology in its original, classical sense involves a conscious, deliberate departure from the
ways of loving service of God and neighbor. Speaking about and thinking within the confines of ideology are therefore never an indifferent
academic exercise. Genuine ideologies always try to seize control of an
entire society.

Ideology and Modernity

The foregoing raises two questions. First, what did the ideologies of the nineteenth and twentieth centuries introduce that was actually new? And second, what made their rapid emergence in Western society possible? Perhaps their novelty lay in turning the pursuit of a specific social objective into an absolute, life-defining project. But that hardly seems possible, for forms of goal obsession have been present throughout history. The so-called Christianization of Europe under the emperor Constantine took place through military coercion, because for Constantine the "righteous" end justified the most abominable means. And to this day in the Middle East, many people, among them Christians, remember the victims of the subsequent Crusades. "Dieu le veut! [God wills it!]," shouted the Crusaders as they stormed villages, sowing death and destruction. There too the goal sanctified the most ghastly, macabre means.

Then is the elimination of myth or of every mythical influence what sets the ideological pursuit apart from earlier endeavors? After all, Enlightenment philosophers such as Marquis de Condorcet declared that the Enlightenment had irrevocably banished superstition and irrationality.[7] But that claim does not stand up to scrutiny either, even granting John Ralston Saul's legitimate point that "none of the modern ideologies can be considered great mythology."[8] Undergirding the ideologies of both the French Revolution and Communism were deeply utopian dreams and images. The architects of these ideologies were utopian thinkers, eagerly anticipating the return of a golden age, a paradise that had vanished shortly after the dawn of human history. Similarly, Nazism was firmly rooted in the German myths and sagas of old, which depicted people struggling and dying heroically in a world where the gods ultimately betrayed them (the "Twilight of the Gods" sagas). So much did these myths become inscribed into the people's consciousness that, for the Nazis, possessing courage and unfailing loyalty to the very end, even to death, defined the real value of a human being.[9] Finally, even the Western faith in endless progress—which Marquis de Condorcet articulated as "the rise of a new doctrine, the doctrine of the indefinite perfectibility of the human race"[10]—has mythical elements. As Ronald Wright observes in his *Short History of Progress*:

> Our practical faith in progress has ramified and hardened into an ideology—a secular religion which, like the religions that progress has challenged, is blind to certain flaws in its credentials. Progress therefore has become "myth" in the anthropological sense, . . . an arrangement of the

past, whether real or imagined, in patterns that reinforce a culture's deepest values and aspirations.[11]

In our view, Wright's description brings us closer to what differentiates
modern ideology from premodern goal obsessions. Three seminal or key
activities characterize the process of a faith "ramifying" and "hardening"
into a modern ideology: rationalization, radicalization, and instrumentalization. Modern ideologies, which are always dynamic social projects,
are rationally preconceived and constructed, piece by piece; they are
systematically thought through, right down to the chilling calculation
of highly efficient means. They are radical in their totalitarian scope and
depth. And they try to instrumentalize everything available, leaving no
stone unturned, beginning with values. Indeed, in its rationalization,
radicalization, and instrumentalization, modern ideology always seeks
to radically retool the entire spectrum of currently held values, such as
good and evil, right and wrong, truth and untruth. Ideology involves
the "conversion of all values" (*die Umwertung aller Werte*), in the words
of the great nineteenth-century philosopher Friedrich Nietzsche; this
conversion legitimates in advance the systematic indoctrination of entire
populations into a new way of thinking and acting.[12]

But how can people be led to embrace such a complete value conversion, even when it justifies the unconscionable dehumanization of
their fellow human beings? No amount of external pressure or coercion,
whether in the past or perhaps even now, can account for such a shift.

The Myth of the Madman

Our mention of the name Friedrich Nietzsche was not accidental.
Of all Western thinkers, Nietzsche probably has come the closest to ex-
plaining the origin of modern Western ideology, particularly in his book
The Joyful Science. There he tells his famous myth of the madman. One
day, in the bright morning hours, a madman lights a lantern, runs into
a marketplace full of people, and yells, "I seek God! I seek God!"[13] The
bystanders laugh at him and ask whether God has perhaps gotten lost.
But their tone changes when the madman jumps up and screams, "I will
tell you. We have killed him—you and I. All of us are his murderers."

Remarkably, the crowd does not get upset. Instead, it falls completely
silent, particularly when the madman begins to wonder, "How [were we
able to] do this? Who gave us the sponge to wipe away the entire horizon?
What were we doing when we unchained this earth from its sun? Is not
the greatness of this deed too great for us?" But his musing disappears
quickly into an unshakable conviction: "There has never been a greater

deed, and whoever is born after us—for the sake of this deed, he will belong to a higher history than all history hitherto."

Nietzsche's powerful parable revolves around humanity's entrance into this "higher history." The history is higher because, as the madman cries out, "Must we ourselves not become gods simply to appear worthy of [such a deed]?" The madman's question is revealing. It implies that if God is dead—murdered—it is now humanity that must take hold of the rudder and steer. Humanity does not escape from playing God: that is its higher history. With the death of God, the world has been emptied and stripped bare: "Do we not feel the breath of the empty space?" wonders the madman. An emptied world requires re-creation. The world must be completely built up again from scratch.[14] Re-creating society requires new stories, laws, and norms. It even requires new sacrifices: "What festivals of atonement, what sacred games shall we have to invent?" asks the madman. And in what is perhaps its most onerous task, humanity must develop a new, self-made perspective of meaning. It must create a new narrative from which to make sense of things. People must design a different horizon than the one that has been wiped out.

It is precisely this spiritual vacuum that modern Western ideology, by fits and starts, has filled and continues to fill. Western ideology is the perilous adventure of projecting a new story, a new meaning, a new certainty, a new spirit in a world severed from God. The image of the lit lantern in Nietzsche's myth symbolizes the perilousness of the task. Early in the morning the madman comes to the market carrying a lit lantern. Later he smashes the lantern into pieces: "I have come too early," he laments. Nietzsche juxtaposes the lit lantern with the true light of the sun as the nihilist symbol of self-ignited enlightenment. It is the image of enlightened humanity, which must now manage things itself.

As the father of modern nihilism, Nietzsche must have sensed the high cost that later Western ideologies, rooted in this soil, would exact of people and society: "Has it not become colder?" senses the madman. "Gods, too, decompose." But for Nietzsche, the cost seemed worth it. People are now entering a history of the highest order imaginable, one that holds the greatest value, he thought. Indeed, nothing else is at stake than the highest achievement that humanity can ever attain.

We may now draw two conclusions. First, clearly the rise of modern Western ideology is strongly related to the notion of the death of God and, with that notion, to the emergence of a world that is now secular to the core. Western ideology was able to emerge only at the moment when the traditional Christian faith began to fade away in Western society, especially among the elite. Strikingly, it also emerged as the antipode to traditional Christianity.[15] Indeed, genuine ideology is always characterized by imitation. It is intent on replacing the dominant values across the entire spectrum of its activities. Ideology creates the world anew. It establishes new founding stories and new laws. It redefines the meaning of life. And to complete the imitation, ideology requires new redemptive powers, new saviors, whose power is needed for the re-creation of the world.

The second conclusion is no less startling. If the source of genuine ideologies—the desire to enter into "the higher history of humankind," a history of self-redemption and self-actualization—is still alive, then contrary to Francis Fukuyama's declaration that we have now arrived at the end of ideology, we may not exclude the possibility that ideologies are still with us or that they may rebound, even fully, in the twenty-first century.[16] The tap from which they surge, highlighted by Nietzsche's parable, has not been turned off. Even in an entirely secular society people will continue to crave one ultimate meaning or another. And it is in that craving that ideologies take hold and prosper.

Contemporary Ideologies

Our second conclusion begs the question of whether people are inclined to make ends absolute in our own time. Naturally, the ideology of revolution is not the only possible ideology. I may set my heart on attaining a new society by way of the revolutionist overthrow of the old one. But I may also try to preserve an existing society by using every means at my disposal. Then too I will be drawn to conscript the reigning conceptions of truth, justice, and love until they become unwitting collaborators of what I hope to reach at any cost.

So far the examples given may sound familiar, but they do not touch us personally. Few among us feel kinship with the aims of the French Revolution or the dreams of Nazi or Communist barbarianism. But what about the pursuit of our own goals and the fulfillment of our deepest dreams?

Suppose we identify the major goals or ends that occupy people around the world today and then determine whether they have the potential to become full-fledged ideologies. We may find that these goals occupy us too. They may give life fulfillment and purpose to those who pursue them. In our view, there are at least four:

1. The systematic resistance of all exploitative, oppressive, and dehumanizing powers that prevent the arrival of a better society.
2. The survival of one's people, culture, group, or religion: the preservation of one's hard-fought freedoms and/or cultural identity.
3. The pursuit of more material wealth or prosperity and the opportunity for continued material progress.

4. Guaranteed security: the protection of oneself, one's children, and one's fellow human beings against any attack from outside.

No one would maintain that these goals are illegitimate in and of themselves or that they may not be pursued in any way. One goal probably appeals more to one person and the other to another. But an ideology does not arise because of the illegitimacy of a goal. One may even say that the more legitimate a goal seems, the more likely an ideology will eventually anchor itself in the hearts of men and women. Legitimate goals can turn into ideologies.

In the following chapters we shall see that, to varying degrees, today's dominant ends do in fact bear ideological traits. In some cases, the pursuit of these ends has developed into partial or less mature ideologies; in others the ideologies have become full-fledged and complete. But regardless of their developmental level, the pursuits of these ends today show evidence of rationalization, radicalization, and instrumentalization. Indeed, ideologies of revolution, identity, material progress, and guaranteed security surround us. Moreover, ideologies such as these can prosper even in the midst of so-called religious societies. History reveals that those who call themselves Christians or Muslims, for example, are not immune to their lure. Christians ought never to forget that largely "Christian" twentieth-century Europe served as the context for the widespread acceptance of merciless ideologies like Communism and Fascism, as well as for the outbreak of two horrific world wars.

Idolatry

Earlier we noted that, to be successful, an ideology requires a new horizon, a new narrative, a new law, a new framework of meaning. But how does the ideology actually become concrete in the midst of society? Clearly, its protagonists need new or radically revamped social forces and institutions to serve as levers by which to set the ideology in motion. The ideology's advocates recruit and invest certain social forces with significant new power, and these forces then serve as the essential tools used to achieve the prized objective. But for the tools to be effective, people must give them as much sway as possible in the public life of society. Broad swaths of society must raise them up, set them free, and surround them with the institutional framework they require, even if doing so involves making painful sacrifices and even if gradually the instruments themselves begin to assume control in society. To these tools falls the task of actually implementing the promised liberation. They function as powers of redemption and release.

This pattern is so reminiscent of the step-by-step interaction that occurs between people and their objects in idol worship that, to understand this aspect of ideology, we need to explore idolatry in more detail.

We know from the Old Testament prophets and from a number of religious practices today that idols do not arise in a vacuum.[17] Myth serves as the milieu or matrix within which people create idols. In an environment of fear or even life-threatening deprivation, myths depicting the origin of the world, its fall, and the heroic acts of the gods serve as the source or feeding ground from which the gods receive their names and accompanying power.

Within this framework, idol worship invariably unfolds in three steps. First, people objectively *represent* the god in an idol of wood, stone, ivory, or some other material for the purpose of bringing the god closer to people, closer to frail humanity. Because the image governs access or acts as the gateway to the realm of the divine, it must be initiated or consecrated and set up on a pedestal in a special, sacred place.

Next, on a daily basis, people *venerate* the idol by bringing it sacrifices. The assumption here is that the idol possesses its own life, a life whose purpose is to repay the people's homage with happiness, health, military protection, or wealth. So important are these ends or objectives that they often even determine the names of the idols. In the ancient Near East, Mammon (an idol of money) meant "wealth"; Baal (an idol of growth and fertility) meant "lord of much wealth"; while Molech (an idol of military power and dominion) meant "king of kings," with a sinister connotation. At its root traditional idolatry is a mythically embedded contract or exchange. People are mythically driven to devote total trust, reverence, and loyalty to the idol in exchange for receiving what they most deeply crave.

But then, as the biblical view of idolatry makes clear, a third step follows. After representation and veneration, people gradually become reshaped and *transformed* into the likeness of their gods. The Psalms graphically describe this role reversal:

> [Idols] have mouths, but cannot speak,
>   eyes, but they cannot see;
> they have ears, but cannot hear,
>   noses, but they cannot smell;
> they have hands, but cannot feel,
>   feet, but they cannot walk;
>   nor can they utter a sound with their throats.
> Those who make them will be like them,
>   and so will all who trust in them. (Ps. 115:5–8)

Fear is what drives this third, unanticipated step. The god depicted by the image does not present itself: it remains distant and hidden. But its representation in the image is tangible and concrete, and to its devotees the image, like the two-faced Roman god Janus, arbitrarily reveals the power of either favor or punishment. The power that people delegate to the idol is a power that both saves and destroys. As such it instills deeper and deeper anxiety. The slightest misstep can trigger the wrath of the idol, a wrath that may even bring people to ruin. Serving idols therefore always brings with it a form of hypnosis, a hypnotic narrowing of consciousness. People's perception of reality shrinks into a matter of merely finding the right type of interaction with the idol. But by then the god has, to some extent, assumed control; it now largely charts its own autonomous course. When that occurs, fear becomes the chief characteristic of life, and the sense of betrayal is pervasive.

But what purpose does a discussion about the relationship between ancient myth and traditional idol worship serve today? Surely it does not apply to those of us in Western society, for modernity brought with it a radical departure from superstitious religious practices! But that view is dangerously superficial. Nothing in the pattern of traditional idol worship suggests that an idol is by definition a static object or a striking piece of wood or stone. Further, earlier we saw that all modern ideologies have mythical backdrops or aspects. We may therefore not exclude the possibility that even the most modern or postmodern ideology may be related in various ways to forms of contemporary idolatry. Even implementing the new rationalist universe designed by modern man and woman requires forces of liberation and emancipation, powers that people put their faith in.

Technology as an Idol

By way of brief illustration, consider the role of technology in today's society.

Technology, or the art of making tools, is surely a fruit of God's good creation. It is not evil. But both nations and persons, believing in its beneficial, liberating power, can grant technology its own life and set it on its own course. Expecting that technology will supply them with more luxury, more prosperity, and better health, not to mention solutions to a number of current global problems, they may give technology room to blaze its own trail and then follow wherever it leads. They may set technology up on a pedestal and begin to interact with technology as if it possesses a life of its own, capable of defining its own path.

Technology and science have indeed become the shining hope of many people. Against a rising mountain of evidence, many decision-makers are convinced that, if we remove all barriers to further technological development, technology will still end disease, hunger, war, and suffering. They try to grant unrestricted technological development complete sway, creating the social, legal, and financial space necessary for it to become a liberating, prosperity-building, safety-securing force. Such reliance on technology has also produced what is known as "the technological imperative." Convincing themselves that what technology can do it must do, some insist that we adjust indiscriminately to the demands of advanced technology. But then the tables have turned and the roles have reversed. Technology has begun to take charge. Already in 1977 Jacques Ellul highlighted this very process, describing the transition from "technology" to "Technology," by which society in all of its modalities, having succumbed to a truncated, reduced view of reality, submits to a coherent, self-sustaining, universal, and autonomous technological system.[18]

Inevitably, such actions and beliefs reflect a narrowing of consciousness and a change in attitudes. Yet people living in a society gripped by one or another idol will likely not recognize that they are operating out of a narrowed consciousness or that they have become caught in a kind of tunnel vision. Indeed, all the trademarks of idolatry become recognizable in this pattern.

Ideology: The Matrix from Which Contemporary Idols Emerge

In this illustration, the ideological drive for more luxury, more prosperity, and better health enthrones technology, giving it an exalted, directive-giving position in society. And the existence of relationships of this nature leads us to formulate a hypothesis: *if myth is the matrix from which traditional idols appear, then ideology is the matrix, the meaning-framework from which contemporary idols emerge.*

In the coming chapters we test this hypothesis; chapter 3 begins with the ideologies of the nineteenth and twentieth centuries that were designed to spearhead radical societal change. We try to dissect the step-by-step exchange that occurs between people and what they make, conceive of, or produce today, exploring it in the light of what many people in society may believe overcomes oppression, preserves identity, supplies prosperity, or brings ultimate security. But before we do so, consider four implications.

First, if our hypothesis is accurate, it implies that the presence of idolatry—the presence of liberating powers designed to make the ideology concrete—serves as the litmus test for determining when the pursuit of a legitimate goal has turned into an ideology. A genuine ideology is present only when some kind of idolatry has taken root in the pursuit of an absolutized end, for only the power generated by the exchange that occurs in idolatry is sufficient to concretely implement an ideology.

Second, contemporary powers of liberation clearly differ from the gods launched by traditional myths and beliefs. But how? First, we may expect modern-day idols to be stamped by or suffused with the rationality, radicality, and instrumentality of the modern ideologies that give them birth. We may anticipate that they will display signs of being systematically rational or logical in nature, totalitarian in their range and depth, and relentless in their instrumentalization of people and the earth's resources in order to reach the ideology's destination. Second, because of the inherent and built-in dynamism of today's ideologies—within their dynamic orbits always striving to achieve certain objectives through every means available—we may expect that the means applied are not static but instead are powerful, dynamic gods in motion. What then remains applicable are the essentials of idolatry itself. People elevate something they themselves have fashioned to an exalted position in society (representation). Next, people make sacrifices on this idol's behalf, as if it possesses its own life and power (veneration). Finally, decision-makers and citizens follow it wherever it leads (transformation), even if over the course of time the original end fades or seems no longer achievable.

Third, if correct, our hypothesis intimates that modern ideology has the potential to permit and even promote the entrance of a series of dynamic gods or forces into Western society. In the coming chapters we explore whether and to what extent this potential relates to contemporary forces like unlimited economic growth, untrammeled technological development, and power unleashed—along with their eventual accompanying institutions, such as state mechanisms, the market mechanism, military mechanisms, the party, and even the formal democratic mechanism. The hypothesis suggests that historically, driven by absolute *ends*, people (including politicians, economists, and scientists) are capable of recruiting and justifying *means*, such as unhampered technological development and unimpeded economic growth, as the indispensable forces needed to achieve a better society. Moreover, such forces and powers may well remain generally appealing and seductive today, particularly if people see these dynamic forces or powers as the ultimate levers by which to set things in motion. The illusion may then be created that the idol possesses a life of its own—perhaps the very illusion reflected in the comments highlighted earlier by the postmodernist Jean Baudrillard.

Finally, venerating a certain force or type of knowledge as something that by definition brings prosperity or security implies that in specific circumstances we may be prepared to place our lives under the control of such a power, a power that would not exist without our efforts. At the heart of that transfer of control may be a need for certainty, an urge to feel as though there is a power greater than us that can regulate our lives. It may be born out of fear that we have little or no control over our world. And for some today, following the dictates of the market, technology, or the state may offer that sense of security. But then the ultimate irony, the role reversal characteristic of idol worship, has been achieved: what we ourselves have created ends up controlling us. The instruments must be obeyed, even if they require sacrifices—such as damage to health, deterioration of the environment, the loss of privacy, the threat of unemployment, or the perilous undermining of peace.[19] In principle, every ideology is able to summon its own tools or instruments, either forces or institutions, whose exacting demands elude scrutiny and critique.

Ideology and Us

"Ideology," "idolatry"—these words may still sound heavy and miles removed from us and our own world. Perhaps we feel angry at the accusation that we may have something to do with them. Certainly we ordinary people, we Westerners, are not possessed, goal-crazed, or fanatic. Even the mere suggestion goes too far.

But the distance between us and ideology is not as great as we may think. To begin with, an ideology does not need a broad base of support to exist. It can prosper on a small scale in any of our lives. All of us know of times when a certain goal takes on extraordinary importance for us. We may feel threatened by the possible loss of jobs, children, spouses, or money, or we may set our hearts on acquiring something that suddenly seems within reach. Then we utilize everything at our disposal to reach our goals. The goals become something that we pursue with all the strength we can muster. If necessary we adjust our standards a little, just as the dominant ideologies do, in order to give us more room to act as we like. The persons or things whose help we need to reach our goals suddenly become uncommonly important. Gradually we become dependent on them, and because of our dependence, they gain power over us. If they wish, they can manipulate us and even make humiliating demands. If for the sake of our goals we comply, then those persons or things have become our gods. The roles have been reversed: self-governing powers control us for as long as our dependence exists and our goals are not reached.

Furthermore, all the dominant ideologies have their origin in immediate and personal circumstances. They almost always arise in situations where something basic is lacking. An ideology may arise in a situation of horrible injustice, as it did in France shortly before the French Revolution, when the pact between clergy and nobility ravaged the rural communities. Or an ideology may arise in a situation of great external threat, as when a foreign enemy threatens our nation's existence and everything we cherish within it. Or again an ideology may arise in a situation of terrible poverty, which, if not eliminated, would cause the deaths of us and our families. Without such deep-seated causes, an ideology will not generate a genuine movement. It anchors itself in something that is fundamentally wrong or that threatens people mercilessly. Because it offers an alternative, often a utopian alternative, an ideology grips the hearts and behavior of people. From that point on, people will consider legitimate any means of breaking out of their awful impasse.

We must remember the modest origins of ideology, because the dominant ideologies of our time are not small, static systems but dynamic forces whose powerful momentum pushes us along with them.

Since that is the case, let us learn more about how ideologies emerge and gain control, using some of the great ideologies of the recent past as our instructors.

/ 3 /

IDEOLOGIES THAT SPEARHEAD RADICAL CHANGE

In chapter 2 we cited four goals that persons or societies can make absolute. The first one we called the systematic resistance of all exploitative, oppressive, and dehumanizing powers that prevent the arrival of a better society. Oppression in a society can become so rampant that its elimination, by whatever means are available, becomes an all-consuming end for many people. To this day, ideologies of revolution originate in that experience. They belong to a type of ideology aimed at spearheading or inciting radical societal change. The ideology of the French Revolution was born as a response to horrific exploitation, carried out under the existing empire of clergy and nobility (the ancien régime, an oppressive, feudal system). Oppression in the French countryside, particularly by the landed nobility, was so severe that children died like rats. The average life expectancy was about thirty years. Most church leaders and members of the French nobility shrouded this oppression in a resounding silence. It thus is no wonder that the revolutionist bomb detonated at that time. The French Enlightenment thinkers viewed the church and nobility as barriers to the arrival of a better society, and their all-controlling aim was to radically sweep them out of the way. As we saw, the French Revolution ideology conscripted all forces and means into the service of this end, even radically transforming moral standards. It sought to bring the French people into a "higher history."

What was the outcome of this fully developed, radical ideology? The question has utmost significance today because we continue to encounter a number of extreme, violent, revolutionist ideologies in various places throughout the world.[1] But the question is significant for another reason. Earlier we suggested that fully developed ideologies are the birthplace of new, modern idols or gods. If that is true, then we ought to be able to clearly detect the activity of the gods throughout the rise and fall of ideologies.

The French Revolution died as a result of its own violence. The revolutionists put their faith in violence as a necessary but liberating power, and that power betrayed its makers. But is that the case with other ideologies that have spearheaded radical societal change, such as Soviet Communism? Did idolatry play a role there too?

We now trace the history of the Soviet Communist ideology of revolution in an attempt to answer that question. In doing so we discover that ideologies follow a certain developmental time line or timetable. We suggest that each full-fledged, mature ideology has a powerful inner dynamic that propels the ideology through a series of stages or phases. Identifying those phases will help us in the next chapters, where we address today's world and the contemporary ideologies that operate actively within it in different ways. With the help of this time line, we may be able to recognize and distinguish ideologies that are less developed than others.

Marxism-Leninism in the Soviet Union

As Soviet Communism moved through the late 1980s, it marched unwittingly toward its own end. Perestroika and glasnost signaled a sea change in the thinking of many prominent Communists. The Iron Curtain began to wobble, revealing ever more dissent and dissatisfaction. Before long the process culminated in the spectacular implosion of the Soviet Union in 1989 and the later splintering of its pieces into self-ruling republics. The internal inconsistencies of Soviet Communism ultimately led to its demise.

For some time already, a number of Communist thinkers had lamented these inconsistencies. Many distinguished and convinced Communists had gradually become bitter and alienated over the condition of contemporary Communism, especially the state Communism behind the Iron Curtain. They felt that Communism in practice had come into conflict with its own ideals. The Pole Leszek Kolakowski, the Yugoslav Milovan Djilas, and the East German Rudolf Bahro, to name a few, all concluded that the oppression in their countries was never the intention of Marx and his original collaborators.[2] But their thesis presents us with a puzzling dilemma. For if oppression was not the intention of Marx, then where did the oppression within all Marxist countries come from?

Marx himself never wanted to use the word "ideology" to describe the scientific socialism or communism that he advocated. Instead, he used the word to depict the harsh capitalism of his time. He believed that within bourgeois society the elite promotes and upholds a false consciousness, an ideology, in order to justify its own position. The ideology of the ruling class justified the suppression of others. For Marx, the Christian faith was part of the ideology. Christianity was part of a capitalist system that used belief in God to perpetuate itself.

Already with Lenin some things changed. Lenin labeled Communism (or Socialism) itself an ideology. Communism had to be forged into a weapon in the most important struggle in the world: the class struggle. This conflict demanded not just economic means, such as strikes or violence. It also required that the consciousness of the working class be directed ideologically toward the one great ideal: the overthrow of the existing social order and the establishment of a new society based on the collective ownership of the means of production. The element of the human will to achieve the Communist goal played a much more important role for Lenin than it did for Marx. Marx saw the revolution as the closure of an internal development within capitalism toward self-annihilation. He viewed the labor class as a kind of suffering messiah, destined to save the world according to the unbreakable laws of history. Lenin, by contrast, consciously sought to bring about the annihilation of capitalism, and he considered every means permissible to that end. Lenin created a fully developed ideology, complete with an antithesis between good (the proletariat, working class) and evil (the bourgeoisie, middle class), which he took from Marx. All evil in the world could be traced to capitalism.

The ideology also had its own morality:

> Morality is anything and everything that destroys the old exploiting society and unites the working people around the proletariat, those who are building up a new, communist society.[3] The Communists must be prepared to make every sacrifice, and, if necessary, even to resort to all sorts of cunning, schemes and stratagems, to employ illegal methods, to evade and conceal the truth.[4]

Moreover, Lenin taught a doctrine of sacrifice, or sacrificial readiness, saying that revolution is a time to wade through streams of blood. We hear in his statement an echo of what Dostoyevsky a half-century earlier had put in the mouth of Raskolnikov, the protagonist in *Crime and Punishment*:

> But if for the sake of his idea [the destruction of the present in the name of the future] such a man has to step over a corpse or wade through streams of blood, he is, in my opinion, absolutely entitled, in accordance with the dictates of his conscience, to permit himself to wade through blood, all depending on the nature and scale of the idea.[5]

But the goal of a revolution requires means for its realization. Merely transforming morality into class morality, narrowing love to class solidarity, and requiring all art and science to be partisan and side with workers in the class struggle—these were not enough. Lenin therefore called into existence technological, economic, and political means to bring the class struggle to completion. As merely one example, the electrification of Russia held top priority for Lenin; it would help deliver Russia into a new Communist era.

What happened with these means and tools? Under Nikita Khrushchev (Communist Party secretary 1953–64, premier 1958–64), war was rejected as a means for solving disputes between states. He preferred to carry the class struggle forward on the economic plane, the plane of guerrilla and related forms of activity, and the plane of ideology: "The main thing is to keep to the positions of the ideological struggle, without resorting to arms to prove that one is right."[6] The means needed to carry out the broad class struggle were bound together in an all-encompassing Central Plan. Planning, after all, is what distinguishes humanity from the animals, according to the official doctrine of Marxism-Leninism. Only central planning, or planning that exercises complete control, regulating everything, was capable of combining a rapidly expanding production apparatus, constant research and technological development, a monitored educational system, an unrestricted propaganda program, and a political and military apparatus. The Plan (Soviet Communism always wrote "Plan" with a capital "P") summoned all of technology, science, and the forces of production to do their utmost to fulfill the Communist dream of the collective ownership of the means of production under the banner "from each according to his abilities, to each according to his need."[7]

But means so chosen do not remain static. If the Plan was to serve as the indispensable instrument for reaching society's ultimate ends, then it had to be given complete sway in every aspect of society—materially, politically, and ideologically. Indeed, the Plan became elevated to an institution dispensing directives and orders that could not be second-guessed. Everyone was required to obey. Nothing could prevent the Plan from assuming total control. The Plan became a mediator between the ultimate end—the classless society—and the economic and technological means chosen to reach the end.

Historically, within two to three decades after the first five-year Central Plan was introduced in the Soviet Union, the Plan began to dominate the whole of society. Even worse, under the so-called leadership of the Party (also with a capital "P") the Plan became an instrument of terror. The Plan demanded complete obedience. The Soviet State, originally considered a temporary, limited catalyst in the transition phase from Socialism to Communism, gradually became an awesome bureaucracy. The State, in combination with the Party and the Plan, became a self-willed power, and its violence was persistent. The State, Party, and Plan towered over the Russian people as a kind of unholy Trinity, a god. And that god betrayed its makers. The bureaucracy tyrannized, and the revolution slew its own children.

Marx had predicted the death of the State. Indeed, he saw in its annihilation the very end of capitalism. But history shows that precisely the reverse took place in the Communist bloc. In his book *The Alternative in Eastern Europe*, Rudolf Bahro describes in somber detail how the State became a mute power, how the labor party turned into a mere extension of the State, and how the earlier feudal-agrarian despots had simply been replaced by industrial despots:

> "Plan together, work together, govern together!" echoes the slogan from the loudspeakers, meaning that everyone is to show more system-conforming activity in his due place. But as soon as anyone ventures to overstep the limits of the prevailing regulations and institutions, he invariably hears the real message of the government: "Cobbler, stick to your last."[8]

Elsewhere in his book, Bahro draws the conclusion: "The historical course of the Soviet Union [has been] a subjective and moral tragedy for all communists who can be taken seriously at the human level."[9] Bitterly he adds:

> In the year 1900 Lenin expected the impending people's revolution "to sweep all bestiality from the Russian soil." Instead, the tremendous progress of the Soviet Union stands comparison, in the most terrible way, with the "hideous pagan idol" invoked by Marx, who would not drink the nectar but from the skulls of the slain.[10]

A revolutionist State that tyrannized everything and everyone, even its highest officials (to prevent a coup)—how far it had come from Marx's dreams and "scientific" predictions! The revolutionary ideology in action inevitably created idols—Plan, Party, and State—that sought to control everyone and everything.

But the more that Soviet society was completely controlled, and the more it became terrorized, the sooner its end became visible. The Soviet Union, a lesson from our own recent history, passed away. It collapsed and died under the crushing weight of its own obese bureaucracy. It stands as a clear example of a goal-crazed ideology that awakens forces the leaders themselves can no longer control.[11]

Six Phases of Fully Developed Ideologies

We have now gathered enough material to draw some conclusions about the inner logic of fully developed ideologies. We can distinguish six developmental phases in modern ideology. Helping to illustrate these phases are aspects of the Communist ideology, the French Revolution ideology, and the ideologies of Fascism and Nazism.

Conception

The first phase of each full-fledged modern ideology is conception. In the conception phase, the conviction develops that a radical change or intervention is required. Certain concepts and ideas demand different, perhaps more offensive, content. People begin to reflect on the end they wish to attain, and they weigh the strategic and tactical means needed for reaching the end. In the conception phase more and more people accept the idea that a specific concrete goal must be achieved at all costs. The radical Enlightenment philosophers of the French Revolution (Voltaire, Rousseau) gave words like "equality" and "freedom" new, revolution-charged meanings. Already in 1901, in his signature work, Lenin stated that "all human values, including science, art, morals, and social institutions are nothing but instruments of class interests and weapons in the political struggle."[12] Using the distortion of reigning norms and values, the ideology recruits disciples, and the critical moment arrives for potentially successful action.[13] The highly charged, explosive moment for setting the ideology in motion has crystallized.

Actualization

The second phase is actualization. Here the ideology becomes real flesh and blood. The sole object of its disciples is to reorient society entirely according to the fundamental pattern of the end. The ideology's adherents do not shrink from acts of violence because, without question, the end justifies the means. For the French Revolutionists, the end was the arrival of a society of freedom, equality, and brotherhood. For the Communist revolutionists, it was the advent of a classless society. For the Nazis, it was the coming of the Third Reich, cleansed of all non-Germanic influences.

The French Revolution ideology, the Communist Revolution ideology, and Nazism were all designed to spearhead radical social change, and each had a distinct birth date and birthplace. The French Revolution was born in Paris in 1789, when the absolute authority of the French king was renounced during an oath-taking ceremony. The Communist Revolution burst onto the scene in Moscow in 1917, when Lenin grabbed power. The birthplace of Nazism was Berlin in 1933, when Hitler was elected to power as the Reich's chancellor and declared the unity of party and state. Clearly, modern ideologies are tied to concrete reality in powerful, dynamic ways. They will use every means available to come alive, to become incarnate. At such pivotal moments, everything strains toward concrete implementation. All real and imagined power, including rage and intellectual combativeness, is concentrated on that objective.

(Re)construction

After actualization comes (re)construction. Obviously, a new, improved society must now appear. But how can that happen? What strategy will be needed to attain it? At this moment distorted norms and values need to demonstrate their full power. People must be taught to think and behave in terms of reaching the all-encompassing objective. Only after this is it possible to fully deploy the means, both forces and institutions, needed to attain the end. Earlier we saw that, under both Soviet Communism and Nazism, the Party was given a key role as the instrument of change, despite the fact that Nazism would seem to be the polar opposite of Soviet Communism. For both, in practice, the Party was in charge of the state.

The new society receives its form out of chaos; it arises as a creation brought about by the new humanity. In Marxism, as we saw earlier, humanity is by definition a creator: the use of plans and tools distinguishes humanity from animals. The new humanity must differentiate itself from the old. The Nazi terms *Übermensch* (superhuman) and *Untermensch* (subhuman) distinguished the Germanic people as superhuman and the non-Aryans (Jews) as subhuman, and each was treated accordingly. During the French Revolution, the real distinction was whether or not one belonged to the commoners, the citizens. Not being a citizen was the same as being an outlaw. Ideologies always possess different visions of humanity, visions that fill in the blanks of what has been stripped bare.

Domination

After the (re)construction phase comes domination. This phase begins at the stunning moment when the means or instruments deployed
achieve a kind of autonomy or self-sufficiency. In the (re)construction
phase, the means still appear to be entirely subject to the will of their
makers and users. Now, however, the opposite becomes true: the means
appear to coerce their users. And it is indeed coercion. The adherents of
the ideology must allow for autonomy in the reign of the means in order
to enable them to function as redemptive powers. Indeed, it is everyone's
social duty to accept their demands. The Plan binds everyone.

The domination phase is critical because it contains the epiphany, the
revelation of the power of the idols as pseudosaviors. All the hallmarks
of idol worship described earlier apply here. In particular, the means
appear to possess a life of their own. They are able to make demands
from which there is no escape. A narrowing of consciousness or awareness also takes place. In both Soviet Communism and Nazism, massive
propaganda fascinated and mesmerized the whole of society and made
known the so-called will of the State and the Party. People had to speak
well of State and Party and falsely please them. A collection of essays by
former Czech President Václav Havel is entitled *Living in Truth*,[14] because
in such situations living in the lie is a matter of course. Illusion rather
than a sense of reality encompasses all of society, and survival requires
playing by the rules of that grave game.

Terror

Independence and domination then usher in terror. In the terror phase,
the new gods throw down their masks. The objectives no longer seem
achievable. They fade into the woodwork. But the power invested in the
forces and institutions of compulsory progress rave on because they
have reached a point of no return. The obstacles blocking the path to
compassion and solidarity are insurmountable. In the French Revolution, this was the time of the Jacobins and Robespierre. For the Nazis,
it was the time of mass deportations to the concentration camps. For
the Russians, it was the time of the gulags. The demonic becomes visible
in its most ghastly form.

Dissolution

Terror then runs its course and gives way to dissolution. Each mature ideology is not only a powerful, earth-scorching project but also is

always based on a reduced, truncated view of humanity and the world. In the end, the plans devised in the minds of intellectuals and around kitchen tables (think of Nietzsche's image of the lantern) do not square with reality in all of the fullness with which God has created it. In fact, they openly conflict with reality. The distortion created by the ideology becomes so profound that its defenders can no longer prevent the demise of the ideology. Either the world itself would succumb to the ideology and be led to the abyss—in which case the demonic would have won—or the ideology itself dies and succumbs to the claims of reality, thanks to whatever deep resistance people are able to marshal against it. The dissolution or death phase of a full-fledged ideology brings to mind the "Twilight of the Gods" in German mythology, captured, for example, by Wagner in his famous opera "The Ring of the Nibelung." In the "Twilight of the Gods" myth, it is not people but the gods who have become corrupt. When things have gone that far, then people feel they have no choice but to commit suicide, as Hitler did in his death bunker. The declared death of God and God's subsequent replacement by the gods (as in Nietzsche) ultimately lead to suicide.

In summary, a modern, fully developed ideology passes through six developmental stages or phases. They are conception, actualization, (re)construction, domination, terror, and dissolution.

We have paid careful attention to ideology's developmental time line before exploring in the next chapters whether our own age displays any of the powers and influences of ideology. Already we have learned two significant lessons. First, understanding ideology's developmental phases has shown us that modern ideology is, above all, a dynamic power in action. An ideology may begin as an idea or concept, emerging out of profound emotion and the inventiveness of the human mind. But it does not rest until it has shaken and transformed reality itself in the face of significant, powerful resistance. To overcome the obstacles, it requires a high-voltage concentration of energy and sacrifice, and it needs to sustain the absolute determination and engagement of its disciples. As a result, each genuine ideology possesses a thoroughly earthbound, dynamistic character. Like a hurricane, an ideology breaks open a path for itself toward the coast of human civilization and then rushes on far inland. Perhaps the apostle Paul had something like this in mind when he talked about a future in which powers (literally, "energies") of deception would cause people to choose lies instead of truth.[15]

Second, before this discussion we could only distinguish between different types of ideologies—modern and premodern. Now, however, we are also able to detect the extent to which an ideology has ripened. State Communism, German Fascism, and the French Revolution ideologies all displayed phases of terror and disintegration. But people can wake up and call a halt to an ideology before it reaches its final phases. In the coming chapters we shall indeed encounter less-developed ideologies. Core civic values that have not been ideologically distorted are still apparent in society. Such values then act as a brake on the dynamism that propels an ideology through its phases. They restrain the ideology from reaching its bitter end. For at least as long as that brake remains functional, the actual power of the ideology remains ambiguous.

Recognizing the possible presence of a brake is critical for another reason. Sometimes, as we shall encounter in part 3, a situation arises that can reactivate an ideology through its interaction with another ideology. In a diabolical alliance, ideologies may actually summon each other into action. And then, unless God and people step in, there is no stopping the downward spirals that they whirl into motion.

SEGUE 1

FEAR, LONGING, AND TRUST

We began this book by sketching the sense of uncertainty and powerlessness that many people experience in our time. A watershed moment has been crystallizing: much has come to an end, but a new beginning has not yet been announced. On the contrary, the massive, urgent problems of our time, particularly those that play out on a global scale (such as global poverty, environmental degradation, and worldwide aggression), no longer seem to have cures. They have built up immunity against the standard remedies. The solutions, in large part, also seem to belong to the past.

This startling development has led us to advocate for investigating together the deeper, even spiritual dimensions of the paralysis and agonizing uncertainty plaguing our world today. That has led us to probe the role of ideologies in modern and postmodern society, including the influence of the contemporary gods following in their footsteps. We found that, due to terrible deprivation or violence, human beings can come to fear their surrounding world; they then begin to long for an absolute goal that will satiate their fear, and they consequently put their trust in a god who will satisfy that deepest longing and calm their fears.

In part 1 we saw how ideologies and their gods have continually cast a shadow over modern Western history. Society tried to systematically banish all religious factors. It wanted to make a completely new beginning based solely on human intellect. But in doing so, society then became deeply vulnerable to the source of ideologies and to their truncated worldviews, resulting in sometimes abhorrent forms of terror and spiritual enslavement.

In part 2 we return to the concrete. The basic question is this: are ideologies active in our time? If so, how, and where? If we find that, contrary to the many arguments boasting that we have now arrived at the end of ideology, ideological influences still operate today, then we will have stumbled upon something extraordinarily important. Not only would we understand our own time better, but more important, certain new paths toward resolution might open up for problems that currently seem impossible to solve. By now these problems have eaten through the fabric of life so far and so deep that, unless God prevents it, they may drag us and the world itself toward the abyss.

In the final chapter of this book we bear witness to new hope in the sense hinted at above. But at this stage we may state that if today's paralyzing uncertainty and agonizing problems do indeed have deep, spiritual roots (roots that are ideological), then only a spiritual turn or reversal, a turn at the level of people's deepest longings and convictions, will be able to generate practical ways out of today's stubborn dilemmas. Problem-management solutions articulated independently of such a turn will not be effective. Such an approach would merely replicate our current impasse; in its desire to micromanage by using only human intellect to solve the problems, it would reflect adherence to a goal orientation. Consequently, we do not provide such solutions in this book.

PART 2

// CONTEMPORARY IDEOLOGIES IN ACTION //

/ 4 /

IDENTITY UNLEASHED

Ideologies do not arise accidentally. They need deep injustices or threats to take hold. The ideology of identity, which aims for the preservation of group or national identity, is a case in point. After World War I, for example, Hitler used and misused the deep feelings of frustration and injury of the German people to assure the success of his National Socialist ideology. Without a previous history of wounded pride, the German people would not have embraced fascism so enthusiastically.[1] In a similar way, the more recent fascist dictators in South America have appealed to past national resentment to unite the masses behind their corrupt regimes. The collective unconscious of a people harbors motives that can be and often are misused.

The nationalist ideology makes huge gains when a religious element is added to it. One of the original emblems of fascism acknowledges a close link between nation and religion: a bundle of arrows or rods (fasces) is linked to a whole in which the symbols of the church and the state stand at the center. This false link between throne and altar is typical of most nationalist ideologies. The clergy and military work hand in hand to create national unity. "One people, one nation, one leader," said Hitler. The leadership stands against the equality of the people, autocracy resists democracy, and compassion and peacemaking are mocked as forms of weakness and cowardice. Sometimes a prominent military leadership tolerates and uses the church, as in Mussolini's Italy and in some of the military regimes of South America. Or the religious leadership may be dominant, as in Europe in the early Middle Ages and as, in its own way, in Iran today.

Apartheid

In the twentieth century, the ideology of identity played powerfully into the consciousness of the Afrikaners in South Africa, the people responsible for establishing apartheid. White Afrikaners repeatedly feared for their own existence. They first fled English colonialism in the 1830s and then suffered under history's first concentration camps, set up by the British in the Second Boer War (1899–1902). The camps claimed the lives of twenty-six thousand men, women, and children.

In such circumstances it is understandable that maintaining a people's identity, including its language, culture, freedoms, and rights, takes on an enormous, even all-encompassing significance. In the multiracial society of South Africa, where the Afrikaners formed a clear minority, the Afrikaners sought to develop powerful means or tools to protect their people. They created apartheid, a monstrously oppressive and unjust system of complex legal and political measures. A strong security force was designed to quell all opposition and ensure the safety, security, and preservation of the Afrikaners, regardless of the consequences for the majority of non-Afrikaners living in South Africa.

How did white Christian Afrikaners wash their hands of such deep injustice? An ideology captivated their hearts and minds and ruled their consciousness. Indeed, South African apartheid demonstrated the power of a genuine ideology. At its heart burned the deeply mythical conviction that a direct covenant had been instituted between God and the minority white Afrikaner people of South Africa. The covenant had its beginnings especially in what seemed to be a miraculous, divinely ordained battle at Blood River on December 16, 1838, where three thousand Zulus died but not one Afrikaner. The Afrikaners saw their victory as the sign of a new covenant, the beginning of a new exodus from oppression.[2] To keep this covenant, the Afrikaners needed to preserve their identity at all costs. They therefore redirected the biblical concepts of love and justice. They bent love to apply primarily to sustaining an unflagging dedication to their own chosen people and bent justice largely to defending the rights of Afrikaners.[3] But their actions demonstrated unequivocally how far these reconfigured values had moved from the gospel they claimed, a gospel that calls for equal justice for all people and agape, an unconditional love that crosses all boundaries of nation and class.

In apartheid, even the love of self was absorbed into the primary, sacrificial dedication expected of every Afrikaner to ensure the survival of

God's Afrikaner people. When standing in front of the mammoth pioneer monument outside of Pretoria, one feels something of the absorption of the self into the single-minded will of the Afrikaner people to preserve their identity at any price. Every year at noon on the Day of the Covenant, December 16, a tiny hole in the dome allows a stream of light to fall precisely on the central letter *o* in the words *Ons vir jou, Suid Afrika* (We sacrifice ourselves for you, South Africa) engraved in granite.[4]

What strikes one about the South African example is how the means of an ideology can take on their own sinister strength and expand into vicious powers. Eventually, the apartheid legislation became more and more difficult to maintain. Increasingly, it led to unscrupulous injustice and brushed harder against the grain of reality. Even police sympathetic to the government found the laws hard to put into effect. When some people randomly selected black youths to be burned in gasoline, the brutal, all-encompassing demands of the ideology began to turn the hearts and minds of people against it. Ironically, the seeds of apartheid's destruction lay in the very ideology that created and sustained it.

Official Afrikaner apartheid existed in the previous century. What situations present themselves today? Since 1990, in the power vacuum created in the aftermath of the Cold War and especially in situations of chronic deprivation, identity conflicts have erupted in various places around the world.[5] Already by 1993 Ernie Regehr had observed that "some estimates count as many as seventy current political conflicts worldwide that involve groups formally organized to promote collective identity issues."[6] Of the thirty-two armed conflicts that took place in 2004, all but one were identity-driven, intrastate civil wars; the lone exception was the conflict in Iraq.[7] A wide range of commentators predict that conflicts over collective and group identity will dominate the twenty-first century.[8]

Is it possible that ideology occupies a place in some or even most of these contemporary conflicts? To find out, we focus on two of the most deeply entrenched, endemic identity disputes today—the battle of radical Islam against the West and the Palestinian-Israeli conflict—searching for whether ideology plays a role in their stubborn intractability. But first we must offer a caveat.

A Caveat

In 1978 the Palestinian intellectual Edward W. Said published a remarkable book called *Orientalism*.[9] It garnered widespread acclaim. *The New York Times* described it as "intellectual history at a very high level, and particularly exciting." With the aid of numerous examples,

Said showed how the West colors its view of the people and societies of the East with any number of rather useful but false assumptions. He captured that distorted view in the term "Orientalism."[10] Orientalism, he argued, is an ideological creation by which European writers, thinkers, and colonial administrators deal with the "other" of Eastern culture, customs, and religious beliefs. Often, argued Said, the root of Orientalism lies in European imperialism and racism: "Who could deny that they [views of "us" and "them"] were shot through with doctrines of European superiority, various kinds of racism, imperialism, and the like, dogmatic views of 'the Oriental'?"[11]

Does a distortion like this operate only in one direction? In a stimulating essay called *Occidentalism: The West in the Eyes of Its Enemies*, Ian Buruma and Avishai Margalit show that the reverse is also true.[12] On occasion, opponents of the Western worldview see Western culture as, by definition, the essence of immorality and depravity. They sometimes view the West simply as "rootless, cosmopolitan, superficial, trivial, materialistic, racially mixed, [and a] fashion-addicted civilization."[13] Various Islamic writers sharply condemn the West's devotion to the material world as a direct denial of Allah and therefore as idolatrous.[14]

It is not our intention to join the ongoing Orientalism/Occidentalism debate.[15] But we do wish to draw a lesson from it. In a chapter such as this, focused on deeply held identities whose origins are often non-Western, as authors we must not consider ourselves as being free from possible prejudices. Therefore we seek to adopt utmost caution in our discussions and adhere as closely as possible to concrete circumstances. At the same time, especially here, we want to remain entirely open to any serious critique that would expose any potential bias or one-sidedness on our part. Ideologies always predispose one to misconstrue.

Islamism

"Everything changed on September 11." That phrase is repeated by many Westerners and emblazoned on their hearts. On that day, al-Qaeda operatives used three commercial airplanes to attack the Pentagon and the Twin Towers. A fourth plane crashed before hitting its intended target, thought to be the White House. In the few hours that it took to put into action a calculated assault on the symbols of Western power, committed Islamist warriors propelled what had been a regional conflict into the world community's primary topic of conversation. The attackers were dedicated to the elimination of Western influence in historically Islamic lands and to the establishment of pure Islamic nations.

Western eyes were glued to television broadcasts both of people jumping tragically to their deaths to escape the burning towers and of the final collapse of New York City's famous international financial centers. To the viewers, the actions of the hijackers were numbingly wanton. Even before the September terrorist attacks, some Westerners had wrongly viewed Islam as a violent, barbaric, and antidemocratic religion. Such stereotypes have been handed down since the time of the Crusades.[16] For those Westerners, the hijackings were the final gavel proclaiming the collective guilt of Muslims as people who practice an aggressive, virulent, and provincial religion.

That final judgment has produced the improbable consequence that ordinary Muslims are among the primary victims of the September 11 attacks. Sadly, the September 11 attacks have reinforced the unfortunate view of some in the West that most Muslims follow a fanatically violent religion. The proponents of anti-Islamism focus on such a small percentage of Muslims that the vast majority of peace-loving Muslims, who lead pious lives centered on the teaching of the Prophet in the Qur'an, become badly morphed into being adherents of an inherently violent religion.

This reality—the primary victimization of Muslims as a consequence of Muslim extremism—only makes the question more pressing: how could Muslim extremists, who represent such a narrow band within Islam, carry out such horrific attacks? To make the issue even more difficult, Islamist militants do not shy away from totalitarian language; instead, they go on the offensive, systematically attacking their enemy. What could be behind this movement and its leaders such as Osama bin Laden, who speaks about "fighting against the enemy" by doing "whatever you can"?[17] How can this strand of devout Islamist believers justify such diabolical behavior?

Typical answers in the West have included the following: it would seem that many Muslims hate us. They are jealous. They are crazy. Or they are angry at Western/American colonialism or neocolonial economic exploitation.[18] But when we dig a bit deeper by examining what militant Muslims are actually saying, we find something substantially different.

Resuscitating Islamic Greatness

The Glory Days and Their Demise

Basil Davidson, the great African historian, once said that African history is so unknown that it is almost as if it has never occurred. To the Western consciousness, it is almost as if Muslims never once dominated the world. But from the late seventh century until the late seventeenth century, Islam controlled a significant part of the globe. Its influence extended from the western tip of Africa to Europe, the Middle East, and even into Southeast Asia. Islam also controlled major trade routes, a reality that, among other things, forced Columbus to look westward for a pathway to the treasures of the Far East. While Europe struggled through the fairly chaotic Dark Ages, Muslims developed great medieval empires. Islamic civilization preserved the learning of the ancient Greeks and Romans, developed highly complex and efficient governments that united and kept the peace over vast territories and varied peoples, and established schools and universities that produced some of the greatest writers, poets, scientists, theologians, and mystics in history.[19]

But gradually things changed. Defeat followed defeat, and Muslim influence collapsed. Grandeur descended into despair.

The beginning of this shift occurred on September 12, 1683, when the combined military forces of Europe defeated the Ottoman Turks. A succession of other losses followed. In a struggle that took place over the next two centuries, European forces regained their land and moved further into Middle Eastern countries. Yet even despite this and drawing on their own rich tradition, most Muslims at the turn of the twentieth century found much to celebrate about Western culture. Karen Armstrong, a prescient commentator, observes:

> At the beginning of the twentieth century nearly every single Muslim intellectual was in love with the West, admired its modern society, and campaigned for democracy and constitutional government in their own countries. Instead of seeing the West as their enemy, they recognized it as compatible with their own traditions. We should ask ourselves why we have lost this goodwill.[20]

After the Ottoman Empire allied with the Germans in World War I, it finally completely collapsed. In the aftermath of that war, the League of Nations set up European control over Middle Eastern countries, largely in the spirit of the "Orientalism" described by Said. For some, the enemy therefore now controlled Islamic territory. In his November 3, 2001, videotape broadcast, Osama bin Laden said, "Following World War I, which ended more than eighty-three years ago, the whole Islamic world fell under the Crusader banner—under the British, French, and Italian governments. They divided the whole world."[21] The greatest possible catastrophe had now occurred: the enemy, the infidel Crusaders, now controlled the holy lands of Islam. And the occupiers had to be removed.

With the demise of the empire came a profound threat to the identity of the Muslims, who asked, "Who are we as Muslims?" The answer had been clear for a millennium, even alongside Western civilization. But now Western modernity threatened to undo Islam altogether. In its encounter with modernity, the Ottoman Empire not only ultimately failed to accommodate itself; it also was literally defeated. The empire was unable to fit into the modern world after the Peace of Westphalia inaugurated the nation-state system in 1648. Then, after humiliating defeat at the end of World War I, a sense of alienation, hopelessness, and despair set in.[22]

How do people respond when their heart, who they are, their very identity, is at stake? For a few Muslims, a new goal crystallized: we, the militants, must restore the original grandeur of Islam. We must resuscitate the Pax Islamica, based on Sharia law. We may justify any violence in the name of this goal. The promises of Muhammad had been realized for nearly a millennium, but now they are lost. We must return Islam to its rightful place and restore the identity of the Muslim people. Achieving that goal requires removing, with the use of any available force, the invaders who dominate the holy lands of the Middle East.

But this development raises disturbing questions. It is not merely a distortion or alternative interpretation of Islam. Perhaps here we observe the absolutization of a goal (preserving Islamic identity) and the sweeping justification of any means needed to realize that goal. The means consist of using calculated violence to remove unfavorable regimes, enforcing strict Islamist (Sharia) law, and creating as much instability in the modern international system of nation-states as possible. "Islamism," to use a phrase coined by Bassam Tibi, a Muslim expert on Islam at the University of Göttingen, is "a *modern* phenomenon dressed up in traditional symbols."[23] That raises the possibility that Islamic extremism, which seeks to radically overhaul the international system of nation-states and replace it with an Islamic order, actually employs modern, totalitarian ideology. Tibi claims that Islamism is not "an expression of religious revival, but rather a pronouncement of a new order," an order that "is nothing less than a vision of totalitarian rule." He concludes that Islamists "are far more dangerous as ideologues of power than as extremists who kill."[24] As unexpected as it may seem, we may then not exclude the possibility that Islamism is a modern ideology, an identity ideology birthed in modernism's attempt to eradicate the Ottoman Empire.

Enemy #1: The Crusaders

Suppose we explore whether a number of trademarks of ideology are present in al-Qaeda's pursuit. The restoration of a pure, unadulterated

Islam—the objective that drives al-Qaeda—can certainly function as an ideological goal. In pursuit of that objective, Osama bin Laden calls on his followers to engage in an all-out conflict of Islam against its enemies. In a 1998 Al-Jazeera interview, he said, "There are two parties to the conflict: World Christianity, which is allied with Jews and Zionism, led by the United States, Britain, and Israel. The second party is the Islamic world."[25] His belief is that the only cure for Islam's fall to Christendom is to throw out the infidel and return Islam to a puritanical form, for it is the apostasy of Muslims themselves that has contributed to their downfall. And restoring Islamic greatness first in the homeland and then globally requires defeating today's powers, for they represent a barrier to the vision of Islamic greatness.

Militants dedicate themselves to this cause with singularity of purpose. Indeed, they have become possessed by the goal of Islamic resuscitation. This goal drives them to warn their enemy to stay away or, as al-Qaeda put it in a letter, "Leave us alone, or expect us in Washington and New York."[26] The militants regard such warnings as not only permissible but admirable. They are fighting a holy battle, a war on behalf of Allah himself. Here we detect the smug air of self-righteousness found among ideologues.

We notice too that the cause of restoring Islamic grandeur is so significant that it sanctions any and all possible means to bring it about. In the aftermath of the September 11 attacks, bin Laden said, "It is our religious duty to resist this [Western] occupation with all the power we have and to punish it, using the same means it is pursuing against us."[27] Violence, no matter how ghastly, becomes the key means by which to overthrow the occupier and reinstall legitimate Islamic regimes. This spirit is captured in the full name of al-Qaeda: The World Islamic Front for Holy War against Jews and Crusaders.

Moreover, historical progression and dynamism characterize Islamism's call to violence. Originally, the call to violence was oriented toward the goal of liberation from the enemy, the Crusaders. The means have now evolved to include an element of violence for mass destruction. Apparently any means are now not only justified but also required, and not only for victory but also to inflict as much pain as possible onto the enemy. On September 11, Osama bin Laden clearly wanted to hit as many people as he possibly could. The attacks of that day betray an ideological devotion.

Finally, the cause of overthrowing one's enemies and reinstituting proper governments also sanctions any and every sacrifice. Osama bin Laden honored the dead hijackers of September 11: "We hope that these brothers are among the first martyrs in Islam's battle in this era against the new Christian-Jewish crusade led by the big crusader Bush under the flag of the

Cross; this battle is considered one of Islam's battles."[28] He similarly vener-
ated those who died in earlier terrorist attacks: "I hold in great esteem and
respect these great men . . . when they carried out the bombings in Riyadh,
al-Khubar [both in Saudi Arabia], East Africa, and elsewhere."[29]

Enemy #2: Moderate Islamic Regimes

The Crusaders are not the only enemies. So also are moderate Muslim
regimes. The primary enemy among today's militant Islamists is the
present regime of Saudi Arabia. The Saudi government has done the
unthinkable: it has united with a Crusader, the United States, by forming
a long-term strategic alliance with it for security and energy reasons.
Perhaps worst of all, the Saudis have allowed American troops—infidel
troops—to station themselves on the holy soil of Saudi Arabia, home to
Islam's two holiest sites, Mecca and Medina.[30] The militants interpret the
American-Saudi friendship as sanctioning the occupation of the holiest
places of Islam, a source of deep anger. Osama bin Laden explained the
horror of Crusaders in Saudi Arabia with these words: "Now infidels
walk on the land where Muhammad was born and where the Qur'an
was revealed to him."[31] The enemy is within the gates.

A Non-Western Ideology?

In the actions of al-Qaeda it is therefore not difficult to see signs of a
living ideology. If we consider the degree of violence used, its systematic
planning, and the willingness to sacrifice human lives for the final cause,
then that conclusion is even unavoidable. But the conclusion is also
remarkable, for Islamism appears to be vigorously opposed to modern,
Western influences! How then might an absolute ideology be present in
it? A new, self-created, absolute meaning can arise only by means of a
modern, Western process of emptying the world of meaning and then
reconstructing it according to entirely new principles. Each ideology
requires a context of deep secularization. Yet Islamism, so viciously
opposed to Western, modern influences, is ironically not an exception
to this rule.

While Islamism draws upon its own origins and resources, something
far more than a distorted interpretation of the Qur'an is at work in it.
The basic faith and attitude of Islamic militancy is actually inspired by
varieties of Western thought. As Buruma and Margalit explain, "What
makes their terror so lethal is not just the religious hatred borrowed
from old texts, which is in any case often based on distortions, but the
synthesis of religious zealotry and modern ideology, of ancient bigotry

and modern technology."[32] Indeed, the diabolical acts of the Islamists reflect nothing less than a full-fledged ideology in the nihilistic Western sense, as anticipated by Nietzsche.

In his recent book *Al Qaeda and What It Means to Be Modern*, John Gray powerfully captures this theme: "Like communism and Nazism, radical Islam is modern. Though it claims to be anti-Western, it is shaped as much by Western ideology as by Islamic traditions."[33] In a later interview, Gray explains: "It is exactly the Enlightenment which has made possible the apocalyptic terrorism of al-Qaeda. In the Islam of Christendom in the Middle Ages, it was unthinkable that people would establish with their own hands a paradise on earth—that lay in the hands of God. That is the reason that I say that al-Qaeda is modern."[34] Al-Qaeda is not a relic from a backward past but rather a globalized, multinational ideology. Militant Islam therefore represents much more than a protest movement, an outburst of a strongly revolutionist group of people.

Muslim militants studied in the West, adopted the Western under-standing of ideology, and formed their entire approach to life around an ideological reshaping of Islam. Educated in a modern world and in modern ways, Muslim militants are shaped as much or even more by the Western world as by traditional Islam, of which, some suggest, they are largely ignorant. The potent mix of deep injury and Western ideology gives Islamic militancy its explosive power.

As we have argued, ideologies always call forth idols. The radical Is-lamist identity ideology summons the idol of power unleashed: violence. Particularly when it links violence to the glory of martyrdom, the Islamist ideology even seems to sanction prostration before violence. As with all idols, however, the god ultimately turns the tables and becomes the con-trolling force. Here the god demands more and more sacrifices and greater and greater violence. Not long after the Coalition invasion of Iraq, Islamic militants engaged in a campaign of beheading foreigners there in order to achieve their own goal of ridding that country of enemy influence. Many in the West were horrified in the summer of 2004 when they watched the video of American Nick Berg being beheaded.

What is particularly shocking is the repeated blend of diabolical vio-lence with calculated rationality. The use of passenger airplanes as bombs for one's own devastating purposes is as demonic as it is rationally cal-culated and coldheartedly planned. Neither Islam nor Christianity can sanction that chilling combination. Religions like Islam and Christianity are oriented toward "ways" of life, especially to taking beginning steps of faith down such ways; Islamism, like all ideologies, is oriented to achieving an "end" or "goal."

In Islamic militancy, therefore, we find the end (goal) of Islamic gran-deur made absolute, the subsequent value conversion of Islam's norms and principles, the redefinition of evil as those who oppose the cause, and the elevation of violence into a redeeming force, even to the point where the ideology's adherents sacrifice human life to the idol and venerate those who die for the cause.

Earlier we recognized the tragic irony that Muslims themselves are among the primary victims in the aftermath of the September 11 attacks. In the following chapters we explore some of the ideological backdrop behind the West's perpetration of this victimization. But here let us highlight the paradox that so many Muslims suffer at the hands of Islamist terrorists, even though both claim the Qur'an as their guide and Allah as their Source. It is specifically the presence of a modern, nihilist ideology among the small but growing strand of Islamist extremists that sheds light on this seemingly impossible contradiction. The discrepancy arises because Islamism has profoundly transformed the values outlined in the Qur'an to suit the purposes of the terrorists, just as Lenin once altered "truth" and Hitler once transformed "right."

The Palestinians and the Israelis

The Palestinian-Israeli conflict, a situation where peace seems elusive, is one of the most enduring conflicts of our day. As authors living in the West, we enter into this discussion fully aware of the difficulties and challenges of understanding the dynamics at work. In Romans 11 the apostle Paul describes a fig tree in which Christians are "grafted" or "artificially implanted" into the original tree, people of the Jewish faith. With great humility in our hearts, we affirm the Jews, with Paul, as "the root that supports [us]" (Rom. 11:18 NRSV). As Christians we long to acknowledge the sins of Christians against Jews and others, acts of horrific injustice and evil deeds, knowing that the beam in our own eye is far greater than the speck in our older sibling's. In its expression historically, Christendom has shown inexcusable evidence of arrogance and acts of horror (from the Crusades through to recent times, including broad support for Nazism, apartheid, and open bombardment of civilian centers). We examine the identity ideology in this context: as faithful seekers, poignantly aware of the weaknesses and limitations of the Christian community. We seek to probe, not to declare.

Overarching Trends

Acknowledging the risk of oversimplification, we characterize with broad strokes some of the main features of this conflict.

First, at one level the Palestinians and Israelis hold fundamentally different worldviews. When it comes to time, family, individuality, community, and religious practices, each side views reality through quite different lenses. It is exceedingly difficult to reconcile with others when one group operates under paradigms that keep it from knowing where the others are coming from. Nevertheless, both sides are aware of joint historical roots, and they share a kinship of brotherhood dating back to the ancient Semites. Yet conflict between brothers can run deep, even reaching the level of hatred.[35]

Second, Palestinians and Israelis each have deep, legitimate, and passionate claims to the land. The Palestinians lived on the land for millennia, and they were not consulted in the legal decisions made in the late 1940s that dispossessed them from the land. They are descendants of the land's first inhabitants, and the third holiest site in Islam is Jerusalem. Meanwhile, so-called secular Zionists argue that historically the land rightfully belongs to the Jewish people, while so-called religious Zionists claim that God gave the Jewish people the land in ancient times. In the modern era, since 1920 Jews increasingly bought land in Israel, and shortly after World War II, the UN partitioned Palestine, giving Jews the land. They have now inhabited it for over half a century. At many levels, therefore, it remains their promised land.

Third, it is even more difficult to reconcile with people against whom your group has fought. There have been six major wars since the birth of modern-day Israel in 1948.[36] These wars have not only given the Israelis control over more land and water, but they have also significantly intensified Palestinian frustration, especially in the Occupied Territories. Conversely, from an Israeli perspective, when suicide bombers wantonly kill innocent children and loved ones, the deepening layers of trauma make the possibility of reconciliation even more elusive.

Finally, all of this is happening in a country roughly the size of Connecticut. Not only is there intense hostility between the people, but they also are forced to live in close proximity. Closeness can breed contempt.

Threatened Peoples

It comes then as no surprise that, despite their many differences, both groups perceive themselves as threatened, vulnerable peoples. The Israelis see themselves surrounded by hostile forces, some of which—Hamas, the governing party of the Palestinian National Authority; the president of Iran; and Hezbollah—have declared their explicit intent to eliminate the State of Israel. The Palestinians have witnessed Israel brutally killing their men, women, and children, bulldozing their homes, and building security walls. At their core, both have reason to believe that they are fighting for their survival, for their very existence.

Israelis

The Israelis are now defending what they had sought for more than half a century: a homeland where they would be safe from persecution. Zionism, whose dream has been a homeland for the Jews in Israel, "originated in Eastern and Central Europe in the latter part of the nineteenth century."[37] Because of the rampant anti-Semitism raging through Europe, especially in the Russian pogroms, Jews throughout Europe began to dream of a place where they could be safe and protected and where they would no longer experience vulnerability. The land would be Palestine, a land where at least some Jews had lived for a very long time. After all, from the Zionists' perspective, the land was historically and rightfully theirs.

The Zionist dream began to take on flesh and blood when, in the Balfour Declaration of 1917, the British declared that the Jews should have a homeland of their own in Palestine. At the Paris Peace Conference in February 1919, Chaim Weizmann, president of the World Zionist Organization, foresaw mass waves of Jewish immigrants heading toward Palestine. There the new country of Israel would be "as Jewish as England is English," he declared.[38]

Meanwhile, a religious Zionist movement had begun in the 1890s, but it did not gain momentum until the 1930s, when, as David Berlin reports:

> Rabbi Abraham Isaac Kook first articulated arguments that allowed religious Jews to embrace the Zionist project. Before Kook, most religious Jews held that there ought to be no state unless the Messiah declared it. Kook, on the other hand, argued that Zionism was not merely a political movement by secular Jews, but a tool of God to promote a divine scheme initiated by the return of the Jews to the promised land.[39]

Notice the dream crystallizing in this confluence of Zionist impulses: behind it lies not merely the creation of a new state but also the deliverance of a people from its enemies, a new Jewish exodus from all the Egypts of the day. Perhaps an ideology is not far away, one born out of a mix of unparalleled injustice and religious impulses. The creation of a state may refill a world emptied of meaning by indescribable suffering. What began as suffering and the destruction of meaning is taking shape in the new encompassing belief that all will be made right. Perhaps an ideology is emerging from a mixture of secular convictions about the historic rights of the Jewish people and religious belief in the centrality of the Jewish people as God's own people and of the land as God's own land.

Indeed, the Zionist desire for a place of sanctuary slowly altered traditional Jewish concepts of justice and morality. The demand for a homeland was so strong that many principles, even those regarding the treatment of fellow human beings, were gradually altered in order to accomplish the goal. In 1937 Chaim Weizmann said, "In the course of time we shall expand to the whole country. . . . This [partition] is only an arrangement for the next 15–30 years."[40] The next year David Ben-Gurion, later Israel's first prime minister, asserted, "After we become a strong force, as a result of the creation of a state, we shall abolish partition and expand to the whole of Palestine."[41] One was left to wonder what would become of the Palestinians. Ominously, Israel Eldad wrote: "Can this rich [Jewish] existence be compared with the Palestinian nation? Who is that nation? What is it? Where and when was it born? What is its identity? What are its physically and mentally distinctive features? And except for the fears of its marauding gangs, what has it ever been known for?"[42]

Shortly after Ben-Gurion's prediction, six million Jews were slaughtered at the hand of Adolf Hitler. The Holocaust created a tidal wave of global opinion declaring that the Jews needed a country of their own. The systematic, unconscionable massacre of the Jews by the Nazis helped to catapult the idea of an Israeli homeland into a reality. Let there be no doubt: the dream of a Jewish state was born out of unspeakable, unimaginable suffering. That suffering took place even before the onslaught of World War II and often at the hands of Christians, justified by a false but powerful appeal to the gospel. Beginning a half century before the Holocaust, the ideology of statehood developed as a real historical force until it led to the birth of the State of Israel in 1948. No longer would the Jewish people be dispersed and slaughtered: now they would be unified and safe. Deliverance was at hand.[43]

The significance of this history cannot be overestimated. The Holocaust was far more than a pogrom; it was genocide. It is altogether understandable then that some surviving Jews viewed their return to Palestine as nothing less than a resurrection from the dead. Many religious Zionists viewed the return to their ancestral homeland as the fulfillment of a number of Old Testament prophecies, such as Ezekiel's vision of the valley of the bones, where dead bones come to life (see Ezek. 37:1–14). To them, the Israeli people were given a new life.

Nevertheless, religious Zionists tended to remain apolitical both before and after statehood was established, perhaps because Rabbi Kook (a good friend of Ben-Gurion) taught that the cause of redemption is served by the individual, not the state. As David Berlin observes, however:

> All of this changed in 1967, when the agent of redemption suddenly became the State of Israel itself. "To us [religious Zionists] the Six Day War seemed like a miracle." . . . Rabbi Razael told the media at the time, "The Egyptian air force destroyed in a few hours; the whole land of Israel ours in a few days. It was beyond anything natural, the hand of God in the process of redemption." Within months of the war, religious Zionism, once a largely apolitical force, consolidated on the right and became more directly involved in matters of state.[44]

How then would the realization of the Zionist dream square with the people already living there?

Palestinians

Today's Palestinians are also suffering. They have been dispossessed of their land, culture, history, and citizenship. They have been stripped of their dignity and their identity. And it is the Israeli occupation of Palestine that has brought this about. Palestinians see their suffering as the direct result of the creation of the State of Israel and the subsequent military and political actions of the Israelis. They point to the original words of Theodor Herzl, leader of the First Zionist Congress, who stated: "We shall try to spirit the penniless population across the border."[45] A half century later Israeli leader David Ben-Gurion said, "With compulsory transfer we [would] have a vast area [for settlement]. . . . I support compulsory transfer. I don't see anything immoral in it."[46] Golda Meir, Israeli prime minister from 1969 to 1974, said in an interview with the *Sunday Times* in June 1969, "It is not as though there was a Palestinian people in Palestine considering itself as Palestinian people and we came and threw them out and took their country away from them; they did not exist."[47] And Herzl once remarked that the Jewish community in Israel could serve as "part of a wall of defense for Europe in Asia, an outpost of civilization against barbarism."[48]

Today's Palestinian suffering is therefore related to yesterday's Jewish suffering.

As we write these words, the suffering continues daily and incessantly. The Palestinian people live under the constant humiliation and oppression of occupation. In the West Bank, many now believe that this substantial interference with fundamental rights and the basic tasks of day-to-day living will lead only to even more resistance. Israel's military occupation of the West Bank and, until September 2005, of the Gaza

Strip has provided almost daily evidence of injustice to the Palestinian militant. Consequently, many Palestinians in the Occupied Territories see little hope for their future. Israeli closures prevent them from seeking meaningful employment. Palestinians languish in refugee camps and in blockaded cities, where they watch their livelihoods and homes slowly squeezed and destroyed by Israeli "retaliation" for terrorist attacks.[49]

It is hardly surprising that such circumstances have prompted often brutal and violent resistance. Ideologies are always self-righteous. Numerous Palestinian resistance organizations have developed with the aim of ending the occupation at all costs. From their perspective, their meaning as a people has been destroyed, their culture is now ruined, and their subjection continues. The unjust infidel occupation must be stopped, period.[50] A Palestinian militant ideology has therefore emerged, one that has taken hold amid grave injustice.

On January 25, 2006, Hamas, perhaps the best-known Islamic militant group, staged a stunning upset of the ruling Fatah faction and took control of the Palestinian Authority after winning a majority of the seats in the parliamentary elections. Endowed with electoral legitimacy and the power of government, Hamas set up a cabinet described by many as dominated by hard-liners instead of moderates. In March 2006 Hamas released its governmental platform. It calls for (1) the right of return for all Palestinian refugees to their land, (2) a release of Palestinian prisoners, and (3) an end to the Israeli occupation. Not surprisingly, Israel reasserted its support for UN Secretary-General Kofi Annan's January 2006 criteria for what Hamas must do: recognize Israel, respect previously signed peace accords, and forswear violence.

Created in 1987 during the first intifada, Hamas combines Islamist and nationalist goals. Initially focused on social reforms and nonviolent resistance, the group gradually incorporated violent resistance against the Israeli occupation in the wake of changing political realities. Indeed, Hamas began to justify any act, even if it violated Islamic principles, in the name of the overarching goal: a free, Islamic Palestine. People without hope therefore began to look to Hamas with hopeful eyes, believing that it could bring them out of the so-called promised land and into their own land flowing with milk and honey. After all, Hamas responds to the social and economic needs of the people through the provision of social services, and at the same time it provides an outlet for political protest in accordance with religious expression.[51] Unfortunately, the hope offered by Hamas comes at the cost of conscripting the prevailing conceptions of justice, truth, solidarity, and love into the service of the overriding objective.

People who had lost hope are therefore now galvanized to act. Empowered by the significance of the goal, they gladly make the necessary sacrifices in order to achieve the goal: a free and independent people. Sacrifices must be made, not only to weaken the will of the opponent, but also, in response to grotesque abuse, to strike back and hurt the enemy.

Ideologies will go to great lengths to justify themselves. After the signing of the Oslo Accords in 1993, greater sacrifices were called for.[52] The type of attacks carried out by Hamas underwent a significant change. Hamas assaults were originally restricted to military targets within the Occupied Territories. Some Muslims could endorse that tactic. But then Hamas began to strike both civilian and military targets within Green Line Israel,[53] a shift that John Esposito links both to altered political reality and to specific events occurring within the West Bank and Gaza, such as the massacre at the Hebron Mosque of the Patriarch.[54] However, the use of unlimited means, including suicidal destruction, runs counter to the principles of Islam. Ironically, in trying to achieve the liberation of Palestine, the ideology of Hamas comes into conflict with the maxims of Islam. Suicide bombers who claim total resistance as a holy duty blend political objectives and religion into the mythically infused ideological framework characteristic of Fascism. Within that framework of meaning, the Hamas leadership judges suicide (or homicide) bombings solely by their effectiveness in creating a free Palestine.

This shift therefore represents far more than an alternative understanding of Islam. It is rather a reinterpretation of Islam shaped by a modern militant ideology. Stanley Humphreys explains this ideological distortion of Islam by referring to the "principle of necessity" used by the militants within the Occupied Territories, a principle used to justify what would otherwise be contrary to Islam. This is the "principle in Sharia's jurisprudence that allows the explicit commands of the law to be violated when the consequences of obedience are unacceptable."[55] In support, he points to Shaykh Nayef Rajoub, an imam in the West Bank, who stated, "The Israeli occupation has deprived the Palestinians of the right to act according to the principles of Islam. We are existing in circumstances outside the usual strictures of Islamic law."[56] Hence, the need to alleviate the extreme situation in the Occupied Territories outweighs the moral calling and guidance of Islam. The defense of Islam requires the violation of Islam.

Hamas now views as an enemy anyone who might threaten the existence of the Palestinian people. It identifies Israel and the United States as enemies; after all, the munitions found in the crumbling structures that make up Palestinian refugee camps are clearly labeled as having originated in the United States. Palestinians hear President Bush refer to former Prime Minister Ariel Sharon, a man responsible for the massacre of numerous Palestinians in the Lebanese refugee camps of Sabra and Shatila, as "a man of peace." Their response is sheer exasperation.

The humiliation and destruction caused by Israel's occupation grates on the Palestinian spirit daily. Many Palestinians not only justify but even embrace anything that will bring them closer to the goal of a free Palestinian people.[57] They believe they must overcome their present weakness with force.[58] Whether the current appeasement efforts between Israel and the Palestinians will lead to an enduring peace therefore remains doubtful.

Driven by the need to overcome weakness with force, supplicants to the god of violence begin to lash out indiscriminately against others, even those who are not Israelis. When controlled by the all-demanding god of violence, soon one lashes out against anyone, even a brother. Fighting occurs in and among Palestinians, and some Palestinians come to suffer at the hands of other Palestinians. Here too we see the dynamic power of an ideology at work, for while the ideology's adherents start out by possessing the god of violence, this god, like all gods, eventually takes control of its makers. The power of violence birthed by the ideology of identity turns upon the ideology's adherents. And there is no shalom in the grip of an idol.

Vulnerability Breeds Force

Given their vulnerability, both sides believe that they need to be militarily strong in order to preserve their existence. Because of their location within the broader Middle East, not to mention Palestinian actions within their own country, the Israelis embrace the need to build power. In the face of real enemies, only the most massive military prowess will preserve the long-sought-after Israeli state. Militarily, what the United States is to the world, Israel is to the region. A potent military is not only a necessity; it is revered as that which protects the people. Many believe that without the military, the enemy would invade.

Vulnerability breeds a similar desire for armed force among the Palestinians. In 1964, against the backdrop of Israeli actions in the first two decades after Western powers recognized the State of Israel, the Palestine Liberation Organization was formed to free the Palestinian people from Israeli domination by any means possible. Three years later, the Six-Day War and the subsequent bullying tactics of the Israelis only reinforced the idea that force is a necessary response to the Israelis' actions. Since the Palestinians do not have an army, the only way to fight back is through suicide bombers, acts of terror, and grassroots uprisings (intifadas). Eventually Palestinians came to revere suicide bombers for sacrificing themselves to strike back against the enemy. Though quite different in size and in killing ability, the Israeli army and the Palestinian suicide bombers are two sides of the same coin: revered power protecting a vulnerable people.

The inescapable conclusion is that both sides adhere to a very similar ideology: the preservation of a people's identity and their threatened land. The Israelis need to be armed because they were a persecuted people for centuries and are now surrounded by enemies. The Palestinians need to be armed because their land was forcibly taken from them without their consultation, and they have suffered under an unjust, brutal reign for over half a century. Though seemingly dissimilar, the entrenched Israeli and Palestinian positions turn out to be flip sides of the same ideological coin.

Yet there is a difference between the head and the tail of the coin. The Palestinians are trying to achieve state status, whereas the Israelis are trying to preserve the State of Israel. This distinction represents two different species or types of ideology. The Palestinian identity ideology seeks to spearhead radical social change, while the Israeli identity ideology seeks to preserve what has already been achieved.[59]

A Spiral of Violence

It is not surprising, then, that a powder keg of violence has ignited. When one side acts, the other must react, and a culture of cyclical violence emerges. In fact, ideologies can become interwoven in such a way that they synergize one another, thereby accentuating the cumulative negative consequences. Even viciously opposed ideologies can become entangled in such a way that they inadvertently collaborate to create powerful, explosive responses in and through each other. But this macabre partnership should not surprise us. Each ideology is built around a concentrated form of energy, a dynamism. In the natural world, when different electrical fields meet, the sky begins to flash. As we see in the Middle East, a similar discharge of energy occurs when ideologies collide.

As we have found, ideologies always summon false gods for the purpose of bringing their adherents what they yearn for. In the case of religious Zionism and Islamism, however, the movement toward idolatry is untenable. The Jewish religion is rooted in the Torah, which on almost every page urges people to avoid every kind of idolatry. We therefore need to proceed with utmost caution and nuance. At the same time, however, we cannot ignore the reality that some of the characteristics of idolatry described in chapter 2 seem to surface here.

First, the need for one's own people and nation to survive is so deep and profound that, if people feel they have exhausted every other way or method, then gradually they come to view the use of unmitigated power as the ultimate remedial force, the final but inescapable means of survival. Second, if the other side reacts on almost equal terms, a certain reactive necessity or double bind sets in, for the other side could easily interpret not reacting as a sign of giving in, of cowardice. An escalation therefore begins in which violence itself seems to move into a kind of natural autonomy, governing the scene and portraying to the outside world an image of a region of endless terror. As if to suit its own purposes, violence tends to dictate the rules of the game, rules in which the boundary line between civilians and noncivilians, or between combatants and noncombatants, begins to disappear on both sides.

Yet that development calls to mind the final phase of each absolute ideology, where people themselves change, hardening their judgments of the other side as the party that deserves to be entirely liquidated, not allowed to live. Here too people can be transformed into the likeness of their idol, just as the psalm we referred to in chapter 2 so vividly predicts. But the direct consequence is that more violence occurs, for this god demands further sacrifices. As in so many other areas riven by violent identity conflicts, a cult of violence has emerged in the Middle East, which people seem powerless to control. And as so often happens in such situations, neither the Israelis nor the Palestinians are more secure today. In an environment of increasing violence, both feel increasingly threatened.

At first glance, one might be surprised to think of a person or group enslaved to violence as an idol. But let us not forget that following the path of violence also has a powerful hypnotic effect, narrowing people's consciousness on both sides. Both sides tend to view violence as the sole response available to the threat, as if the claim "There is no alternative" also applies to the Palestinian-Israeli conflict.[60] Within the confines of this utterly constricted framework, it is most unlikely that the demands of United Nations Resolutions 242 and 338, calling for an end to Palestinian terrorism and the return of Palestinian lands taken in the Six-Day War, will be implemented.[61]

As already recognized, the ideological pursuit has resulted in the sad reality of Palestinian violence against Palestinians. But it also raises the tragic specter of Israelis coming into violent conflict with Israelis. According to David Berlin, to religious Zionists, who comprise up to one-third of Israelis, "redemption will come only when Israel reclaims all of its biblical lands, stretching from Beirut to Baghdad. Only then will the Messiah arrive, will the dead return, and will the world finally accept the primacy of Halachic (Jewish) law."[62] The Gaza withdrawal was a direct affront to this view of Greater Israel, and the debate about possible future withdrawals from the West Bank, which was the central issue in the March 2006 Israeli elections, has revealed Israel's "divided soul."[63] Some predict violent reprisal by Israelis against further Israeli withdrawals. In response to the Gaza withdrawal, Elyakim Haetzni, a lawyer and founder of the settlement movement, declared, "Israel is an ideological project. To undermine Zionism is to challenge the viability of the nation as a whole. This is what happened in Gaza. We are now living in the aftermath of a tsunami from which it is not clear [that] we will ever recover."[64]

Alternatives

Will the identity ideologies in Palestine be given room to move full-blown through the dissolution phase, where the tyrannical gods shut down altogether the prospects for a life-affirming future?

Speaking about tyrannical idols seems to close doors, to take away hope. But precisely the opposite is true: naming idols and their activities actually opens the door to hope. As we describe in more detail in part 4, the hypnotic power of idols can be broken. Enslavement to an idol is never a predetermined fate. And the time to turn to shalom, salaam, is now.

Thankfully, remarkably courageous and even heroic experiments in shalom and salaam already exist in Palestine. They serve as living alternatives to the ideologies of identity, and they provide glimmers of hope in the midst of the vengeful god of violence. For more than twenty years, Palestinian and Jewish families have lived together in Neve Shalom/Wahat al-Salam (Oasis of Peace), a community of peaceful coexistence and equality. Located between Tel Aviv and Jerusalem, people live, work, and educate their families in the way of peace. Elie Wiesel captured some of the hope these families inspire: "When Jews and Arabs get together, live together—they create their own miracle; Neve Shalom/Wahat al-Salam is such a miracle. It deserves our warmest support, for it justifies our highest hopes."[65]

Moreover, six hundred Israeli soldiers have joined the movement "Courage to Refuse," in which Israeli reserve and combat officers refuse to serve in any of the Occupied Territories. The movement began in January 2002, when fifty combat officers and soldiers signed a protest letter after returning from their duty in the Gaza Strip. Such acts of courage in the name of peace provide real hope to even the most ideologically hardened hearts.[66]

Recently a Palestinian Muslim lawyer, Khaled Kasab Mahameed, opened a Holocaust museum in his law office in Nazareth. "What I say to Arabs," he declared, "is that the Jewish people are carrying the pain of 60 nuclear bombs. The Palestinian people just don't understand this. Because our conflict is not about land. If not for the Holocaust, we could live together in peace." Not surprisingly, the Palestinian press has ignored him entirely, but he has carried on with great determination, despite opposition from some Palestinians and suspicion from some Israelis.[67]

Finally, on March 19, 2002, hundreds of Palestinian and Israeli parents who had lost children in the intifada placed over a thousand coffins on the steps of the United Nations, representing children who had died—their children. Parents who might have wanted revenge for their children united together to plead for peace. If mourning parents can unite, then surely there is hope that people can turn from the goal of ethnic preservation to the way of peace.

The Lesson for Us

Advocates of apartheid, militant Islamist terrorists bent on murder, harsh Israeli systems of oppression—these all seem distant, far removed from those of us who live in the global North. But the temptation for we ourselves to embrace an ideology of identity is greater than we may think. Today violence increases, economic worries intensify, and fears of another terrorist attack persist; meanwhile, voices reminiscent of those in Germany in the 1930s cry for a strong, decisive leader to restore order. They call for stronger laws to protect us, our people, our way of life, and our identity. In these appeals lies the kernel of ideology. But if the main goal of a policy is to preserve the greatness and superiority of America,[68] if love is equated with love for America, and if American interests determine what is "good" and "just,"[69] then an ideology of identity—a civil religion—is at work. If people honor a national flag as an expression of what gives ultimate meaning, then it can become a symbol of idolatry.

During difficult times democracy falters and the national urge for a strong leader and tighter security returns. Movements like National Socialism do repeat themselves. When self-preservation becomes our highest goal, then we deem whatever contributes to it as strong and whatever detracts from it as weak. Further, the all-encompassing desire for self-preservation can lead us to redefine good and evil, whereby good becomes whatever preserves us and evil becomes whatever threatens us. In the aftermath of September 11, did not President Bush declare, in a paraphrase of John 1:15, that "the light [America] has shone in the darkness [the enemies of America], and the darkness will not overcome it"?[70] These words have echoes of a nationalist ideology. If this ideological impulse is allowed to progress, its cures will be worse than the illness, and the means for maintaining order will slip out of control. And then it will be too late.

But the ideology of identity is even closer to us than this. The heart of it—the decision to protect one's own identity at any expense—touches more than just national identity. The goal of self-preservation can infiltrate any human group or organization. The ideology can be cherished by ostracized groups of people, political parties, businesses, or even churches that strongly desire to protect their identities. The opportunity for pursuing the identity ideology therefore lies extremely close to home, even literally within the home: playing with fire, we permit violence in the media, including television, movies, and computer games, to implant the idol in the hearts of us all, particularly children. We all belong to various social, political, religious, and racial groupings. Feelings of threat, superiority, or pride can creep into them at any time. We may use the assumed "inferiority" of being poor, black, non-Christian, or uneducated as a demonic instrument for assuring the "superiority" of being rich, white, Christian, or educated.

So much suffering on this earth has its root in this ideological distortion. How else can we explain the many persecutions of Jews throughout history, especially in the midst of so-called Christian nations and communities? How else can we explain the permanent state of misery for the world's most desperately poor? The rich need the poor to enhance their own self-esteem.[71] In a manner of speaking, through this ideological distortion Jesus is crucified again—Jesus, the impoverished Jew who was despised and rejected by the ruling religious elite of his time.

Indeed, the ideology of national or group identity lies within reach of us all.

/ 5 /

MATERIAL PROGRESS
AND PROSPERITY UNSHACKLED

When it comes to ideology and the world of the economy, we face a remarkable challenge. The race for money and possessions is deeply entrenched, especially in Western society. Selfish emotions often flare up when the issue of dividing wealth arises. But does the pursuit of material prosperity in our society carry the trademarks of a real ideology? Surely it lacks the enormous energy, radicality, and bloody extremes of the French Revolution, Soviet Communism, German Nazism, and Islamism. Further, making glib references to a prosperity ideology poses a serious risk. We could be accused of deliberately trying to make the improvement of one's material condition morally and legally suspect by definition.

Indeed, caution is needed here. But let us nuance this caution with two observations. First, full-fledged ideologies can differ profoundly in the way their adherents adopt norms and values and select the means needed for reaching the end. People can opt for relatively peaceful tools, not just violent ones. They will even prefer such means if they prove to be effective. So we should not be surprised if devotees of an ideology of material progress and prosperity use relatively more peaceful means than those characterized by blatant violence.

Second, we have identified differences in the developmental time lines of ideologies. Ideologies that incite radical societal change can flare up in a short period of time but then also may die out relatively quickly. Other ideologies may last several decades or even more than a century. Living ideologies also adapt themselves to changing situations and thus even alter their characters as they march through history. If an ideology of material progress and prosperity exists, it may well be that over the course of time the accent has shifted from an ideology that spearheads radical change to one that seeks to maintain the existing social order with every means at its disposal. After its initial success, such an ideology evolves from radical transformation to preservation.

But the question is still valid: how do we ensure that we not rush into premature conclusions about the presence of a materialist ideology? In our view, only one solution is acceptable. Our point of departure must not be the conceptual ideas developed in the first part of this book, followed by an appeal to reality for some kind of affirmation. Rather, we must take the opposite approach. With open minds, let us begin by daring to listen to the relevant processes taking place in reality today, carefully observing what is occurring in practice in our time. Using that material, we can then explore whether ideology and subsequent elements of idolatry pop up. Reality itself must deliver the decisive proof.

Remarkable Trends

What then do we observe in today's world, especially in the economic and financial domains? Perhaps most immediately striking is its dynamism. Never in the recent past has the average standard of living risen as dramatically as in the last few decades in the West. The West's standard of living has doubled or even tripled, thanks to vigorous growth in productivity. As a result, a number of new technological achievements now lie within the grasp of most people, items that in many respects have made life easier and more pleasant. But that does not tell the whole story. Huge material successes have come at a cost, and the powerful dynamism casts threatening shadows over our time.

Let us begin by describing four economic trends: the rise of socioeconomic paradoxes, globalization, commercialization, and the rapid application of frontier science.

Socioeconomic Paradoxes

Consider a relatively new, startling trend: the rise of a number of specific economic and social paradoxes. On the surface, these paradoxes make no sense; from a standard economic vantage point, they are irrational. Yet it is striking to observe the number of absurdities that now seem to completely confound the current, accepted economic predictions. Consider, by way of illustration, several such paradoxes.

The Poverty Paradox

Despite an unprecedented expansion of wealth, recent years have witnessed unpredicted increases in situations of deepening poverty, not only in the poorest parts of the world but also, remarkably, in the richest. Recent statistics from the United States, Canada, and Europe highlight this tragic irony. According to Bread for the World, in the United States 36.3 million people, including 13 million children, live in households that experience hunger or the risk of hunger. This represents more than one in ten households (11.2 percent) and is an increase of 1.4 million people from 2002.[1] In the United States 15.3 million people live in deep poverty (living on cash incomes less than half of the poverty level).[2] Meanwhile, 20 percent of the jobs in the nation pay less than poverty-level wages for a family of four (less than $9 an hour).[3] This raises a puzzling, unexpected economic dilemma: if material prosperity expands in a country, then why has poverty not been alleviated in tandem with that expansion?

The Care Paradox

Opportunities for extending care are steadily eroding in increasingly wealthy societies. Organizations providing nursing and other care for the elderly, for the handicapped, and for children struggle under the burden of serious financial problems. Essential support services often have huge waiting lists. Every economics textbook still states that a general rise in the standard of living means that the supply of services for people increases as people's buying power increases. Instead, the relative supply of services is decreasing. Where then does the painful care paradox come from?

The Time Paradox

Almost all economics textbooks also claim that more prosperity brings with it more free time, along with an ability to work less intensively at fewer hours. In actuality, however, the opposite appears to be true: a time paradox has now entered our lives. Not only has our pace accelerated, even in the escalating tempo of flitting television images, but also more and more workplaces now confront the effects of stress and burnout among employees, due to the elevated time pressure on them. Where does our increasingly harried lifestyle come from? What has caused "the overworked American" (the title of a book by Juliet Schor) to surface precisely at a time when the majority of people in Western society have never been materially better off?[4] Would not exchanging a small amount of prosperity for lower stress and more free time seem like an obvious alternative?

The Environment Paradox

How startling it is to observe that the application of improved technologies, more economic resources, and a series of international agreements has not been able to turn the tide of environmental destruction. Inexorably, it seems, the global ecosystem becomes more and more unstable. More species disappear each day now than disappeared each week twenty years ago. Accelerating world climate change is creating concern and anxiety around the world, and the rapid succession of heavy hurricanes has its most devastating impact on the poor. Why, specifically in a time of unprecedented prosperity, have the world's environmental dilemmas slipped out of control? Never have the possibilities for redressing environmental deterioration been better than today.

Other Paradoxes

We could mention other paradoxes, such as the scarcity paradox (a rising sense of general scarcity in the midst of unprecedented luxury), the health paradox (increased threats to health in the midst of unparalleled medical expertise), and the industrial paradox (the rising pressure to industrialize even further in the midst of highly industrialized societies).[5] But before we investigate the deeper roots of such paradoxes, let us fill out the picture with three additional trends.

Globalization

The second trend is toward further globalization. Increasingly, national economies, especially those of the West, are opening themselves, or are being opened, to what is now called the global market. Enormous technological development, especially in the information and communication sector, has enabled that process, sometimes also called "the rise of the network society" (the title of a book by Manuel Castells).[6] It has also been enhanced by the partial abolishment of national protective tariffs and the adoption of a relatively coherent monetary system of interchangeable national currencies (the Bretton Woods system). Within this globalization dynamic, what is most striking is the rate of transactions occurring in the currency markets in relation to other markets: billions of dollars circulate every day in the so-called pure financial circuit, a volume highly disproportionate to the transactions taking place in the so-called real circuit of goods and services. While new forms of regional cooperation have also emerged (as in Africa, Latin America, and the European Union), a reaccentuation of national interests has occurred simultaneously, both inside and outside of these forms of cooperation, and the role of the United States, through the pursuit of its own "vital interests," has expanded.

Commercialization

The third trend is toward growing commercialization and monetarization. Increasingly, more domains of life, such as recreation, leisure, health, and cultural activities, are being drawn into the sphere of commerce and subjected to the calculations of money. Television and the Internet have become important media for transferring messages and images designed to broaden and influence consumer tastes. With the striking increase in financial criminality, even violence is becoming monetarized. In addition to highly publicized corporate scandals involving companies like Enron, WorldCom, and Nortel Networks, consider the manner in which the Russian Mafia operates in Russia today. The Mafia creates insecurity, terrorizing inner cities and urban neighborhoods. Then, in the chaotic situation it has created, it offers economic security, particularly to small business entrepreneurs, in exchange for a sizable fee. Currently a substantial portion of the business done in Russia goes to the Mafia. Finally, billions of dollars are spent each year in the global arms industry, due in part to the relentless, overwhelming sales pressure in that industry (as at its Arms Bazaars).

Frontier Science

The fourth trend is toward frontier knowledge. More than ever before, science has stepped out of its so-called ivory tower. It is now primarily operational and paid to be such, particularly in the economic, social, and military spheres. Science has always possessed a frontier aspect in its drive to surpass old forms of knowledge. But the frontier thrust is now entirely operational, so much so that the ethical debate about scientific discoveries has become largely a debate after application, a postdebate.

The Root of the Paradoxes

Against the backdrop of the dynamism behind these four trends, let us examine the deeper source of the paradoxes. In one way or another, each paradox involves tension between what can progress and what can scarcely progress, if at all. It is the tension between dynamism and preservation. Certain things in life cannot succumb to the dynamic forces of production. We cannot produce time. Similarly, the environment around us and the culture we live in are more or less givens, like our bodies. From a socioeconomic standpoint, poverty in modern society is usually rooted in the inability of a number of people, either physically or mentally, to adapt to the demands of our dynamic, ever-changing society in employment. Lack of training and education also contribute to some people falling by the wayside. Because people in such circumstances cannot participate, they become excluded or disenfranchised, and they can find themselves clumped together into ghettolike environments.

Similarly, as an economic activity, care is characterized by virtually fixed levels of productivity. In the care sectors it is impossible to enforce the productivity increases possible in the advanced sectors of the economy. Demanding increased productivity in hospitals, schools, and social work settings can destroy this relationship-centered work. As a result, every year the gap widens between what the care sectors of the economy must pay employees (because of the wage and salary standards of society) and what they are able to pay them (because of the slower rise in productivity in these sectors). This widening productivity gap means that, as the prices of industrial products are able to remain the same or drop because of increased efficiency, the costs and prices of services in the care sectors increase each year. As we see more and more today, the costs of care become so high that they even become partially unpayable, certainly in terms of available public funds. As a result, in the midst of a dynamic economy and rising material prosperity, care activities become proportionately more expensive than goods and services provided in sectors of the economy where dramatic increases in productivity occur.[7]

Paradoxes like these clearly emerge at the dividing line separating what can expand as a result of the current technological and economic dynamism and what is simply not in a position to expand.

Not surprisingly, then, problems morph into insurmountable paradoxes where and when the laws of the dynamism set the tone. When dynamic forces call the shots, the adaptations they require are strictly one-sided: everything must bend to the unremitting dynamism. Within the perspective of a dynamic universe, society views whatever remains stationary as a form of regression. Using the gauge applied by modern thought and action, society tends to experience whatever has difficulty moving as an obstacle, backward, or even inferior. The dynamism world-view is full of such perceptions and judgments. Poor people and poor countries are stragglers who need to be stimulated to achieve more. In the care sector, the only acceptable answer to all of its problems is that it must increase efficiency. Gripped by the dynamism perspective, society experiences the environment and time as impediments because each regularly imposes new limitations upon us, hindering what we want to bring about. No wonder, then, that the ongoing dialogue about the so-called limits to growth is the starting point whenever the issue of the environment comes up. Similarly, the dynamism worldview recognizes seniors and people who are physically or developmentally challenged as fellow consumers but not as fellow producers. Society therefore experiences them largely as a cost factor, which hampers the development needed. Meanwhile, policy-makers, media, and even nongovernmental organizations (NGOs) label poor countries, which often possess numerous cultures older than Western culture, as "underdeveloped" or "developing" countries.

Inevitably, in a world where society crowns dynamism king and compels people, the environment, and culture to adjust solely in the direction dictated by the dynamism, paradoxes emerge. The paradoxes remain in place no matter what supposedly progressive measure a government or institution might implement, because more money, technology, or science will not resolve these paradoxes. On the contrary, the more likely scenario is that paradoxes flow from the excess of the forces of unlimited development. Indeed, the spreading scourge of paradoxes in our society is a sign or signal that our society does not allow the negative and even risky consequences of paradoxes to overrule the belief that, above all else, the current dynamism must be sustained and expanded.

It is then legitimate to conclude from this diagnosis that, at least to a certain degree, a contemporary ideology of endless progress pervades our society. Clearly the dynamism of the means—technology, the economy, science—toward the goals society once established and still subscribes to has acquired such importance that the instruments have become self-sufficient. We increasingly allow the means, as a deity, to take the measure of everyone and everything. The means therefore indicate the presence of ends that have once become absolute and remain absolute to this day. All this reveals the presence of a vital, living ideology.

Further Testing

Is this conclusion also warranted in relation to the other trends we noted as dominant tendencies in our time?

The second trend we named was accelerated globalization, and the third was the expansion of commercial and monetary interests and pressures. Both take place primarily in already wealthy Western societies, through which they influence countries that are less wealthy. Now one can well imagine why poorer countries give priority to the growth of production and consumption: too many basic needs remain unmet in their countries. But why does expanding the economic domain receive the highest priority in countries that are already rich? The message conveyed through many political speeches is that society needs economic expansion in order to battle the remnants of misery and poverty that still exist in wealthy countries. But that is hardly the primary motivation.

Consider the third trend: the rise of commercial and monetary pressures, pressures that border on coercion. What creates the need to drive people to ever-higher levels of consumption, even when they already possess so much? If the answer is that most people simply desire conspicuous consumption, that in and of itself could indicate the presence of an absolute goal and therefore an ideological impulse. But the flip side is that today's economic producers simply cannot grow or expand without a rising demand for their products. Consumer desires, at least to a certain extent, must be artificially "produced." Giving complete sway to increasing commercial pressure is then merely another sign of an ideological influence, an influence that now has structural features. Perhaps we detect here something of what means can do when powerful interests elevate them in the midst of our society as powers that enforce their own will: they begin to reign like idols.

Within this trend we hinted at the expanding role of money and finance. In chapter 1 we observed that money and finance ought to serve the real economy. In our time, however, they seem to have begun to govern the real economy. Businesses substitute annual corporate reports for quarterly reports, and corporate takeovers increasingly occur simply to satisfy the demands of the financial markets. Irrespective of whether or not society views these developments as progress, financial markets have become empowered to assume the role of an exacting decision-maker, one that we must please under all circumstances. The considerations of money have now become decisive.

As an illustration, consider that developments in international currency speculation have gradually led to the volume of international trade in money and money products now being forty to fifty times greater than the total volume of international trade in goods and services. Presently less than 2 percent of worldwide financial transactions cover actual goods and services; the rest, about 98 percent, cover mostly pure financial currency speculation.[8] Money is therefore not merely the flip side of the goods-and-services coin. It is an independent good or product in its own right. And trade in currency-derived "products" is becoming more and more independent from trade in goods.

Money has therefore acquired a different role. While money once was primarily a medium of exchange representing the value of goods and services provided, today money is primarily a commodity from which one can make a large profit. For banks, trade in this commodity has become their most important source of income. But the production of goods and services has not increased accordingly.

Perhaps the financial markets assumed their privileged position as the guardian angels of money because they are the most dynamic of all markets and therefore the best suited to enhance the competitive struggle. Today they stimulate perpetual competition not just between corporations but also between nation-states, which fear losing the capital and investments they so badly need. Here too we notice a higher degree of the autonomy of the means than we can rationally comprehend.

Finally, consider the transformation caused by the increasing attention given to particular national or vital interests, especially when those interests require military protection. The word "vital" implies life and sustainability over the long term. Vital interests ought to relate primarily to care for people, for the well-being of society, and for the environment. Regrettably, however, political references to vital interests today are instead to material interests and to corresponding areas of domination; this shift makes a profound difference, especially considering that the word "vital" now often legitimizes protection and even action by means of force. The philosopher Adorno once described full-fledged ideology in one word: legitimation. Today, the legitimation granted by the expression "vital interests"—sanctioning even the inhumane treatment of opponents—reflects the impact of certain ideological influences.

Therefore, paying careful attention to the facts and data of our time, we cannot honestly escape the conclusion that we live, to a greater or lesser extent, in the grip of a powerful, largely Western ideology: the ideology of a restless commitment to unlimited material progress and prosperity.

But where did the ideology come from? And how does it connect to the prevailing economic institutions in Western society, such as the market?

The Developmental Time Line of the Ideology

To locate the sources of the ideology of material prosperity and progress, we must look back to the time period of Destutt de Tracy (1770), though more in Anglo-Saxon than French territory. At that time, Western society suffered not only under political oppression but also under abysmal social and economic misery. People felt a compelling need to escape hunger and deprivation. Almost every Enlightenment philosopher shared that deep desire, so much so that it consumed the practical branch of Scottish and English Enlightenment thinkers: the classical economists. Most of them devoted themselves to finding a solution to the struggle against human deprivation. They were fascinated by the possibility of creating an ongoing expansion of material prosperity in Western society, and they fully supported the gradual adoption of that goal by Western society as the decisive, overriding objective for its further development. Indeed, Western development would derive its meaning from it. It was therefore no accident that the bible of classical economics, written in 1776 by the Scottish philosopher Adam Smith, was entitled *An Inquiry into the Nature and Causes of the Wealth of Nations*. It was also not an accident that, as a good friend of the French Revolutionist Marquis de Condorcet, Smith wrote part of the book in de Condorcet's home in France, as his guest.

Classical economists were convinced that achieving the objective required nothing less than a kind of economic revolution. The existing guilds had to go, and new forms of industry had to be built up. New markets had to be developed entirely free of the intervention of the state. Most economists and politicians viewed these steps as unavoidable if society was to achieve its goal. Smith's work sharply underscored the cry for profound changes in society, changes we now know as the industrial revolution.

But how far can one go in the pursuit of an important, even essential goal before it becomes transformed into a real, living ideology?

A number of historical facts suggest that the legitimation of the industrial revolution lay deeper than simply overcoming technical problems. The traditional order of production and consumption was broken down completely. As social cooperatives of production, the guilds were abolished, often by law. The enclosure movement ended the practice of allowing peasants access to the pastures, which gave them the means for basic subsistence. The common land began to be used exclusively by the lords for the production of wool instead. This resulted in the massive uprooting of countless farmers and their families to the rapidly emerging slums of the new cities, where they became a willing arsenal from which the new industrial enterprises could draw their laborers in return for often extremely low wages. Indeed, the new industrial firms began to compete vigorously in the new labor markets to obtain labor at the lowest price possible.

Much more was at stake than an external change of circumstances. An active political will created far-reaching social and economic reconstruction, built on the new concept of the free market. This free market was to be implemented everywhere. Decision-makers understood the new market mechanism as possessing nothing less than the "invisible hand" of God himself (the concept of Adam Smith). Using this unique mechanism, the invisible hand would transform economic self-interest into the wealth and well-being of the whole of society.

What tells us that nothing less than a deeply rooted faith was at stake here? Those who implemented the program or project enhanced and strengthened it despite its overwhelming shadow sides: immense urban poverty, abysmal working conditions that included workdays of over ten hours daily for women and children as young as age six, environmental devastation, and massive disease. The revolutionists possessed an unshakable belief in a blueprint that, from their perspective, simply could not fail. Their plan prescribed the rational reconstruction of economic life according to the laws of an impeccably operating market mechanism. Adam Smith described universities as "homes of obsolete prejudices," because they were artificially protected from "the blast of competition."[9]

In order then to achieve society's new ultimate goal—the growth of the wealth of nations—the primary instrument for reaching it became institutionalized and granted a life of its own. The free market was established not only for consumption goods but also for all factors of production: land, labor, capital. Increasingly, therefore, the market mechanism was seen and accepted as the ultimate coordinator of all economic effort. It became elevated to the high authority designed to competitively stimulate further economic growth and implement every new technological advancement. Indeed, the trap of idolatry was not far away.

But even as we offer criticism of this historical development, let us make our intentions perfectly clear. We are not saying that each market is an institution that by definition ought to be mistrusted. A market has no inherent power to mislead. Neither a market nor an economic plan possesses that kind of potential. On the contrary, if they are handled and treated responsibly, both can be good and valuable social institutions. John Calvin thus saw the market not just as an "expression of human solidarity," but even as "a sign of the grace of God." Yet people can elevate even good institutions like the market and beneficial forces like economic growth into artificial saviors. Some grant them the highest degree of autonomy imaginable because they see them as the ultimate, unerring compasses by which all of society's actions, under all circumstances, must be governed. At that point, such forces or institutions become idols, and people's relationship with them carries all of the trademarks of idolatry.

Ever-larger degrees of domination exercised in society as a whole signal the development of idolatry. But so does the conscription of the reigning norms and values into ones that legitimize the goals selected and pave the way for idols. As illustrated in the book *Capitalism and Progress*, already in the nineteenth century one can trace adjustments to currently held values like freedom and justice.[10] Freedom became freedom to act in one's own self-interest, regardless of the harm done to others, yet within existing laws and contracts. Freedom became almost entirely property- and contract-based. Justice shrank to mean obedience only to existing contracts and rights. It became individualized and formalized, resulting in the possibility that thousands of people could suffer at the same time that one could claim that justice had been done.

The Ideology in Its Present Features

Value shifts of this nature have not occurred only in the past. Today also, Western society easily redefines a number of reigning values, altering their content, in order to pave the way for infinite progress and the unfettered operation of all markets. For example, the law of the pursuit of self-interest permeates the interpretation of solidarity. Solidarity now applies nationally and internationally only if enough (which usually implies "more") economic results are achieved first. Similarly, consider the yawning distance between the term "economy" today and the biblical word *oikonomia*, from which we get our word "economy." *Oikonomia* means "the caring administration of all that is entrusted to us," while "economy" today refers to the "cult of efficiency" (after the title of a book by Janice Gross Stein).[11] Finally, sustainability, instead of criticizing and judging present-day realities, serves as a goal for the future, requiring for its fulfillment primarily economic growth and technological innovation.

The paradoxes that have surfaced in our own time appear to be extensions of what we have just described. Behind their obvious economic irrationality we now recognize their hidden ideological logic. How else, other than as the outcome of a vigorous, living ideology of material progress and expansion, can one understand why decision-makers pursue and promote strictly market-driven economic growth where it clearly makes no real sense? Only an ideological compulsion can explain why societies that already experience unparalleled wealth intensify the pressure of commercialization in noneconomic sectors. And only by it can we comprehend the strange prioritization of finance and financial markets in a society where one would expect the significance of money to gradually decrease.

But even these do not complete the test for ideology established at the beginning of this chapter. The presence of at least some influences that narrow people's awareness also betrays an ideology. We therefore conclude with some remarks about these influences.

In relation to the means or instruments used by a materially progressive, market-oriented society, money plays a special role. How do most people speak about money today? Do they see the possession of money only as a means or instrument for meeting their basic needs, or do they see it as the basis for their whole lives, allowing them to achieve every goal they have? Biblical texts clearly warn that money can turn into an idol for persons and groups. As Jesus warns, "You cannot serve God and mammon" (Matt. 6:24 RSV). Money can become an ultimate standard for society as a whole, the instrument society uses to assign value to persons, professions, the environment, and culture.

That impulse has led to the dominant role that financial markets play today. Financial markets no longer really serve objectives beyond themselves. George Soros explains: "It is market fundamentalism that has put financial capital into the driver's seat."[12] The president of the German Federal Bank once declared that "politicians have now been brought under the control of the financial markets."[13] In addition, a remarkable sense of fear radiates from these markets, fear of what they might do to us. The predominant question today is, How do we behave as a corporation or as a nation so that our actions become acceptable in the eyes of the financial markets? The question in and of itself suggests that money and financial markets have taken on a life of their own: a feature of idolatry. Fear also captivates so-called developing countries in relation to flows of short-term international capital. They often see financial markets as higher than themselves, as a power they must please and obey under all circumstances.

The language used today is also instructive. Increasingly, religious terminology has crept into the debate. People speak not only of the saving power of the market but also of the sacrifices needed. "We must follow the dictates of the market. . . . Only further economic growth can save us. . . . All groups in society need to make sacrifices for a better future." Such statements are common. They remind us of what Andrew Carnegie wrote more than a century ago in an essay deliberately entitled *The Gospel of Wealth*: "We accept and welcome, therefore, as conditions to which we must accommodate ourselves, great inequality of environment; the concentration of business, industrial and commercial, in the hands of a few; and the law of competition between these, as being not only beneficial, but essential to the future progress of the race."[14] He concluded his reflections with a declaration: "Such in my opinion, is the true Gospel concerning wealth, obedience to which is destined some day . . . to bring 'Peace on earth, among men good will.'"[15]

Religious language like this is not accidental. It hints at decisions made about ultimate meaning, done either openly or unconsciously, without which people do not see life as feasible. Imitation saviors still move among us, and we see them as entitled to demand sacrifices.

Finally, a glance at most daily newspapers and television messages today suggests that contraction of the mind is occurring simultaneously in a number of ways. Time has shrunk to the present and the near future; long-term concerns scarcely enter the public debate, just as long-term scarcities do not register in the market.[16] World events narrow down to only what connects with our own largely national needs. And monetary interests outweigh almost all other interests. Newspapers, magazines, and television stations are owned by large corporate interests. The media are seen to present news coverage in line with the major interests of the owners. As a result, genuine protection of human dignity in the face of existing economic and political powers falls increasingly outside of public purview.

As we saw earlier, the contracting of the mind accompanies the practice of idolatry in an ideological setting. Our perception of the world becomes crimped because idols cast spells. Though first we set idols up on pedestals, expecting that they will deliver us from misery, later they exact punishing demands. Indeed, both people and societies can become possessed by what they feel must be preserved at all costs or obtained in the near future.

No doubt the emerging narrowing of consciousness to prioritize only dynamic material remains the greatest threat of all. In the context of the paradoxes, the narrowing of the mind results in interpreting all of the shadow sides of the advancing dynamism—rising poverty, increased stress, underfed people in the midst of overfed people, environmental deterioration, and eroding care—as either inevitable or as necessary sacrifices, essential for our progress. Progress consists of higher consumption levels, more economic growth, higher profits and returns, and dramatic rises in productivity. And the march to greater material progress must move forward at any cost, even if it draws us closer to the abyss.

/ 6 /

GUARANTEED SECURITY

Protecting a country against attack is not just a legitimate goal. In times of real threat it can also be a moral and political duty. In the 1930s Dutch defense efforts were virtually absent, even though the militarist Nazis had accumulated vast power and had publicly declared their intention to expand German territory. The Dutch people were also spiritually unprepared for what brewed across their border. Many people, including Christians, claimed that Hitler had merely restored authority in Germany with a strong arm and simply wanted to take up the gauntlet against onrushing world Communism. The right wing minimized the significance of protecting Holland by dismissing the dangers of the rising Fascism; the left wing did the same by advocating a specific, widely held brand of total pacifism. The Netherlands entered World War II spiritually and militarily unprepared. Tragically, Holland's experience roughly mirrored that of the other countries that later allied themselves against the Nazi threat.

The horrible trauma of World War II became etched indelibly in the minds of many. People resolved "never again" to face a threat unprepared, and they quickly organized themselves to ensure that their freedom would never again succumb to tyranny. Almost immediately on the heels of World War II, a new threat surfaced: the Soviet revolutionist dream of world domination. In 1948, at the inaugural address of the North Atlantic Treaty Organization (NATO), Paul Henri Spaak declared, "We are all afraid." The Cold War had begun.

What was the outcome of that resolve, rooted in the experience of the indescribable suffering of World War II? The Cold War period (from about 1948 to 1990) witnessed the most profound militarization in human history. By the end of the Cold War, as the result of an arms race pursued at breakneck speed, the United States and the Soviet Union possessed approximately seventy thousand nuclear warheads, which together represented destructive power more than one million times greater than the bomb dropped on Hiroshima.[1] Only a few hundred were capable of destroying the entire globe. More firepower was consumed in the Vietnam War (a proxy conflict of the Cold War) than in all prior wars in human history combined, including World War II.[2] The Cold War also created structural imbalances. According to reliable estimates provided by the Brookings Institution, the cost to the United States for the research, development, and production of nuclear weapons and their delivery systems has amounted to an astounding $5.48 trillion since 1940.[3]

When the Iron Curtain collapsed in 1989, the Cold War came to an end, thus removing the spur that had stimulated an ever-faster, frenetic arms race. Commentators engaged in enthusiastic dialogue about an imminent "peace dividend." It did appear that, while maintaining more than enough capacity for defense, a substantial portion of military spending could be redirected toward meeting basic human needs, particularly in the poorest countries of the world. By 1980 annual weapons expenditures in the world as a whole were higher than the gross domestic products of the poorest half of the world's population.[4] And the United Nations report *The Relationship between Disarmament and Development* had already definitively established the link between disarmament and poverty alleviation on the one hand and between rising armaments and rising impoverishment on the other.[5] Surely, with utterly modernized defense systems in place and with the threat removed, the world would now withdraw from its commitment to absolute security and guaranteed freedom.

But the baffling reality is that the peace dividend did not materialize. Today, over fifteen years later, nuclear deterrence remains an essential, integral part of NATO's strategic concept, even though the threat that gave birth to NATO's doctrine has disappeared. Despite relative reductions, tens of thousands of nuclear weapons still exist, 16,500 of which remain deployed.[6] Together they still represent one million times the blast that pulverized Hiroshima.[7] And currently the United States alone spends $100 million each day to maintain its nuclear weapons.[8]

To make matters more baffling, consider a few of the remarkable developments that unfolded instead of a peace dividend. By 2000, at the conclusion of the Clinton administration's tenure and before the September 11, 2001, attacks, 41 percent of the US fiscal budget, or more than a half trillion dollars, was spent on military purposes and $2.9 trillion of the total US debt of $5.6 trillion was militarily related.[9] Also under the auspices of the Clinton administration, the Space Command issued its *Vision for 2020*, advocating "full spectrum dominance," with outer space as the final part of the spectrum requiring weaponization. In the absence of a tangible threat, President Clinton earmarked several billion dollars toward space-based antiballistic missile shield development.

Moreover, again before 9/11 and despite the end of the Cold War, President George W. Bush's administration threatened, undermined, or scuttled a number of long-standing arms control agreements. By 2003 the US military budget was larger than those of the next fifteen nations combined, most of which were US allies.[10] When the interest on past military debt is factored in, currently the US government spends over $2 billion each day on military matters.[11] To give a sense of scale, Bread for the World, a Christian relief organization, has estimated that $4 billion per year in poverty-focused development assistance would cut hunger in Africa in half by 2015.[12] Finally, in March 2003 the "Coalition of the Willing" invaded Iraq in a preemptive war.

These developments raise new, puzzling, and troubling questions. Why did the peace dividend not materialize? Why did the shocking escalation of arms in NATO countries, particularly in the United States, continue almost unabated after the threat that created NATO had disappeared? Even when well-intentioned, neither the political left nor the right seemed able to rein in the powerful momentum of arms escalation. Indeed, it seems to have a mind of its own. Eluding the grasp of the currently accepted approaches, that momentum now seems unstoppable.

These questions introduce ideology into the picture. Is it possible that an ideology has crept into our own thinking and behavior? Have we perhaps allowed means to slip out of our control, and now they loom over us as gods, dictating their will as they please?

Peace and Conflict in History

To answer these questions we must begin far back in Western history. We do not understand our current strategic problems, including those in Iraq, in part because we have lost a sense of history.

How have people understood war and peace in the past? At least three historical developments stand out.

Renaissance and Enlightenment Transformations

The first important development is the rise of the "Renaissance man" more than five centuries ago. During the Renaissance, people wanted to unburden themselves from the yoke of the authoritarian medieval church and create a new world. They would achieve this through new techniques not only in art, science, economics, and world exploration (Columbus's travels were a fruit of the new attitude), but also in warfare. Besides being a great artist and scientist, Leonardo da Vinci was the ingenious designer of new weapons of war, including a submarine and a helicopter. For him, the style of war was one of the new arts of autonomous man, who through reason and intellect could force peace on his enemies. At about the same time, Machiavelli wrote his famous book *The Art of War* (1521). For the Renaissance person, peace and economic prosperity were the end products of human ingenuity and accomplishment. They were manufacturable, seen as the results of humankind's own self-directed efforts.

Scientific progress grew by leaps and bounds, and with it came the emergence of a new science ideal. The Renaissance gave way to the Enlightenment urge to rid the world entirely of the supernatural and replace it with the rational certainty of scientific inquiry. The new ideal affected the style of warfare no less than the style of economics and other human activities. According to military historian Michael Howard, "Military thinkers sought for rational principles based on hard, quantifiable data that might reduce the conduct of war to a branch of the natural sciences, a rational activity from which the play of chance and uncertainty had been entirely eliminated."[13] In words that bear an uncanny resemblance to some current Pentagon strategic thinking, the Welsh soldier Henry Lloyd (1720–83) summarized the conventional wisdom: "Whoever understands these things is in a position to initiate military operations with mathematical precision and to keep on waging war without ever being under the necessity of striking a blow."[14] By 1795 the great German philosopher Immanuel Kant had developed this thinking further in his book *Zum ewigen Frieden* (On Perpetual Peace); it was an integral part of his overall work and provided a perspective taught at military colleges well into the 1800s.

During the Renaissance and Enlightenment periods, then, war and peace became inseparably bound up with the belief in human progress accomplished through scientific and technological achievement, which pervaded Western culture. People thought they could secure peace through the achievements of reason. And they fought a host of national wars according to the new rules.

During this period the Dutch jurist Hugo Grotius tried to set limits on warfare. Using the principle of natural law and the just-war principles of Greco-Roman legal theory, he justified armed defense and formulated guidelines to which all warfare should adhere. To warfare he fixed two main conditions: the purpose of any armed conflict must be peace; and people must limit the means. In any war situation, armies must spare women and children, abstain from cruelty, and respect existing property. Contrary to the trend then current, Grotius's guidelines pointed toward the God-given requirements of justice and love of neighbor that ought to apply even during periods of conflict.

Total War

The second development occurred during the French Revolution. In 1793 the French National Convention issued a mass conscription (*levée en masse*) proclamation, drafting the entire French population into the uprising against their oppressors. It mobilized men and women, young and old:

> The National Convention, having heard the report of its Committee of Public Safety, decrees:
>
> Article 1. From this moment until the time when the enemy is driven from the territory of the Republic, all Frenchmen are drafted into the service of the army.
>
> Let the young men go into combat; the married men forge weapons and transport provisions; the women make army tents and uniforms and serve in the hospitals; the children tear up linen; and the elderly be put in public places in order to stir up the courage of the soldiers and preach the hatred of the kings and the unity of the Republic.[15]

The concept of total war, using any and every means, was born.

A half century later, Carl von Clausewitz, a Prussian military officer, developed the theoretical concept of total war. His complex thought had an enormous impact on subsequent military strategy. He was revered as much by Marx, Engels, Lenin, and Trotsky as he is today by Washington military planners. Indeed, one of the ironies of the Cold War is that each side could claim the same strategist as its mentor—reflecting, no doubt, the strategic mirror image that each side formed opposite the other during the Cold War.

Clausewitz rejected the Enlightenment scientific ideal rampant in the military colleges of the day. Instead, he insisted on scrupulously maintaining an intimate link between political policy and military means, in all instances insisting that military means remain subordinate to political policy. This meant that war became an additional item on the menu of options available to a government for implementing its policies. War became a normal and indispensable instrument for carrying out government policy:

> [War is political policy] conducted by fighting battles rather than by sending diplomatic notes.
> . . . It is apt to be assumed that war suspends [political] intercourse and replaces it by a wholly different condition, ruled by no law but its own.
> We maintain, on the contrary, that war is simply a continuation of political intercourse, with the addition of other means. We deliberately use the phrase "with the addition of other means" because we also want to make it clear that war in itself does not suspend political discourse or change it into something entirely different. In essentials that intercourse continues, irrespective of the means it employs. . . . Do political relations between peoples and their governments stop when diplomatic notes are no longer exchanged? Is war not just another expression of their thoughts, another form of speech or writing?[16]

For Clausewitz, the practice of war itself, while limited by political policy, could be nothing less than absolute or total, for life and death itself were at stake. The French Revolution changed everything for him; with the overthrow of monarchy, "suddenly war again became the business of the people."[17] Clausewitz and particularly his followers described modern warfare as a conflict between nations requiring a total deployment of all possibilities and forces. Nations should commit to the struggle all their labor, their whole system of production, all their natural resources, their whole culture, and all other means of assistance. Literature and art must promote victory, and so must the news service and propaganda. But as simply subservient means to a greater political end, military means offered no criticism of the end itself, remaining strictly "neutral"—no doubt accounting for the Soviet Union and NATO equally embracing Clausewitz's approach.

Clausewitz's total war strategic thinking remains utterly relevant today. Consider an excerpt from a book entitled *Shock and Awe: Achieving Rapid Dominance*, published by the Pentagon's National Defense University in 1996.[18] The book advocates the overwhelming bombardment strategy later used partially in the 2003 invasion of Iraq. Harlan Ullman—whom Colin Powell, former US secretary of state and chairman of the joint chiefs of staff, credits with "enlarging my vision several levels"[19]—is a principal author, and his work makes for chilling reading:

> One recalls from old photographs and movie or television screens, the comatose and glazed expressions of survivors of the great bombardments

of World War I and the attendant horrors and death of trench warfare. These images and expressions of shock transcend race, culture, and history. Indeed, TV coverage of *Desert Storm* vividly portrayed Iraqi soldiers registering these effects of battlefield Shock and Awe.

In our excursion, we seek to determine whether and how Shock and Awe can become sufficiently intimidating and compelling factors to force or otherwise convince an adversary to accept our will in the Clausewitzian sense, such that the strategic aims and military objectives of the campaign will achieve a political end.

Security Powder

The third feature of this history is the invention in 1866 of dynamite, or "security powder" as Alfred Nobel called it. Nobel's invention stimulated an enormous expansion of the technology of warfare, thanks partly to the rapidly growing natural sciences.

What inspired Nobel to call his sinister invention "security powder"? And what caused him to allot vast sums of money, earned by his weapons factory, to the Nobel Peace Prize? Do not Nobel's actions suggest a form of schizophrenia?[20] Undoubtedly they do. But Nobel reconciled these impossible tensions in his life by maintaining that the expansion of the military's destructive possibilities would make peace on earth an incontrovertible fact. "I hope," he once wrote, "to discover a weapon so terrible that it would make war eternally impossible." Hence the invention of security powder and the financing of the Nobel Peace Prize with money made from weapons.

Eighty years later the first atomic bombs fell on Hiroshima and Nagasaki. Was that the fulfillment of Nobel's long-cherished dream?

Lessons of the Past

This brief historical sketch suggests several things. First, already far back in history the waging of war and/or the defense of one's territory were seen as ends for which God-given ways of justice, as brakes against violence, do not hold. Humankind's own ends were too important or too decisive. Hugo Grotius began a countermovement, later elaborated by jurists like Cornelius van Vollenhoven. It led to a few international treaties and conventions, such as the Hague Peace Conferences (1899 and 1907), which outlawed the bombardment of open cities, and the Geneva Conference of 1925, which declared that the development of chemical weapons violates international law. But today these principles of justice, including the noninvolvement of the civilian population and of women and children, are a vague memory. In a real conflict situation, noncombatants may be erased entirely. The Nazis bombed Rotterdam (an open city), and the Allies bombarded the civilian population of Dresden. Conflict, menace, and war write their own law: the law of the strongest. Around 1900, about 5 percent of those killed in war were civilians; by 1990 that figure was 90 percent.[21] And now, with the possibility of using weapons of mass destruction, has it not become meaningless to speak of forbidding the killing of innocent women and children?

Second, long ago a contrast developed in the order in which people thought about peace, security, justice, and love. The biblical order has always been: do justice, love your neighbor, respect the Torah, and then you will have life. Seek first the kingdom of God and its righteousness (thus taking care of the poor and of the earth), and all that remains, including peace and prosperity, will be added to you. In the Renaissance, however, peace became a product of human technology and science. Since then, the Western order has been different: put peace, security, and prosperity first; and then freedom, equality, justice, brotherhood, and sisterhood will be added to you as the harvest of your labors. Biblical ways are quite nice in one's private life, but they must not hinder human progress toward prosperity and peace in the public square.

Finally, building up technology in order to coerce peace has increased the means of military destruction and the probability of their use. The increase was both in range and in depth. The circle of persons and areas of life involved in military conflict became larger (today it envelops all citizens and all sectors of life), and gradually modern weapons technology itself took control over the problem of peace and conflict. Weapons technology today is hardly restricted by the principles of international law. The schizophrenia of Alfred Nobel generated a split in all Western culture: more weapons—the more destructive the better—will create peace.

Strategic Shifts during the Cold War

Let us now look at more recent history. In reality, more weapons threatened peace. In the years after World War II, our civilization acquired full command of the technology of splitting the atom: an instrument for waging war and maintaining peace. Shortly after the formation of NATO in 1948, the atomic bomb was added to its arsenal. How would NATO, conceived in the reality of Soviet aggression and aware of the lessons of history, handle this new totalitarian weapon?

NATO's first strategy was to plan for massive retaliation against a conventional attack by the Soviet Union. Some years later, however, the Soviet Union was believed to be approaching the production of nuclear weapons. Because of the Soviets' advancing technology, NATO developed a new strategy under the title "mutually assured destruction" (MAD). From that point on, the Soviet Union and the United States tacitly sought to hold each other's population hostage, as it were, in order to ward off the danger of a nuclear war. Each knew that after receiving a first blow, it needed to have enough remaining power to destroy a large segment of the opponents' civilian population. Each country needed second-strike capability. The United States in particular devoted itself to maintaining and building up this capacity. During this time (from 1948 until around 1970), something of Alfred Nobel's dream seemed to be realized. New weapons were available, weapons so terrible that war seemed impossible. In line with Enlightenment thinking, politicians began to view peace as the result of technology and science. The nonuse of these means of destruction stood at the forefront of their strategizing. Presumably the arms race would end when a weapons ceiling was reached that would guarantee the total elimination of the enemy and its population in the event of a first strike. After that, more weapons would surely be unnecessary and useless.

Around 1970 that ceiling was reached. One American nuclear submarine then had the capability to destroy 160 Soviet cities simultaneously. Any nuclear submarine that survived a Soviet first strike could therefore accomplish the necessary total destruction. Consequently, a further increase of strategic weapons was no longer necessary. Sufficient deterrence had been reached regardless of whether the Soviet Union wanted to strategically arm itself further.

But the dismal story is that during the 1970s the world staged a greater arms race than ever before. After 1970 both sides, the Soviet Union and NATO, multiplied their capacity to destroy the world ten times. Why did this happen?

In his memoir, *The White House Years*, Henry Kissinger suggests why.[22] In 1969 Kissinger summoned the Joint Chiefs of Staff for the US military forces to explain that the United States could not escape adjusting its strategy of MAD. Armaments and weapons technology in the East and the West had advanced to such a stage that strategic nuclear weapons could now be aimed more and more at both tactical targets (on the battlefield) and also directly at well-defined military targets, such as missile silos. Prompted by a strategic direction adopted already in 1962 by then-Secretary of Defense Robert McNamara, Kissinger wanted to create room for this realignment in American strategy, particularly to lessen the chances of total eradication of the American population in case of a general conflict.

This was a moment of tremendous significance. Kissinger's proposal was to break through the existing weapons ceiling. No longer were we to view strategic weapons as weapons whose nonuse is primary at all times. On a limited scale, these weapons could be deployed, if necessary, against military targets to prevent more serious destruction. Kissinger believed that second-strike capability had to become at least partially preemptive strike or first-strike capability. In Kissinger's proposal the existing ceiling for strategic weapons would therefore disappear. By choosing military objects as points of possible attack, the arms race could naturally continue.

What did the Joint Chiefs of Staff do?

> The Joint Chiefs of Staff cooperated because they understood that the doctrine of assured destruction would inevitably lead to political decisions halting or neglecting the improvement of our strategic forces, and in time reducing them. We therefore developed in 1969 new criteria of strategic sufficiency, that related our strategic planning to the destruction of military targets as well.[23]

You have to rub your eyes to believe it. The arms race continued because otherwise the "improvement" of American strategic forces "threatened" to stop.

Later Developments

From that moment, the arms race again moved ahead furiously. The possibility of beginning and even waging a "limited nuclear war" on European soil with strategic nuclear weapons worked its way into NATO planning, causing a rift between the United States and the European members of NATO. The United States pressured European countries to install short-range nuclear missiles in Europe. The NATO members played a poker game on a global scale, and the lives of millions were the stakes. The January 1, 1984, headline of *Die Zeit* quoted German Chancellor Helmut Schmidt: "Do Not Be Afraid. Fear Has Overcome Us, But Reason Can Conquer It."[24] Reason, whose most spectacular achievement was the creation of nuclear weapons, was now supposed to cure us of our fear of them: a tall and impossible order.[25]

Between 1970 and 1980 weapons trade across the world more than doubled.[26] Like cancer spreading through the body, the capacity to build nuclear bombs spread to many countries. In the image of an old story, Pandora's box had opened. The world began to live in fear over what could come from this staggering proliferation of means of destruction.

Meanwhile, negotiations over arms control continued, leading to the result that under SALT I America and the Soviet Union gave each other permission to build two nuclear bombs per day. Under the SALT II accords in which many people said that America went "too far," that number was expanded to three and a half bombs a day. Weapons control became a camouflage allowing both sides to maintain a relentless arms race, extending even into outer space: on March 23, 1983, President Reagan delivered his famous "Star Wars" speech, in which he called on the scientific community "to mobilize its efforts and resources in quest of an impenetrable antiballistic missile shield over the entire nation—without triggering perilously destabilizing countermeasures, both offensive and defensive, on the part of the U.S.S.R."[27]

A Complete Ideology

In these developments we detect all the hallmarks of a full-fledged ideology: an ideology of guaranteed freedom from tyranny. In a struggle in which the end justified every conceivable means, the "free" West became pitted against the state-sponsored terror of the East.

Many nations and groups of people became possessed by the goal of guaranteed security. Their obsession gave them the impulse to use any means at their disposal to create new strategies for reaching their all-encompassing end.

Also evident were the means: instruments of total violence. The end justified threatening others with their possible use. Weapons development was judged by no other standard than maximum precision and destructive power, to the point of absurdity. We did this in spite of the early warning of Eisenhower:

> It happens that defense is a field in which I have had varied experience over a lifetime, and if I have learned anything, it is that there is no way in which a country can satisfy the craving for absolute security—but it can easily bankrupt itself, morally and economically, in attempting to reach that illusory goal through arms alone.[28]

Consider the radical adjustments that took place in the means. From the mouth of Henry Kissinger, an impeccable witness, we heard what happens when a nation deems the goal of guaranteed security to be of paramount importance. It develops the most modern technological means possible and gives that development free rein in its economic system. At a certain moment those means begin to govern themselves. For their own "improvement," they demand new possibilities of use;

they coerce their users to develop new strategies that will again give them room to maneuver. The means take control. The strategy no longer holds the weapons in check. Instead, the progress of weapons technology determines the strategy.

The final step of idol worship—the role reversal of idol and idol worshipper—was therefore also present. This reversal indicated that the range of the ideology was absolute. Though initially we thought ourselves able to use and control weapons technology, the reality was that increasingly it controlled us. We surrendered to the further testing and expansion of the arsenal of destruction, an arsenal that years earlier had eluded our grasp. A god arose, and fear and hypnosis were its tools of terror. Today, many years after the end of the Cold War, we tend to forget the palpable fear under which the world lived. The world was a hair breadth away from unmitigated disaster. At the height of the Cold War, Robert Jay Lifton, a visiting professor of psychiatry at Harvard Medical School, conducted studies of American young people in which he found that many did not expect to live out the full course of their lives, due to the likelihood of a nuclear catastrophe.

We trusted in this god for our security. In 1978, in the thick of the Cold War, the French-American social theorist René Girard observed: "Humans have always found peace in the shadow of their idols—that is to say, [in the shadow] of human violence in a sacralized form. This is still true, as humanity looks for peace under the shelter of ultimate violence."[29] This idol required unbearable financial sacrifice and demanded even human sacrifices, like the Old Testament Molech, for whom the people of Judah "sacrificed their sons and daughters in the fire" (2 Kings 17:17). Why else did the systematic accumulation of means of mass violence continue?

Annihilation belongs to the very nature of these demonic means, even though our intention was never to use such weapons for the purpose of annihilation. But if nuclear deterrence, still part of NATO strategy today, is to be effective, it requires credibility. And credibility demands the actual readiness to use such weapons. The real question was therefore whether in critical situations we would have the freedom to act in accordance with our intentions. During his first tenure as secretary of defense (1975–77), Donald Rumsfeld stated brazenly, "We do not exclude the possibility that for the defense of our interests we will be the first to use nuclear weapons."[30]

We must realize that gods never loosen their grip on people. If nations choose gods, they become slaves to their gods. Gandhi once said that the personality of a man changes when he acquires a weapon, and Churchill observed that if the military could run its course, it would fortify the moon. At some point those who want to protect life at any cost may feel that their weapons systems leave them no choice but to use them. No doubt that feeling is a form of illusion, of hypnosis. Weapons systems do not live and cannot force us to use them. But in genuine idolatry, they do function in this way. Consider the history of NATO strategy: we first considered the use of nuclear weapons impossible (1948), later improbable (1970), and still later probable (with the rise of the concept of a limited nuclear war in 1979). Only an ideology that has aroused a full-fledged idolatry can accomplish this reversal.

The ideology also conscripted the currently held values of truth, justice, and love for its own purposes. Commonly known mandates of international law inscribed in authorized treaties did not interfere with the further development of weapons technology or even with the renewed production of chemical weapons. The law of self-protection at any price replaced international law. Political parties, and some Christians, sometimes publicly and unashamedly advocated a double morality. They admitted that the use or threat of use of nuclear weapons is morally and ethically objectionable and even absolutely forbidden. But they argued that in the political reality then current, such weapons were indispensable. "Goal morality" won out. Morality and ethics were adjusted to the pursuit of national security.

Finally, the ideology of guaranteed freedom also formed an image of the enemy. The image became most obvious when the ideology legitimated the deployment of every military means available because of the desire to battle a demon, the Communist ideology. Are not all means legitimate when resisting the devil? We no longer thought in terms of the possible mass destruction of Russian citizens, including innocent women and children. Instead, we thought only of smashing an intolerable demon. Against that demon we permitted ourselves to use the most hideous means of destruction. We fought totalitarian ends (Soviet Communism) with totalitarian means (weapons of indiscriminate, total destruction). But did we not then fall prey to an ideology no less totalitarian than Communism?

Countermovements

No doubt the implosion of the East Bloc, under the weight of its own idolatrous terror, prevented the West from taking the final step in the role reversal instigated by idolatry: the inevitability of the use of nuclear weapons. But a second brake also acted as a restraint.

As the Cold War increased in intensity and as its built-in madness became more and more evident, many people from across the political spectrum began to eloquently protest and oppose. Using just-war criteria, many church denominations and bodies (such as Catholic Bishops' Conferences in many countries) publicly and courageously urged their government leaders to renounce their nations' reliance on nuclear weapons. Former apostles of the Cold War, among them Robert McNamara and George F. Kennan, publicly sounded the alarm.[31] Policy alternatives were articulated under such rubrics as the Freeze movement. Delegations of ordinary citizens from NATO countries and the Soviet Union exchanged visits with one another to symbolize concretely their commitment to peace. And a number of people, such as Daniel and Philip Berrigan, engaged in active nonviolent protest against the arms race. Many of these now largely forgotten activists, driven by their faith in God, often did so at significant personal cost.

Post–Cold War Developments

Much of the Cold War era itself is now fading from memory. Does that mean, as some commentators have boasted, that the ideology that gripped so many people during that period has also faded? Or has the West as a whole, despite the profound change in world circumstances and despite the countermovements against the once-dominant Cold War tendency, chosen to keep intact its commitment to guaranteed freedom and absolute security? What prevented the West from repairing the structural imbalances created by the Cold War, thereby creating the "peace dividend" that was so desperately needed around the world?

The answer lies in tracing Western military strategic developments after the Cold War. Here again, three historical developments stand out.

The Changed Nature of Conflict

First, almost immediately the nature of conflict profoundly changed. Identity conflicts, driven by identity ideologies, quickly emerged around the world (with identities sometimes coalescing across national boundaries). Like a lit match on a powder keg, these "localized mini-holocausts" were inflamed by the surplus of arms that suddenly became available.[32] The West was ill equipped to deal with them. Its lack of preparedness became hazardous because the new identity conflicts quickly threatened the "vital interests" of the West. Within a year after the fall of the Berlin Wall, the first Gulf War, Desert Storm, took place—a war whose intensity of firepower surpassed all previous wars, including the Vietnam War.[33] And shockingly, the resulting enormous arms buildup in the Middle East almost outpaced the earlier arms race between the East and the West.

This global return of military insecurity was not an accident. Its roots lay in the conduct not just of some people in the Arab world but also of some in the West. Economists have shown that access to the mineral resources of the world contains potential for conflict, whose scope is entirely unknown.[34] Indeed, with Desert Storm a new element surfaced: now it is primarily the affluent nations, not the poor ones, that find themselves compelled to acquire, with whatever degree of violence is required, guaranteed access to the world's oil fields. Some rich countries, especially the United States, are enormous oil producers themselves, but their own production cannot match their much greater consumption. At the time of Desert Storm, though the United States ranked second in the world in oil production, 40 percent of all the oil it consumed was imported, which accounted for 60 percent of its staggering trade deficit.[35] The enormous economic power of the rich nations therefore rests on lame feet. Without guaranteed access to economic resources from other parts of the world, their economies shake at their foundations. The giantism of the world's rich nations increases the possibility of international conflict.

The gravity of the first Gulf War lay also in the fact that it preempted the use of scarce resources for the sustaining of life in other parts of the world. This occurred on two sides. The countries of the North did not earmark the scarce resources freed up from the former arms buildup for peaceful ends, a task that the leader of the Soviet Union, Mikhail Gorbachev, had urged in a major address at the United Nations (in which he pinpointed reversal of the trend of worldwide pollution as one of the most important items requiring action). But the bitter reality for the South was that the poor countries that did not produce oil were forced to help finance the Western arms buildup in the Gulf because the conflict inevitably inflated the price of imported oil and because Western governments refrained from raising taxes for this purpose. Thus, the poor countries had to help finance the startling arms buildup, even though they themselves could not provide the basic necessities of life for their own people.[36]

Iraq and the West

The second critical post–Cold War strategic development involved Iraq. Here too, lack of knowledge of recent history clouds our ability to understand current strategic issues regarding Iraq.

The first observation to make is that, using even strict military definitions, the Coalition of the Willing did not begin a war against Iraq with its invasion in March 2003. Properly speaking, it merely intensified a conflict begun particularly by the United States and Great Britain shortly after the end of the first Gulf War.

After Desert Storm, under the auspices of the United Nations, the West imposed strict economic sanctions on Iraq, designed in part to turn the Iraqi people against Saddam Hussein. The result was that by 2003, the prevalence of poverty in Iraq was greater than in India, though in the early 1980s Iraq enjoyed near–First World economic prosperity. Iraq's infrastructure was decimated, and Iraqi oil production was not near capacity.[37]

As a result of sanctions, it is estimated that one million Iraqis, half of them children, died between the end of Desert Storm and the attack against Iraq in 2003.[38] To give this figure some scale, roughly 214,000 people were killed in the bombings of Hiroshima and Nagasaki. When confronted with these numbers in a television interview, Madeleine Albright, then the US secretary of state, did not deny them but stated, "It's a hard choice, but I think, we think, it's worth it."[39]

In addition, after Desert Storm the United States and Great Britain unilaterally established no-fly zones over Iraq. These zones covered 60 percent of Iraq's air space. Ostensibly, the no-fly zones were to protect the Kurds in the north and the Shiite Muslims in the South from Hussein and the Sunni Muslims in the middle. However, it became clear that the zones also had military purposes.[40] Further, the *Mirror* reported:

> In March [2002], RAF pilots patrolling the "no fly zone" in Kurdish Iraq publicly protested for the first time about their enforced complicity in the Turkish campaign [against the Kurds living in Iraq]. The pilots complained that they were frequently ordered to return to their base in Turkey to allow the Turkish air force to bomb the very people they were meant to be "protecting." . . . In addition, American pilots who flew in tandem with the British were also ordered to turn their planes around and turn back to Turkey to allow the Turks to devastate the Kurdish "safe havens." "You'd see Turkish F-14s and F-16s inbound, loaded to the gills with munitions," one pilot told the *Washington Post*. "Then they'd come out half an hour later with their munitions expended." When the Americans returned to Iraqi air space, he said, they would see "burning villages, lots of smoke and fire."[41]

According to UN personnel and other independent reports, confirmed by mainstream media and not denied by the US government, the United States and Great Britain also bombed Iraqi "military establishments" an average of three to four times per week from the end of the Gulf War until 2003, using cluster bombs, not precision-guided bombs. These figures are a matter of public record.[42] The United Nations reports that at least three hundred civilians were killed by these bombs between 1998 and 2002, and many more injured, leading, in part, to the successive resignations of three senior UN officials in protest.[43] One of them, Hans von Sponeck, former UN assistant secretary-general and humanitarian coordinator in Iraq, stated: "If you want to be very cynical then you say that what has in fact resulted from these zones is death and destruction. . . . On average, during the time I was in Iraq, there were bombing incidents every three days. The casualties were in the very areas that they allegedly established to protect people."[44] Sometimes "military targets" were located in population centers, killing the very people that the no-fly zones were designed to protect.

The Pentagon estimated that each of these missions cost $750,000. In 2000, the Pentagon-reported bill for the southern zone alone was $1.4 billion.[45] This was the longest-sustained US bombing campaign since the Vietnam War.

In the view of many observers, the economic sanctions and bombing amounted to nothing short of crimes against humanity. Mairead Corrigan Maguire, who won the Nobel Peace Prize in 1976, said, "In fifty years, the next generation will ask: What were you doing when the children of Iraq were dying?"[46] On this matter, the policy of the United Nations, Great Britain, and the United States was, by its own definition, a colossal failure. It had a significant negative impact on the view of the West held by many throughout the Muslim world. And it did not turn the people of Iraq against Hussein.[47]

US Military and Defense Policy after 2000

The third development brings us squarely into the present debate and requires us to situate ourselves within it. Recent presidential elections in the United States (2004) have also been among the most polarized. The so-called Democratic Left poured its energies into trying to unseat the so-called Republican Right.

But in our view, the notion that the Democrats would introduce a basic change of direction was fundamentally misguided. One needed to look no further than the Clinton administration to ascertain that. In the same vein as President Bush, President Clinton claimed for America the right to "unilateral use of military power" to ensure "uninhibited access to key markets, energy supplies, and strategic resources."[48] A staggering, unconscionable, and almost unimaginable number of innocent people were killed as a result of the UN policy against Iraq, actively endorsed by the Democratic Clinton administration. And as if in lockstep, Democratic and Republican presidential candidates appeared to be outdoing each other in their pledges to raise defense spending after the election.

There may be differences in degree or nuance between the Republican and Democratic parties. But it would seem that there are no clear differences in principle and vision. And it is at that level that genuine alternatives can emerge.[49]

A second comment follows naturally from the first. It is our deep conviction that, if alternative perspectives and policy proposals are fueled by "anti-Americanism," they merely exacerbate today's polarizations and do not contribute to peace. Such opposition is itself ideological. It serves only to pull opponents into the same force field they wish to oppose. Regrettably, on occasion it has seemed that the quality of some people's anger against the United States over its Iraq policies has not been terribly different from the same impulse toward revenge that may have inspired, in part, US policy.[50]

Against this backdrop, consider the significant developments in US military and defense policy since 2000.

In a speech, President Bush once declared, "Today's tyrants are gripped by an implacable hatred of the United States of America. They hate our friends, they hate our values, they hate democracy and freedom and individual liberty."[51]

What is noteworthy is the date that President Bush made these comments. They were spoken on May 1, 2001, at the National Defense University, when he announced that America was withdrawing from the Anti-Ballistic Missile Treaty. They thus were uttered before September 11, 2001.

The point is that September 11 has had a negligible impact on US military and defense policy. Clearly, 9/11 shifted some attitudes and sponsored some changes. But it scarcely affected US military and defense policy.[52]

Indeed, in the nine months before 9/11, the Bush administration showed itself to be perhaps the most militarily driven administration in US history, more so than Ronald Reagan's and likely Richard Nixon's. Before 9/11, the Bush administration threatened, undermined, or dismantled the following:

1. *The Biological Weapons Convention.* The US government scuttled a major six-year effort to reach an agreement on procedures to verify and monitor compliance. The government gave two reasons. First, astonishingly, the protocols would not adequately protect US pharmaceutical and biotechnology companies from having to divulge information that might compromise their economic edge in a highly competitive environment. The second was that the proposed protocols would not adequately deal with "rogue" nations.[53]

2. *The Chemical Weapons Convention.* On November 25, 1969, President Nixon said, "I have decided that the United States of America

will renounce the use of any form of deadly biological weapons that either kill or incapacitate." Before 9/11, the US government began to try to ensure that biological weapons that "incapacitate" were acceptable.[54]

3. *The Anti-Ballistic Missile Treaty.* This was one of the only truly successful arms control measures. In violation of this treaty and the Outer Space Treaty, President Bush announced the implementation of a "Missile Defense" plan, despite rather colossal testing failures and despite the weaponization of other countries that this initiative will clearly sponsor and already has so sponsored.[55] The policy is justified in part by a false statement that more nations have nuclear weapons and even more have nuclear aspirations. In recent years, the number of states in possession of nuclear weapons has in fact decreased.[56] Seven countries have abandoned their nuclear programs and joined the Nuclear Non-Proliferation Treaty as nonnuclear states.

The word "Defense" in "Missile Defense" is a euphemism. *Vision for 2020*, a Pentagon strategic plan that partly animates the Missile Defense plan, calls for the weaponization of space. It begins with these words: "U.S. Space Command: dominating the space dimension of military operations to protect U.S. interests and investments. Integrating Space Forces into war-fighting capabilities across the full spectrum of conflict." This report was followed up by a classified, May 2002 Pentagon planning document, about which military analyst William Arkin concluded, "No target on the planet or in space would be immune to American attack."[57] Such plans are historically unprecedented.

4. *The Outer Space Treaty.* President Eisenhower conceived and implemented the Outer Space Treaty. In 1958 Eisenhower said: "I propose that we agree that outer space should be used only for peaceful purposes. We face a decisive moment in history in relation to this matter. . . . Should not outer space be dedicated to the peaceful use of mankind and denied to the purposes of war?" This was a crucial moment in history: the Soviets had just launched Sputnik. Eisenhower was successful in this endeavor.[58]

5. *The Nuclear Non-Proliferation Treaty.* The Bush administration reintroduced the concept of a first-strike, winnable nuclear war in violation of the treaty. For several years, in keeping with the concept of a nuclear preemptive strike—reinvigorated before September 11, 2001—President Bush's budget submissions included millions of dollars for the development of so-called nuclear bunker busters, each of which is seventy times more powerful than the atomic bomb dropped on Hiroshima.[59] Stymied by congressional

pressure to bury this initiative, the Bush administration proposed the development of a "Reliable Replacement Warhead" instead, designed to replace current nuclear warheads.[60] So significant are these developments that some commentators have begun to describe our time as the Second Nuclear Age.[61]

September 11, 2001, came after these developments, and in its aftermath came the declaration of *The National Security Strategy of the United States* (September 2002). This document brought to full expression the impulses behind the Bush administration's unprecedented changes in US military and defense policy before 9/11. In her testimony before the congressional commission examining American preparedness for 9/11, Dr. Condoleezza Rice claimed that nine months (prior to 9/11) was not long enough for the Bush administration to become truly oriented to al-Qaeda's terrorist threat. But it was long enough to undertake the most significant militarization of US policy in modern history.

A Reinvigorated Ideology

What brought about this profound intensification in military force? *The National Security Strategy* (2002), amplified by more recent statements made by President Bush, provides a clue. Together they represent a repristination, a vigorous recommitment to the ideology of guaranteed freedom. They sing a paean, a hymn of praise to freedom, but freedom defined according to the Enlightenment faith in individual human progress and autonomy. They revel in America's "manifest destiny" to spread freedom throughout the world. Consider a sampling:

> We seek to lift whole nations by spreading freedom. . . . This is the work history has set before us. We welcome it.
>
> Today, humanity holds in its hands the opportunity to further freedom's triumph over all these foes. The United States welcomes its responsibility to lead in this great mission.
>
> As the greatest power on the face of the Earth, we have an obligation to help the spread of freedom.
>
> America is leading the civilized world in a titanic struggle against terror. Freedom and fear are at war. And freedom is winning.
>
> The United States possesses unprecedented and unequaled strength and influence in the world. Sustained by faith in the principles of liberty, and the value of a free society, this position comes with unparalleled responsibilities, obligations, and opportunity.
>
> The National Security Strategy must . . . look outward for possibilities to expand liberty.

I believe so strongly in the power of freedom.

We understand our special calling. This great Republic will lead the cause of freedom.

All of us are called to share the blessings of liberty, and to be strong and steady in freedom's defense.

We will serve the cause of liberty, and that, always and everywhere, is a cause worth serving.[62]

More recent statements amplify the praise. In President Bush's second inaugural address (Jan. 20, 2005), he exclaimed:

There is only one force of history that can break the reign of hatred and resentment . . . , and that is the force of human freedom. . . .

One day this untamed fire of freedom will reach the darkest corners of our world.

We go forward with complete confidence in the eventual triumph of freedom. . . . Freedom is the permanent hope of mankind, the hunger in dark places, the longing of the soul.

We are ready for the greatest achievements in the history of freedom.[63]

The United States was born by becoming free of tyranny, and it is commendable to want to share that freedom with others. Further, the United States and other NATO nations do good things internationally that are not ideologically driven. But when freedom becomes absolute, when freedom is not subject to the requirements of justice, mercy, compassion, solidarity with one's neighbor, and care for the poor and for God's good earth, then an ideology has arisen that takes on the dynamic and damning power of an alternative religious drive.

The point is that the ideological impulse for freedom made absolute, born in the aftermath of the suffering of World War II, found new articulation after 9/11. It was never abandoned after the Cold War. It accounts for the actions of Western governments in the 1990s and for the unprecedented intensification of military force by the US government in 2001, prior to September 11, 2001. It then found new expression after the attacks on the Twin Towers and the Pentagon. Since 1989, our society has left virtually intact the feeding ground, the meaning-structure, the matrix, the ultimate commitment that sustains the unrestricted expansion of the means of destruction. Only a fundamental change of conviction at the level of ideology could have slackened the relentless momentum of arms escalation. Hence, only a shift at the level of ideology could have created the flexibility needed for the restructuring that would have generated a "peace dividend." The unflagging control exerted by the means to the end meant that the world suffered under a built-in, structural inflexibility.

In *The National Security Strategy* of 2002, just as in *The National Security Strategy* of March 2006, the end (goal) of freedom possesses ultimate significance.[64] Together, most Democrats and Republicans hold that "truth" to be self-evident. Their joint adherence to the ideology explains the inability of Democrats to differentiate their position from the Republican one on the invasion of Iraq. And it directs both Republican and Democrat attention to ensuring that America's "vital interests" are protected at all costs.

President Bush publicly professes his faith in Christ. But a signal failure of the current religious discourse is that it has failed to discern the syncretism that has driven recent decision-making at the most senior levels in Washington. *Webster's Dictionary* defines "syncretism" as "the combination or reconciliation of differing beliefs or practices in religion, philosophy, etc., or an attempt to effect such compromise." President Bush and his administration have tried to form a profound and fundamental religious syncretism, an amalgam of irreconcilable basic tendencies.[65] They seek to merge values of the gospel with a modern obsession with individual freedom, driven by a modernist, Enlightenment faith in human ingenuity and accomplishment.

Freedom and Control

In the current context, then, what happens when freedom is made absolute? By this point we can predict the effects. In an intensely biblical irony, pursuing absolute freedom results in the loss of freedom. Just as "all who draw the sword will die by the sword" (Matt. 26:52), so too those who live by freedom engage in and experience the radical curtailment of freedom.

Absolute freedom requires absolute force to accomplish, secure, and guarantee that freedom. The end (freedom at all costs) justifies every possible means, including unprecedented force (such as unlimited military power, a profound curtailment of civil liberties, and the violation of international law). The requirements of that force gradually diminish, curtail, restrict, and ultimately destroy freedom. The ideology of freedom at all costs therefore possesses a basic internal contradiction or tension that cannot be resolved, a schizophrenic tension between freedom and control. Thus it is ironic that the doctrine of preemptive strike, rationalized as essential in today's environment in order to spread democracy throughout the world, is entirely dependent upon Congress giving the president sweeping powers to act based on information that must remain secret. Congress had to abandon its democratic function to approve the policy of preemptive strike. Within the framework of freedom made absolute, the act of spreading democracy requires at its core the abandonment of democracy. By reason of that schizophrenia alone, the strategy will fail.[66]

Further, absolute freedom even contains within it the seeds of terror. President Bush is sadly mistaken when, at the beginning of *The National Security Strategy* (2002), he contrasts his definition of "freedom" with "totalitarianism": "The great struggles of the twentieth century between liberty and totalitarianism ended with a decisive victory for the forces of freedom. . . . In the twenty-first century, only nations that share a commitment to . . . guaranteeing . . . freedom will be able to unleash the potential of their people. . . ."[67] But guaranteed freedom is not the opposite of terror or totalitarianism. By no means are they reflections of different value systems. On the contrary, when the means to the all-consuming end are given full sway, terror and freedom are siblings in the same family.

Means Unleashed

To illustrate, let us track the momentum and the radical adjustment to means that the adherents of the ideology have unleashed. In today's post–Cold War world, what do societies do when they embrace the ideology of guaranteed freedom?

First, they support puppet dictators who serve the cause of freedom. They fund tyrants like Saddam Hussein in order to support his resistance against Iran. After the unconscionable Hussein gassed to death about five thousand Kurds, US arms trade with Hussein increased. They set up Osama bin Laden: the West recruited bin Laden and others and urged them to start an Islamic holy war, a jihad, against the Soviet occupation of Afghanistan. The United States partially funded bin Laden's efforts. Al-Qaeda's current Islamic jihad was originally partly activated by the United States in the name of freedom.[68] Sadly, the United States has a checkered history of actively supporting tyrannical dictatorships in the name of freedom.

Second, the military has now become the core, almost the sole instrument, of foreign policy. Numbers tell the story:

- For 2007 President Bush proposes to spend $463 billion on the military, not including the costs of the military presence in Afghanistan and Iraq.[69] That is more than the military budgets of the next 25 countries combined.[70] It represents a 43 percent increase since 2000 (again, not including the military costs of Iraq and Afghanistan).[71] In 2005 42 percent of federal funds were spent on current and previous military expenditures.[72] If the pattern of 2005 continues, in 2006 almost half of the accumulated US debt, which is expected to surpass $8.6 trillion or 66 percent of gross domestic product (GDP) that year, will be due to past military spending.[73]

- The president's proposed military budget is over twenty times greater than the State Department and foreign aid budgets, which represent many of the other possible instruments of foreign policy. President Bush's 2006 budget submission allocated $14.2 billion for development and humanitarian aid, programs designed to address the root causes of deadly conflict.[74] It is estimated that 10 percent of the US military budget would take care of the basic needs of the world's population, and the US ranks last among the developed countries in foreign aid as a percentage of GDP.[75]

As we saw, in the nineteenth century Clausewitz developed the total war concept of the French Revolution to be simply one additional item on a menu of foreign policy options available to governments. Today the military option has been transformed to become the core instrument of foreign policy.[76]

Third, guaranteed freedom sanctions the use of weapons and weapon systems that violate international law and the principles of justice. Consider the use of depleted uranium in Afghanistan and Iraq. There is controversy over the effects of depleted uranium. But there is so much anecdotal evidence—including some by US Army Major Doug Rokke, a medical specialist who directed the army's Depleted Uranium Project during Desert Storm—that in our judgment its use must at least be suspended until adequate health testing is completed. The Pentagon and the UN estimate that the attack against Iraq used 1,200 to 2,200 metric tons of depleted uranium, largely in densely populated urban centers.[77] This does not include the depleted uranium dropped in the bombings before March 2003. Depleted uranium has a half-life of 4.5 billion years. Inconceivable as it may sound, thanks to the use of these radiological weapons of indiscriminate effect, the deadly impact of depleted uranium could be felt for that long in both Afghanistan and Iraq.

The ideology also redefines truth. Truth morphs into whatever serves the cause of freedom, as we saw graphically with the remarkable shifting, contradictory series of rationalizations for the invasion of Iraq.[78]

Finally, the ideology creates its own image of the enemy. After 9/11, President Bush unequivocally named a new "axis of evil" and with it a new definition of "good," one that brings with it its own legitimizing power. In a speech in September 2002, President Bush declared a supremely ideological redefinition: "And the light [America] has shone in the darkness [the enemies of America], and the darkness will not overcome it." At the Washington Cathedral on September 14, 2001, in a statement suffused with ideological hubris, he declared, "Our responsibility to history is already clear: to . . . rid the world of evil."[79] For this task, the newly defined "light" overcoming the reconceived "darkness," sacrifices are required: the erosion of democracy, the loss of the humanity of others, the curtailment of basic rights and freedoms, and even economic viability.[80]

So it is that while "democracy" is demanded of Iraq, in a marvelously retouched image of the "enemy," democracy is not demanded of Saudi Arabia, one of the least democratic nations in the Middle East. Similarly, many Muslims testify today that they have become subject to abuse simply because of their faith or nationality. And the horrific prisoner abuses in Iraq and Guantanamo Bay are not aberrations but merely logical extensions of the ideology. Such abuses require belief that the detainees are less than human.

Truth, justice, righteousness, care for the earth, compassion, love of one's neighbor, even freedom itself—the relentless requirements of absolute freedom trample upon all of these.

The Consequences in Iraq

Not surprisingly, the contradiction between freedom and control has been playing itself out in Iraq. One can trace the history of the Coalition's intervention in Iraq according to the freedom/control contradiction. How is this freedom, more and more Iraqis began to ask, if we are occupied? At no point did the US administration consider the loss of control permissible. The first US administrator in postinvasion Iraq, Jay Garner, stated that he was fired because, though he wanted to hold elections, the Bush administration insisted that he first open doors for American corporations.[81] Had it not been for massive pressure exerted by Iraq's Grand Ayatollah Ali al-Sistani, spurred on by the US administration's decision to cancel municipal elections across Iraq in June 2003, the historic election that took place on January 30, 2005, would have been for an indirect, tightly controlled caucus system rather than the direct "one person, one vote" election that it became. Ironically, we can view the courageous Iraqi balloting that took place as a vote against occupation and for freedom.[82]

Indeed, as Garner warned, the handover to the UN-picked Iraq authority on June 30, 2004, was about the appearance of giving up control, not the fact. The *Los Angeles Times* reported that, on his final day in office, Proconsul Paul Bremer ensured that the "100 Orders" he had earlier issued remained intact after the transition. They locked into place sweeping advantages to foreign corporations, at the expense of enterprising Iraqis. The Orders granted foreign contractors complete immunity from Iraqi laws, including environmental laws. They suspended all tariffs and duties, which devastated local producers and sellers, who could not compete with the massive influx of cheap foreign goods. They required the placement of US-appointed auditors in every government ministry—auditors with five-year terms and sweeping powers over contracts, programs, employees, and regulations. They allowed for 100 percent foreign ownership of Iraqi businesses, prescribed no incentives in support of local over foreign businesses, and offered forty-year ownership licenses. In what *The Economist* called "a capitalist dream," foreign corporations could buy and set up Iraqi businesses and suffer no penalty for moving 100 percent of the profits out of the country.[83]

As Lord Goldsmith, the British attorney general, warned in a leaked memo to Prime Minister Tony Blair, the Orders violated international law, specifically the Hague Conventions of 1907 (of which the United States is a signatory) and the US Army's Law of Land Warfare.[84]

Finally, the tension between freedom and control is behind the United States and British inability to comprehend the most basic tenet of peacebuilding. Peacebuilding requires immediate handover of control to a neutral or nonaligned third party. The Geneva Convention requires it. But that option is inadmissible within the ideology of guaranteed freedom because it means giving up the guarantee.

The purpose of freedom is freedom, not slavery or control.[85] Yet we have witnessed the expanding yoke of control and slavery in the ongoing, deteriorating occupation; in the massive, violent rise in anti-American sentiment in the Middle East; in the unconscionable deaths of tens or even hundreds of thousands of Iraqi civilians, mostly women and children, and the likely poisoning of many more; in the tragic, increasing collapse of civil society; and in the disenfranchisement of millions of able-bodied, unemployed Iraqis. Is it any wonder that Iraq, though it had little such prior history, has become a breeding ground for terror?

Countermovements

Earlier we stressed that all ideologies are born out of an experience of genuine suffering. The ideology of guaranteed freedom is no exception. But the ironic, tragic effect of the post–World War II resolve to guarantee freedom was that it overstepped the bounds of genuine justice, morality, and love. As a result, it unwittingly spawned a culture of violence, a culture for which all of us must acknowledge responsibility. That culture is now all-pervasive. In the words of René Girard, "No slightest section of nature—now that science has cleansed it of all the ancient projections of the supernatural—has not been reinvested with the truth of violence."[86] The ideology of guaranteed freedom has let violence loose; it has set violence free to follow its own self-determined course in the illusion that, in exchange, violence will grant us freedom. But violence set free as an autonomous power is indifferent to truth, international law, and respect for life. If the West was spiritually unprepared for the Nazi onslaught of World War II, then how much more so are we spiritually unprepared to confront terrorism today! Indeed, violence is knocking at our door, calling our name, urging us to enter its spiral of death. But this god has betrayed us.

The ideology of guaranteed freedom today bears all the traits of the alternative "religion" touted in Nietzsche's parable of the death of God. It is a belief system complete with its own prophets, oracles, articles of faith, history, orthodoxy, mythic rituals, and body of self-evident truths. Most significantly, it possesses its own powerful incarnational drive: the activity of violence in all of its manifestations. Violence is the ideology's word become flesh, *the* preeminent means recruited to achieve the end (goal) of guaranteed freedom. As we saw, violence belongs to the very nature of weapons of indiscriminate destruction. Violence is the essence of the nuclear weapons on which NATO still actively relies, it is the heart of the military means used against Iraq from 1991 until today, and it is the soul of the violent exclusion and rampant death caused by the economic sanctions against Iraq.

Thankfully, however, just as throughout the modern history of war and peace, there is evidence of remarkable countermovements against this false god. Massive worldwide protests, galvanized at the grassroots level, spoke powerfully against the 2003 invasion of Iraq before it took place—an event unprecedented in scale. This included significant, if often unreported, protests in the United States. Few may know that by January 2003, over thirty US city councils—including Detroit, Baltimore, Seattle, Washington (DC), Philadelphia, Kalamazoo, and others—passed official resolutions opposing US military intervention in Iraq.[87] Many courageous dissenting persons spoke out, including members of the US Congress and the US military, both current and retired. Many church officials, including the bishops in President Bush's own United Methodist denomination, publicly and eloquently opposed the planned action against Iraq.[88]

In addition, in the spirit of the countermovements of Hugo Grotius, Cornelius van Vollenhoven, and the Cold War, enormous disarmament activity is happening, particularly due to citizen pressure from nongovernmental organizations (NGOs). In 1997 the terms of the Convention to Ban Land Mines were finalized, driven by unflagging grassroots and

NGO pressure, and aided particularly by the government of Canada. The need is desperate: there are more land mines in Cambodia than people, and land mines are intrinsically indiscriminate in their destruction. The convention has carried on despite the refusal of the United States to ratify it. Under the auspices of the United Nations, significant strides have recently been taken to curtail the trade of small arms and light weapons (SALW) and to address the scourge of child soldiering. Further, over the past twenty years, a great deal has been learned—and practiced, often in the most ethnically riven conflicts in the world—about conflict transformation and peacebuilding.

All of these creative, courageous efforts give cause for hope. They point to the possibility of alternatives to the ideology of guaranteed freedom. Will such efforts sponsor a new direction away from the ideology of guaranteed freedom and toward life? Are there ways to begin slowing the momentum of rising insecurity in the world? If so, what are they? Does hope actually awaken life?

We address these questions in our final chapter. But first we must do more preparatory work.

Segue 2

Two Paths before Us

We have now studied four ideologies in action: ideologies of revolution, identity, material progress and prosperity, and guaranteed freedom. Ideologies are spiritual forces that direct and lead us, often at an unconscious level. We may now draw at least one conclusion.

In our view, no goal or end, however lofty or worthwhile, may allow us to elevate the means to achieve it outside the reach of genuine truth, justice, and the love of God and neighbor. This principle holds whether the goal is maintaining a culture, eliminating the most malicious powers, protecting our deepest freedoms, or even pursuing disarmament. As soon as the means become independent, they also become our gods, gods that will ultimately destroy us.

Our society has two paths before it. The first is to commit our lives to God-given ways: to live justly, to love our neighbors, and to take care of God's creation as good stewards. This is the path of obedience, the way of God's law, the torah.[1] It does not mean that we renounce all personal and societal goals. But as soon as our goals do not square with these deepest life principles, then we must either let our goals fall by the wayside or else drastically readjust them.

The second path is to commit our lives to our own ends. Such a course will redefine God-given standards and rules for life. It will determine what freedom and justice are and even how we read Scripture. The means that we use to accomplish our purposes will then torment us unceasingly. We will nevertheless embrace them, whether we admit it or not. We will convince ourselves that we have no other choice or that no one in life ever escapes getting one's hands dirty. We will justify our behavior because our overarching goal hangs in the balance.

No other paths exist, either personally or politically. Either we give God-given norms priority and relativize our goals, or we give our goals priority and relativize God-given norms.

For Christians, a great tension therefore exists in our day between the gospel and ideology, between following Jesus and serving idols. The contrast is razor-sharp. There was only one way that Christ could conquer the powers of this world and make "a public spectacle of them": he did not seek his own well-being, he distanced himself from every pursuit of power, and he preferred to obey God's commands rather than to look after his own identity as the Son of God (Phil. 2:6–11; Col. 2:15).

Many of us as Christians have systematically suppressed this knowledge of the Savior. We have selected our own goals, delivered ourselves over to various ideologies, and thus have unwittingly worshipped demonic powers. We have built our own empire rather than serving God's kingdom. Following that course has been the deepest cause of our political fragmentation. It has been the ruin of the Christian church.

In part 4 we address the question of how genuine hope, in contrast to the tortuous perspectives of the gods, can awaken new social, political, and economic alternatives in the flesh and bone of contemporary life. But before doing so, we must first explore the monstrous alliance: the insidious interactions that occur at various levels between today's ideologies.

In part 2 we probed the ideologies that are most active in our time. We discovered that a number of concrete circumstances contradict the declaration that "the end of ideology" has arrived in our time. On the contrary, in many respects ideologies of the past live on, and others have moved in.

But exactly how do they worm their way in? Do they operate independently, or do they interact in some ways? It is not difficult to understand that the awe-inspiring and all-consuming dynamism of one ideology can interfere with and even destroy other ideologies. But remarkably, mutually hostile ideologies can actually summon and even reinforce each other. In a kind of monstrous or diabolical alliance, they then collaborate in an apparent joint effort to destroy life and/or the earth. Consider the Palestinian-Israeli conflict. There we saw that the ardent ideological convictions on both sides have set in motion a spiral of violence that has led to a profound impasse. The need to react with violence is now self-evident on both sides. Ideologies can therefore evoke or reinforce each other not only when their objectives clash, but also when they use the same means to accomplish diametrically opposed ends.

But what kind of relationship describes the interaction between ideologies that at first glance seem to process smoothly down the same aisle, such as the ideologies of endless material progress and guaranteed freedom and security?

Naturally, this question draws us to reflect on today's Western society. Currently the ideologies of material progress and guaranteed freedom appear to be compatible, perhaps even complementary. But remember that an ideology imposes few, if any, restrictions on the pursuit of an objective. Subjugating everything to its absolute will belongs to the essence of ideology. And because an ideology, by means of its dynamism, demands everything, ideologies that at first appear to collaborate eventually clash.

With these observations as the backdrop, part 3 begins by sketching the intricate relationship between the ideologies of material progress and guaranteed security.

// OMINOUS SPIRALS //

/ 7 /

COLLIDING IDEOLOGIES

In chapter 5 we examined the West's unrelenting material progress, and in chapter 6 we described its untrammeled quest for a guaranteed living space. Are these pursuits sustainable? To what extent can these two ideologies coexist?

The term "living space" (*Lebensraum*) immediately brings to mind thoughts of the 1930s, when Hitler came to power in Germany and successfully exploited this ideological combination. The rearming of Germany provided an enormous stimulus to the economy. It meant that Germany's detested massive unemployment melted away like snow on a hot day. Conversely, the economic surge that resulted also acted as a hidden stimulus for more arms. The higher the economic growth, the more things needed to be militarily secured, and the easier it was to finance the increased military expenditures required. Hitler's minister of finance, Hjalmar Schacht, possessed an outstanding grasp of this relationship.

On an entirely different plane, history now appears to be repeating itself. As we saw in chapter 5, the core of the material progress ideology lies in subjecting society to the requirements of endless economic growth and to its accompanying rise in productivity. The financial markets in particular oversee this streamlining and stimulate the further productivity growth required. But this dynamist process also contains a built-in impulse to embrace constantly upgraded weapons technologies. Industry profits substantially from political-military-technological initiatives (such as "Star Wars"), as well as from the foreign government contracts signed because of the pursuit of arms-trade export markets. The resulting economic spurt then helps create more room for higher military expenditures. "California's Economy Could Grab Back Old Defense Jobs in a New Surge of Military Spending," the *Los Angeles Times* announced in 2004.[1] Clearly, a mutually beneficial interaction between ideologies is present in these developments.

But is this form of mutual reinforcement sustainable? Most certainly it is not. At a given moment an irreconcilable rupture will take place in the relationship between them. After that, not only will the ideologies find it more and more difficult to live in harmony with each other, but increasingly, according to evidence already emerging, each will even threaten the existence of the other.

That should not surprise us. When economic, military, and communication technologies become clumped together on a global scale, something like an empire emerges. Then doubts inevitably arise as to whether such an empire can secure its future and at what price. Such concentrations of power and technology always require a base, a foundation to support their expansion. Over the course of time, the base can crumble or collapse under the weight of the colossus that the empire has become. The biblical metaphor for empire is that of a giant supported by clay feet, as Daniel saw in his dreams about the empires of his day (Dan. 2). Let us now investigate what is taking place on the vulnerable underside, at the weak base or foundation of the giant superstructure.

Resource Vulnerability

Neither burgeoning economic growth nor an expanding military power structure can exist without the availability of enough material means, especially resources and energy. The vigorous pursuit of both expanded consumption and increased defense consumes ever-increasing quantities of energy, such as oil. Over the course of time, a nation or bloc of nations (such as the G8, the bloc of rich industrial nations), caught in the web spun by the ideologies, is increasingly unable to extract enough resources from its own stocks. As a result, the nation's or bloc's dependence on energy supply from foreign countries rises. In the book *Jihad vs. McWorld*, Benjamin Barber reports that in 1970 some 88 percent of the United States' energy use came from internal sources, but already by 1994 this figure had dropped to less than 50 percent.[2] About 60 percent of the sharp increase in energy imports came from the Middle East, a region well-known as an area of tension. Historically speaking, the conflicts in the Middle East exist because certain animosities have dominated the area for a long time. But could the need for higher energy flows also have introduced certain tensions from the outside?

To find out, let us review the ideological context, particularly in relation to the ideology of guaranteed freedom discussed in chapter 6. There we paused at the US Space Command's *Vision for 2020* issued in 1996. It contends that the Outer Space Treaty, ratified in 1967 as a result of US initiative and safeguarding outer space from military activities, is antiquated.[3] The report's argumentation, beginning with its front cover, is crystal clear: the United States must militarily dominate space in order "to protect US interests and investment." Because "the gap between 'have' and 'have-not' nations will widen—creating regional unrest," the US Space Command must dominate space militarily, using "space-based strike weapons" that enable "the application of precision force from, to, and through space." Elsewhere *Vision for 2020* declares: "Into the 21st century, the US Air Force needs to be . . . globally dominant, . . . selectively lethal, . . . virtually present."[4] An echo of this vision reverberates in the report of the Rumsfeld Commission, which in January 2001 baldly stated that policy needs to "ensure that the president will have the option to deploy weapons in space to deter threats to and, if necessary, defend against attacks on US interests."[5]

The reason for revisiting *Vision for 2020* is that it explicitly links the vital economic interests of the United States around the world (including the need for investments elsewhere and for the protection of raw material supply lines to the United States) with the need for advanced military protection—and even, where necessary, military attack. The report assumes, with cynical "realism," that the tension between the haves and the have-nots will intensify around the world, and it concludes that, as a result, more military power will be required. Thus, the resource initiative recommended by the report no longer involves closing the gap between the rich and the poor.

Here we face what we can call the paradox of power: precisely because the United States and its allies lack the power to vigorously enhance their material prosperity by means of their own resources, they require the world to serve as their economic platform. That implies that if any world bloc or state wants to keep expanding its power, sooner or later it brings itself into a situation of increased dependence and powerlessness. Eventually it will not be able to enhance its power and prosperity by means of its own resources, which will compel it to forcibly guarantee an adequate supply of resources from outside its borders. In turn, however, this will either increase its dependence on others or tie up its military power in the pursuit of that specific goal. If the nation or bloc chooses the military option, then it will be ideologically compelled to position overwhelming military force everywhere, even in outer space, to answer threats to its vital interests.

But the outcome of a scenario so ideologically suffused (pushing inevitably toward the ultimate span of control) is not difficult to imagine. The need for ever-expanding resource and energy flows will lead, ironically, to increasing difficulties with supply. This tendency is already apparent today. Even where finite natural resources, particularly energy, are not threatening to dry up at the moment, they are already increasingly becoming the object of a highly pitched competitive rivalry on a world scale. And what persuasive message to the world can an "empire" offer that might help it win this major competition? In an important interview in 2001, René Girard observed, "Competitive relationships are excellent if you come out of it as a winner, but if the winners are always the same, then one day or the other, the losers overturn the game table."[6] And then, at the level of resource vulnerability, a destructive, ideologically created spiral—not unlike a cyclone created by the collision of irreconcilable weather systems—will make its first devastating downward turn.

Financial Vulnerability

A second form of rising dependence lies in the area of finance. We have seen the degree to which the financial markets now form the command center of the global economy and how their erratic conduct arouses concern and even acute anxiety in many areas of the world. The financial markets finance today's extensive economic expansion. But will enough money remain available—will there be enough capital—to keep financing ever-increasing Western material prosperity and mounting military expenditures, both of which are already astronomically high?

At first glance the ongoing availability of capital appears possible. Since World War II, Western countries have held a monopoly on the creation of new international currencies or liquidities. Not only do their so-called key currencies, especially the US dollar and the Euro, serve as the accepted means of payment in international trade, but Western banks and governments can also create them as they please.

Yet the appearance is deceiving, as the current situation of the US economy starkly illustrates.

Over the course of the years, the US economy easily expanded both its consumption and its defense expenditures through issuing new dollars and new government bonds (US Treasury papers). The result, however, is that it is now plagued by a twin shortfall, the so-called double deficit. An enormous, ever-increasing deficit in the US government's budget is accompanied by an unparalleled, massive deficit in its balance of trade.

Year by year the US government expenditures far outstrip government revenues; at the same time, year by year the United States imports more goods than it exports. The US Department of Commerce reported that the deficit in the US balance of trade reached a record $726 billion in 2005 (an 18 percent increase over 2004), while in the same year the US federal government budget deficit climbed to $459.3 billion.[7]

It is not difficult to see that this double deficit is unsustainable over the long term. In its obsession with material progress, the United States treads in boots that are much too large: its economic growth is clearly not financed sufficiently by its own resources, but rather by the infusion of foreign capital. Add to that the enormous loans to finance burgeoning military expenditures, since the government prefers not to raise taxes to cover the costs. Hence, the reality emerges that the United States is now the world's largest debtor nation. Huge amounts of foreign capital continue to flow to the United States, particularly from China, a reality that helps veil the two gaping holes at the center of its economy.

How long will this situation last? In the area of finance, the United States is deeply vulnerable. It displays a rising dependence on other countries in general and on the speculative behavior of the suppliers of capital in particular. If the suppliers of capital lose faith in the US economy (if they anticipate that the United States can no longer pay back its debts), then a devastating financial spiral will appear: speculation will arise against the dollar, and the fate of the US economy will inexorably turn downward.

Moral Vulnerability

We have just seen that, while initially the prosperity and security ideologies seem to reinforce each other, in the long run they actually undermine one another and even block each other's path. If the economy fails, then where will the resources for guaranteeing military security come from? And if the cost of guaranteed security continues to have no bounds, then what financial room will remain for economic growth?

Other elements of vulnerability also lie hidden at the heart of ostentatious power. They become evident when we introduce the ethical or moral dimension. Those who must retreat in the face of power, or who become subjected to power, accept the impact of that power only to a certain level or degree. Beyond that point, the more people experience the use of power as disproportionate and unjustified, the more the counterreactions become deadly. A piece from ancient Chinese wisdom literature says it all:

A state becomes powerful when it resembles a great river, deep-seated; to it tend all the small streams under Heaven. . . . Thus a great state attracts small states by meeting their views, and small states attract the great state by revering its eminence. In the first case this Silence [or Humility] gains supporters; in the second, favour. The great state unites men and nurtures them; the small state wishes the goodwill of the great, and offers service; thus each gains its advantage. But the great state must keep Silence.[8]

When the great state does not nurture the small states, the risk rises that the victims of power feel humiliated, a feeling that then, all too often, finds expression in irritation, opposition, resistance, sabotage, and violence. And then a grotesque spiral of violent reaction and counterreaction begins to gyrate out of control.

Regrettably, the developments described here are not just theoretical. Already they involve real people and actual events. The lesson of the spirals is that the unchecked expansion of power can drag along entire populations in its wake. At the same time, it can also lead to the gradual breakdown and even fall of an empire.

But surely, one might ask, is not our world working hard to prevent both outcomes as, step by step, it opens itself up to a single global market, allowing poor countries to participate in the benefits of globalization?

This question sets the stage for chapter 8, where we examine today's globalization process in all its aspects, including its possible ideological backdrop.

/ 8 /

GLOBALIZATION

The theme of globalization has set many pens to paper. Indeed, globalization is one of the most commented-on realities of our time: an almost unbroken stream of books and articles floods the marketplace. Yet it is striking how few observers seem prepared to explore the ideological or spiritual underpinnings of globalization. Notwithstanding a few exceptions,[1] commentators are quick to attach stereotypical labels to globalization, such as "neoliberal," "capitalist," or "neocolonial." Epithets like these are seldom the result of serious investigation.

Here too we begin with the concrete, focusing especially on events occurring at the surface of globalization, in order to put into our hands the key needed to burrow down into globalization's spiritual and ideological roots.

Globalization as a Satellite

In its most direct sense, globalization refers to companies or institutions expanding their reach to embrace what occurs in the world or in the global market. Because for many producers the national economy no longer serves as an adequate economic platform, more and more entrepreneurs have begun to pursue business opportunities and possibilities in the world as a whole. Their new orientation has been stimulated by the relaxation of trade barriers and, particularly, by the rapid advancement of modern information and communication technologies.

But what is actually new here? Is "globalization" simply a description of the fact that international trade has rapidly expanded and that many national economies have gradually opened themselves up to the influences of the world market? No, there are more dimensions of globalization to disentangle. The expansion of international trade and the revolution in communication technologies are best seen as preconditions for globalization, not as globalization itself.

What then does "globalization" refer to? A few years ago *Time* magazine made reference to globalization as "The Global Awakening of Mankind."[2] "Awakening" suggests stumbling upon another kind of reality. Modern consciousness seems to want to come alongside a new dimension of reality. And in that new reality the "global" no longer lies at the end point of human initiatives and activities. Instead, increasingly the "global scene" serves as the beginning point. Globalization refers specifically to the processes that from the outset are worldwide, processes that have a global character from the very beginning.

Perhaps an illustration will help. Globalization is like a satellite launched into space by certain booster rockets, such as the emancipation of world trade, the information technology revolution, and the existence of a coherent international monetary system. Once it has reached its appropriate height, however, the satellite turns and circles the world autonomously under its own power or dynamic. It follows only its own orbit. And from that circuit, it exerts its increasingly powerful influence on the world.

Consider a few examples:

- A number of decades ago, the multinational corporation appeared. Using its motherland as its home base, a multinational opened up places of business (its daughters) in various other countries. But more recent decades have witnessed the emergence of the transnational corporation. The transnational company has no specific ties to a mother country; it no longer seeks such loyalties. For the sake of efficiency, it moves its head office relatively easily anywhere around the world. Rather than belonging to a specific country, the transnational corporation is a citizen of the world. It operates out of that global optic from the outset. Its home base is the globe.
- A second example is the rapid emergence of so-called global capital. Global capital refers to short-run capital circulating in enor-

mous quantities around the world. It is largely portfolio capital of a speculative nature. Johannes Witteveen, former managing director of the International Monetary Fund, identifies three types of private capital flows occurring: (a) foreign direct investments, which cannot be easily withdrawn; (b) portfolio investments; and (c) short-term bank loans in foreign currency.[3] If the prospects or expectations of profit-making are favorable, global capital can arrive in a country in huge quantities. But it can also leave overnight. At the least rumor, such as a possible devaluation of the relevant currency, capital can abandon a certain country wholesale, like a herd of animals that has just heard a shot. It then touches down somewhere else. Global capital constantly ricochets around the whole world, driven by its quest for maximum short-term financial gain in a climate of changing expectations. Here too the world has become the decisive context: this capital has no specific loyalty to a particular national economy. In fact, no country, not even the rich ones, has any guarantee that sufficient capital will remain within it. Global capital belongs only to its own autonomous circuit around the globe.

Global capital is primarily virtual. Yet it plays a coordinating or governing role over the process of globalization itself. Our time has seen an enormous growth in the amount of virtual money. A rough calculation suggests that the amount of credit provided by banks today is about two times the size of their actual financial resources. At the same time, new information technologies have led to the creation of virtual financial markets, which permit the easy transfer of people's expectations into tradable objects (so-called derivatives, such as options and futures). These show fantastic growth rates, approximately 120 percent over the past three years. In turn, these derivatives add to the high degree of turbulence that already exists in most financial markets because of the sharp increase in the mobility and volatility of international capital flows. The remarkable degree of vulnerability of most real economies to the whims of virtual global capital then starts to become apparent. Several years ago *The Economist* highlighted the growing subordination of political and economic life to the regime of financial markets: "The financial markets have become the judges and the juries of all economic policies." And recently Witteveen expressed his concerns by stating that highly volatile global capital increasingly induces national governments to alter their tax structures to favor hospitality to capital rather than the fair fiscal treatment of labor and the protection of the environment.[4]

- A third example can be found in patterns of consumption and communication. Globally specific symbols of consumption have now materialized; globalization has been called McDonaldization. Popular culture has also become global: universal Top 40 hit parades and blockbuster movies released simultaneously around the world are now the order of the day. At the same time, in tandem with English becoming the leading medium of communication around the world, we now also participate in global electronic intercommunication: the Internet. The Internet may have been launched at a national level (in the United States), but its very nature makes it a global network. Not only does it weave economies together into one strand; it also braids together various expressions of culture in infinite variations.

Globalization is therefore bound up with the emergence of both new financial markets, such as currency markets, share markets, and option markets, and new technologies, such as new information and communication technologies. It assumes globally functioning and modernly organized companies and their related institutions. And it is inseparably coupled to the rise and partial fall of the new economy, the economy that focuses on the global information technology circuit. Indeed, in recent decades the global financial system has become hugely bloated by the growth expectations of this new economy, while, conversely, the new economy has required gigantic quantities of new capital.

We may therefore describe globalization as the emergence of a global ellipse with two foci: a financial center and a technological center. Globalization proceeds dynamically from within the force field these two foci create. Moreover, this expanding and increasingly dynamic universe requires the poor countries to expend immense effort to avoid being left permanently behind, and a number of them, by their own admission, have already missed the opportunity.

These observations generate at least three basic conclusions. Though a number of commentators describe globalization in various ways, their analyses likewise generate the same basic findings.[5] First, globalization is an interlocking and highly dynamic phenomenon. Second, modern technological and economic developments are clearly at the center of the process. And third, the process itself is not confined to economy and technology: from the outset, globalization has important social and cultural impacts.

In light of the above, we offer our first observation: *Globalization presents itself as a global, modern phenomenon; from the outset it is a form or method of modernization on a global scale.*

Globalization and Modernization

At first glance, this observation may seem to add little to what we already know. One might question whether it proves helpful to drill down to deeper levels. But the appearance is deceiving. "Modern" and "modernization" are not neutral words. Most readers of this book would consider themselves to be modern or postmodern people. But what do we actually mean by the word "modern"? This question has endlessly fascinated philosophers of all stripes, because they link it to the arrival of modernity in Western society.[6]

It is not possible to explore the philosophical debate in detail here.[7] But we can observe that the modern worldview had already surfaced in the West in and around the sixteenth century, well before the eighteenth-century Enlightenment. The sixteenth century was a time of huge uncertainty. People no longer knew which country they belonged to or which faith they should claim. They heard tales of strange peoples from entirely different cultures. And they could no longer rely on their own perceptions. Even what they saw with their own eyes was suspect: clearly the sun rises and sets; surely the sun revolves around the earth, not the other way around. During that time of profound political, social, religious, and intellectual crises, leading thinkers in the West sought new forms of ultimate certainty. If certainty could no longer be found in the surrounding world, then perhaps it could lie in the simple fact that I doubt, or I think, and therefore I am (Descartes's *Meditations*). Or perhaps the insights of the new natural sciences could provide anchorage; perhaps they might even furnish the material needed to construct new forms of certainty in politics and society (Hobbes's *Leviathan*). Somewhat later John Locke postulated that we are born with a blank slate in our minds (the tabula rasa), which in turn led to the notion of a blank world (in the second of his *Two Treatises of Government*, Locke spoke about establishing a new society *in vacuis locis* [in empty places]). This blank world could be filled by people, in culture, applying the rules of free contract and private property.[8]

During this period of unsettling confusion, a new, rationally determined, modern worldview arose that relied on the value of mechanical or physical insights, mathematical methods, and new principles of social order, such as private property and social contract. In the modern perspective, the accent fell heavily on the significance of the free-thinking and free-acting individual person. The free individual was like everyone else and superseded all existing relationships.

Our second observation follows: *The word "modern" is not neutral; it cannot be divorced from a specific view of life, humanity, the world, and ultimate meaning.* But this implies that, to the degree that globalization is a modern phenomenon, from the outset it is value-determined and value-laden. Indeed, we cannot understand globalization or apply it apart from its roots in a modern Western worldview.

Before we embrace this observation as correct, let us test it against what we know about the actual process of globalization.[9]

First, from its beginnings modernity was driven by the desire for rational social-economic (re)construction. Borrowing the principle discovered by the new natural sciences that we can break reality down into its smallest parts (numbers and atoms, with individuals being their social counterparts), modernity sought to rebuild reality in thought according to the rules of functional rationality. Modernity, or more precisely the modernization process, is therefore intrinsically bound up with the construction of programs and projects for our general well-being, especially in empty spaces.

If we consider the current appeals to expand globalization, we already notice a striking similarity. Think of the adage that traditional markets must "of course," without question, give way to modern markets, regardless of how deeply traditional markets are embedded in their own cultures and woven into innumerable social relationships. Underlying the globalization appeal is the vision that the globe is an empty space suitable for modern economic activity.[10]

Second, from its beginnings modernity also clung to the mathematical-mechanical method, again derived from the natural sciences, as the best way to obtain certainty and security. Today we often hear attempts to capture our globalized world in figures or to describe it in terms that remind us more of a well-functioning machine than a living organism, such as a human body. Thus we hear references to "the market mechanism" and "the democratic mechanism." The word "derivatives" similarly betrays a mathematical-operational orientation. Moreover, people usually see financial markets as complete and self-regulating, the ultimate aim of any well-operating mechanism.

Finally, modernity fundamentally embraced autonomous individuality. The only potential restraint against it was pursuit of equality. In this respect much of the present style of globalization is permeated by the logic of the autonomous will and individualist self-determination of its most important actors. So overwhelming is the element of power and domination that the respected Group of Lisbon, in *Limits to Competition*, even speaks of "a new type of war: the competitive techno-economic war for global leadership."[11] "The new global economy," they claim, "looks like a battle among economic giants where no rest or compassion is allowed to the fighters, in a world where competition [has become an] . . . imperative."[12]

This deep, seamless relationship between the present pattern of globalization and the original spirit of modernity and modernization brings us to our final observation: *Possibly never before has modernity achieved higher expression than in today's process of globalization.*

Globalization and the Formation of Ideologies

Thanks to the important insight that globalization and modernity are deeply entwined, we can now also establish the relationship between globalization and ideology. Three elements of that relationship stand out.

The first element contains both a caution and an observation. Globalization, we have stated, is the paramount expression to date of the ongoing process of modernization. But that does not mean, as some authors have suggested, that everything about modernization is therefore ideological.[13] As a cultural phenomenon, modernity is broader than ideology. Modernity does not by definition require the embrace of absolute goals or ends.

Yet on the other hand, how utterly close the modernization process lies to the development of contemporary ideologies! The Enlightenment arrived on the heels of modernity, and it then served as the cradle for the emergence of all subsequent ideologies. The contemporary globalization process serves in a similar way: it prepares the way or sets the stage for the activity of a number of different ideologies, even ideologies that oppose each other.

Globalization easily latches onto an express prosperity ideology in this manner. Here it is helpful to distinguish between the process and the project of globalization. The globalization process refers to the actual, value-driven course of globalization through time. The project refers to globalization's objective: the pursuit of an unfettered, market-driven expansion of one's own material prosperity. Where the project compels us to embrace this pursuit—about which Margaret Thatcher once famously declared, "There is no alternative" (TINA)—then the partnership between globalization and today's materialist ideology is unmistakable. Under that dictum, all nations and peoples have no choice but to adapt themselves and the environment to the project of expanding freedom, prosperity, and democracy.

Second, earlier we saw that the emphases within modernity and modernization are uniform or narrow. The quantitative or measurable wins out over the qualitative or unmeasurable. In the new global framework, people today see global society primarily as a system of mechanisms—such as the market mechanism and the democratic mechanism—not as an organically connected whole. Similarly, modernity begins and ends with the individual, with the result that it pays scant attention to the value of human communities. Moreover, the modern perspective regards the environment as an object of use; the ecosystem is more an empty space than something that possesses intrinsic value. Now, if globalization does not rein in all of these modern mechanist, individualist, and instrumentalist tendencies—not just in its global project, but also in its process—then there is reason for concern. In a world rich with cultural and natural diversity, what happens when such a narrow, modern uniformity is in charge of the household? Is not the loss ultimately greater than the gain?

Third, the West launched globalization, which is rooted in Western culture. If a certain culture (Western, in this case) tries to expand its dominance throughout the world, regardless of how peaceable its intentions might be in its own eyes, will not cultures that pursue the protection of their own identities above all else interpret such actions as threatening? And will that not evoke aggression?

Direct Confrontation

We have identified three elements in the relationship between globalization and ideology. First, the globalization process sets the stage for the formation and progression of ideologies, particularly the Western materialist ideology. Second, the globalization process bears the characteristics of the narrowed perspective of the modern worldview. And third, the globalization process imposes Western culture onto other cultures around the world. Suppose we now combine these elements and permit them to interact. Then we find even more than simply cause for concern: we actually find it difficult to suppress a foreboding sense of shock. We have seen the degree to which ideologies are active in today's world, ideologies that aggressively pursue, even at all costs, the preservation of identity, the expansion of material prosperity, and guaranteed freedom. In chapter 7 we showed that even ideologies that seem to be compatible, such as unrestricted prosperity expansion and absolute protection, can eventually generate massive tensions and create ominous spirals, spirals not unlike tornados that lead to destruction and even death. Ought we then not anticipate a profound clash between the spirals of the ideologies when it is the narrow, even aggressive process of globalization that has been laying the groundwork?

These concerns are not academic. On the contrary, tragically, to a large degree the explosive collision sketched here has already been corroborated. The violent clash between spirals came to light in the unfathomable depths of what occurred on September 11, 2001, in New York City, Washington (DC), and the fields of Pennsylvania. There for the first time, the virulent spirals created by the dominant ideologies of our time—the rigid identity ideology of militant Islam, Western prosperity growth, and the guaranteed security demanded by the West—furiously collided. Helping to ignite the firestorm was a difference in developmental phases: in a shocking manner, the radical Islamist ideology managed to penetrate deep into the heart of the force field and power of the dominant prosperity and guaranteed freedom ideologies, ideologies that had already been laying the groundwork for such a radical attempt. Inevitably, the act immediately set off high-voltage reactions that ricocheted off the newly charged centers of all three ideologies. It was as if Islamism had thrown a spark onto a highly combustible mixture, which had been created especially by means of the ongoing globalization process. Have we not seen how the rigid identity ideology of radical Islam arose in response to an identity crisis sparked by Islam's internal confrontation with Western modernization?

All the signs point in this direction:

- The absolute cold-bloodedness with which this attack was rationally planned and executed and the absolute morbidity of using another country's passenger airplanes as flying bombs for the purpose of killing thousands of unknowing and unarmed people. This indicates the presence of an end that sanctioned every possible means in advance: the chief trademark of classical ideology. It displays a cold-blooded cruelty quite similar to the deadly systems of the French guillotine and the Nazi Holocaust.
- The objects of attack selected: the centers of the enemy's material prosperity and military and political power. The choice betrays an undisguised hatred for Western materialism and American domination, which is not unique to Islamic fundamentalism but supported more broadly in the Arab world.
- Finally, on the other side, the implicitly aggressive character with which many actors in the West pursue the contemporary globalization project. The 9/11 attack cannot be divorced from the unspoken arrogance by which the West favors its own so-called vital interests over securing genuine life interests within the impoverished countries in the East and the South. Have we not already underscored the blatant cynicism in the *Vision for 2020* report, which simply accepts as a given that in the coming decades the gap between the haves and the have-nots will increase and then advocates for increased military effort to deal with the escalating tensions?

If this analysis is correct, then dismissing the events of 9/11 as an aberration would clearly be a grave miscalculation. On the contrary, here, for the first time in modern history, the world staggered under the explosively charged collision of highly developed ideologies. But this means that within the climate created by the uniform process of globalization, further all-consuming, life-destructive spirals will have the opportunity to develop at a furious pace as shock waves from the initial conflagration.

Is that a form of doomsday thinking? We radically reject the perspective that such a scenario is inevitable. But there is reason to sound the most urgent warning about the enormous dangers of a self-generating dynamism that has overshot the mark. That dynamism can launch deadly spirals, as is apparent from the immediate reactions to 9/11. Consider, even beyond the reinforcement of the Western goal of guaranteed security that took place after 9/11, the willingness of many people to overstep the boundaries of justice by adopting the policy of preventive military action. Adoption of that policy was sparked by readjusting people's vision of good and evil (as in the "axis of evil") and by brazenly shoving aside the norms of international law. This step is ideological through and through. Clearly, direct mutual confrontation recharges each ideology; in a spiral of response and counterresponse, each sharpens the other's knives, with all the consequences that follow.

Indirect Confrontation

In addition to direct confrontation, ideologies can also react to each other indirectly. And these increasingly close encounters today are also having the effect of discharging energy into life-threatening spirals. The indirect clashes between ideologies are less visible but exceedingly dangerous. People feel the impact in areas of life that are intrinsically vulnerable, areas to which the dominant, onrushing ideologies pay little or no attention. Specifically, ideologically generated spirals today afflict three areas of heightened vulnerability: the environment, people who live in deep poverty, and individual languages and cultures on every continent that people have built up across the centuries. The poor, the environment, and the lingual and cultural diversity all seem to be "soft" matters, and the ambitious project of globalization so easily treats them as trifling. But if they go under or are even deliberately destroyed, they can manifest a terrible boomerang effect.

Consider for a moment each of these precarious vulnerabilities.

Poverty and Exclusion

As reported in chapter 1, in 2000 government leaders from all parts of the world met and officially endorsed the so-called Millennium Goals.

The goals include cutting world poverty in half by 2015, creating universal access to clean water and primary education, and reducing infant mortality by two-thirds. Since then, various sides have concluded that the endorsing nations will not meet these objectives. Even the United Nations Development Program (UNDP) reports publicly express that apprehension. How can that be? Some people attribute this failure to a lack of political will. But is that entirely the case?

The answer becomes clear when we investigate a new paradox: the paradox of rising global exclusion. Global exclusion today is indeed paradoxical, because globalization is by definition a process of inclusion: it spreads to all countries and all areas of the world. It brings with it new technologies, new markets, and new methods of organization, all of which have resulted in economic benefits for a number of countries. However, many countries, as in Africa, describe more and more articulately and forcefully a pattern of persistent exclusion, an exclusion that leads to increased poverty. They consciously hold the current pattern of globalization responsible for that exclusion. But how is it possible to connect worsening poverty (exclusion) to expanding globalization (inclusion)?

In chapter 5 we observed a similar paradox at a national level: the stark reality of rising impoverishment precisely in the midst of the wealthiest societies. There we recognized that the number of households in the United States at risk of or experiencing direct hunger is high (more than one in ten) and rising.[14] These households fall further and further behind partly because of an economic process that is part and parcel of today's rapidly expanding, dynamist economies. In the present environment, the economy's advanced, directly productive sector (which orients itself to producing products for the market) puts increasing pressure on the economy's care sector (whose activities, both paid and unpaid, focus on the care and keeping of people, social relationships, and ecosystems through time). This occurs in two ways. First, in its production process, the directly productive sector easily damages the existing stocks and stores of resources, ecosystems, human health, and cultural heritage—areas that then require additional support from the care sector of the economy. Second, in the economy's care sector, it is impossible to replicate the dramatic increases in productivity that occur in the advanced sector. The widening productivity gap between these two sectors means that, as the prices of industrial products remain the same or drop (because of increased efficiency), the costs of care become proportionately more expensive and even partially unpayable. The outcome is a painful paradox: rapidly expanding modern economies simultaneously increase care needs even as they reduce the ability to meet those needs.[15]

Today's poor and working poor households bear the brunt of the resulting exclusions. They find themselves increasingly unable to receive a good education, appropriate training, or adequate, affordable healthcare. They often cannot find suitable jobs that pay living wages. Frequently they are deemed unworthy of credit because of mounting debts. They encounter increasingly insurmountable barriers to finding promising ways out.[16]

The modern economy's inclusion of people in the process of rapid industrialization brings with it, for those who find themselves in difficult positions, rising exclusion from its benefits. Economic inclusion today means that essential opportunities or resources are systematically eluding a growing number of people. In the midst of rapid, continuous economic expansion, a relationship therefore exists between becoming poorer and becoming richer. It is then no coincidence that they emerge simultaneously. As an example, on January 16, 1999, *The Economist* reported: "The gap between America's rich and poor has grown in the past 20 years. Whereas the average earnings of the top fifth of male earners rose by 4% between 1979 and 1996, those of the bottom fifth fell by 44%."

A comparable process is taking place globally. Here we bump up against a reality that is partly hidden from the Western public. More or less regularly the press reports on the amount of so-called development assistance granted to poor countries, as well as the investments made in them by Western countries. The Millennium Goals were based on the performance of those efforts. Now and then the news media, along with some politicians, also voice criticism, urging their governments to increase the money and capital streams flowing from the North to the South. But what is scarcely discussed, if at all, is the reality of today's capital flows. As reported in chapter 1, according to official figures, the stream of capital flowing from the North to the South does not even come close to matching the money and capital streams that the poor countries of the South send each year to the countries of the North. For many years now, there has been no net transfer of official capital from the North to the South. Quite the opposite: the net transfer of money tends to travel from the poor to the rich, not the other way around. Already by 1992 the UNDP reported that "the current debt-related net transfer from the developing to the industrialized countries stands at $50 billion a year."[17] In its *Human Development Report 2002*, the UNDP noted that in 2000 all of the developing countries combined received 0.6 percent of their GDP in the form of development aid and donations, and 2.5 percent in the form of direct investments (see table on facing page[18]). But in that same year not less than 6.3 percent of their GDP flowed to the rich countries of the North in the form of interest payments and the amortization of their existing debts:

**Exports and debt service dominate resource
flows to and from developing countries:**

Type of flow	Percentage of developing countries' GDP, 2000
Exports	26.0
Debt service	6.3
Net foreign investment	2.5
Aid	0.5
Net grants from NGOs	0.1

The year 2000 was not an exception. On balance for several years now, a substantial portion of total domestic income in the South has flowed *net* to the rich countries and their banks. This net reverse transfer is an altogether chilling manner of exclusion: it reflects a pecking order that, on balance, systematically excludes those on the lower rungs from genuine economic benefit.

But how can such a pattern continue year after year? It renders impossible the effective alleviation of poverty in the poor countries of the world.

The answer is simple, but it is steeped in ideology. The structural persistence of the debt burden shouldered by the poorest countries, which continues despite every gesture of reduction or cancellation, is created by a fundamental imbalance within the international monetary system itself. In the international monetary system, the rich countries and their banks exercise a complete monopoly over the creation of so-called key currencies, those used in international trade (the dollar, the euro, and the yen). If one's own monetary unit serves as an accepted means of payment in international trade, then one's own country has a relative economic advantage.[19] Not only are the poor countries not allowed to create currency acceptable in international trade; they also are not given a single share in the process. If a poor country requires goods from outside its own borders, it must borrow money to purchase them, unless it chooses to vigorously increase its exports. The enduring, huge debt burdens of the South have arisen as a result; at the same time, the poor countries are permanently compelled to give priority to increasing exports rather than to developing the domestic home markets they so desperately need to meet even basic subsistence needs.

Hence, running parallel to the enrichment spiral in the world as described earlier, focused on the application of more money and technology, is an impoverishment spiral, focused on enduring debt and deficient domestic market development. Globalization is therefore also segmentation where lines of demarcation between rising enrichment and deepening poverty become more vividly defined. It is no wonder that the Severely Indebted Low Income Countries (SILICs) find themselves more and more excluded from the economic benefits of globalization.

This story is discouraging. But it also exposes the deepest reason for the ongoing injustice. Global exclusion is caused by the permanent, ideologically suffused unwillingness of the rich countries to relinquish some of the monopoly over money creation that is so vital to their own prosperity expansion. Blatantly one-sided forms of protection of their own markets are extremely difficult even to discuss with the governments of the rich countries. The rich nations, in both Europe and North America, cling tenaciously to their power and their money monopoly. The ideology of material progress and prosperity obliges them to do so.

But what a notoriously limited perspective this is! Does no one in leadership see what this exclusion awakens in the poorest countries and their populations? History, we saw earlier, testifies to the way virulent ideologies arise precisely in situations of unending subordination, hunger, and oppression. The rich countries are playing with fire. Already now at their borders they experience intensified immigration pressure from the countries of the South. The United States struggles with its Mexican border, and Europe has developed into a kind of bastion, foiling the streams of people who try to reach the West in small boats or by swimming. The pursuit of guaranteed security by the privileged boomerangs and afflicts their own lives.

The repercussions from the South, while already felt, will undoubtedly increase. But then the most probable reaction by the North will not be to turn or reverse direction, but rather to entrench even further. And that will come at the cost of everything vulnerable that must be protected and built up. Ideologies do not embrace wisdom but rather foolishness.

The Finite and Vulnerable Earth

The second illustration has to do with the vulnerable earth and the finiteness of the natural resources that still remain. Various politicians and governments have predicted that ecological and resource issues could lead to considerable problems in the future. Their warnings also partly explain the number of international conferences that have been held about environmental issues: the "Earth Summits" in Rio de Janeiro (1992) and Johannesburg (2002), the Kyoto Conference on Climate Change (1997), the second World Water Forum in the Hague (2000), and numerous others. But here too, as with global poverty, the parties encounter great difficulty in concluding negotiations successfully, much less in implementing them.

Why? The nature of the proposed solutions illustrates the problem. Here too, in addition to a lack of political will, it is striking how time and again at most such conferences the emphasis falls on needing to apply more and better energy- and environment-saving technologies and to giving the market more room to operate (such as through trading so-called emission quotas). Such measures will no doubt help in some situations. But suspicion mounts when the application of more money, markets, and improved technologies—the gods of Western progress—becomes the solution to the entire problem.

The world population is continually growing. As a result, the pressure per world citizen on existing resources, on the soil, and on the environment is continually increasing, as we see in the rapid growth of India and China. Some experts have calculated that if each member of the rising world population now lived at the same level of prosperity presently enjoyed by those in the West, the current environment and stocks of raw materials and energy would be completely depleted in the relatively short period of one to two decades as a result of the accompanying pressure on the environment, energy, and the land.[20] Viewed from the perspective of the earth's limits and the vulnerability of the world's environment, the wealthy nations of the West tromp with boots that are much too large. Their further material progress is actually a parasite on the growth possibilities that other nations and peoples badly need in order to achieve even a portion of the current well-being in the West.

Most international conferences are silent about this harsh reality. The unspoken rule of thumb is that the wealthy nations may not, for the most part, be held in check. The recent report "The Stern Review on the Economics of Climate Change" even argues that desperately needed measures to stablize climate change need not interfere with the growth ambitions of the rich countries: "Tackling Climate Change is the pro-growth strategy for the longer term. And it can be done in a way that does not cap the aspirations for growth of rich or poor countries."[21] But again, what will be the horrific repercussions—perhaps even deadly—if the topic of the material saturation of wealthy Western countries remains taboo? This taboo is ideological through and through. For the West, everything seems open to conversation as long as the dialogue never touches on the preservation of its own power and the expansion of its own prosperity. But these ideological ends create the compulsive urge to latch onto new technologies and to cling to new and often highly risky market solutions as the gods who will save us. Idols remain among us.

Even more so than with the increase in world poverty, the West's refusal to dampen its own power and prosperity in the least is tantamount to playing with fire. Already, conflicts around the world over scarce resources are increasing: Iran's desire for nuclear energy has the

West on edge, and the dispute about fresh water markedly intensifies the Israeli-Palestinian conflict. The endless, narrow drive for more material progress will compel the rich countries to secure, with military threat or intervention, the resources they believe they will need in the future. But that will surely elicit strong resistance in the areas involved, especially if the people there regard the preservation of their identity as an absolute goal. The clash will open up a battle scene of grotesque proportions for people and the environment, and it will usher in deadly spirals of confrontation and violence. And why, really? Because the highest law of life is not the desire to serve life and make life possible for others but rather to protect one's own life at any cost. In that way the world loses its soul.

Threatened Cultures

Too many people in the West, among them various development experts, shrug their shoulders when they hear the claim that the expanding project of globalization brings with it an erosion of cultural diversity in the world. Their indifference stems partly from a sense that their reflections will not change the process. But it also arises partly because, in their judgment, colored by the modernization perspective, such cultures seem antiquated. They appear to have outlived themselves. Experts will sometimes even advance the arrogant position that such societies badly need to modernize as quickly as possible, because traditional ways of life interfere with their "true" progress.

This view is pompous and short-sighted. Cultural diversity, like the diversity between persons, is an integral part of created life. Further, the discussion usually turns on cultures that may be many centuries older than Western, "superior" culture. But the view is also fraught with danger. In all of their diversity, cultures largely house human identity and people's sense of dignity. As people we may possess goods (in larger or smaller quantities), but we belong to a shared culture; culture forms our home. If one culture confronts another culture, and if that culture runs roughshod over the other culture with its own ideas about the development it "needs," then it tramples upon people and their dignity. For that reason, the reaction to a wounded sense of identity can be harsh, malicious, and even violent.

But there is more. Globalization involves more than Western products, technologies, and methods of organization. Western culture comes with it. For many people from different cultures, all too often Western culture strikes them—unfortunately, often correctly—as decadent and degenerate. Western people today happily speak about their technological, economic, and organizational achievements, and they praise their free markets and democracies, but they are conspicuously silent about what accompanies those achievements: violent films and television, sporting a murder a minute; violent video games in which the greatest skill consists of disposing of each other as quickly as possible; and Web sites in which the human body, especially those of women and children, is absolutely degraded. Contrast that with traditional African, Indian, or Arab cultures, where clear codes, sometimes centuries old, prescribe clothing, interaction, and the use of weapons; these cultures established such codes (sometimes heavy handedly) precisely to prevent such excesses. Then we begin to understand something of the deep cultural resistance that flares up in many countries against the current Western, dominant pattern of globalization. We begin to grasp the rising reluctance among broad sectors of the population in such countries and cultures to expel their own extremists and fundamentalists, even though the people themselves shun violence.

In his book *The Clash of Civilizations*, Samuel Huntington advocates the position that differences between cultures will act as the catalyst for the violent conflicts that will increasingly plague the world in the future. In our judgment, he goes too far.[22] But when the ingredient of ideology formation is added to the mix, the element of truth in his thesis comes undeniably to the fore. People belonging to minority cultures can become tremendously aware of and deeply wounded by the malice or oppression foisted upon them by a dominant culture. Their wounds can cause them to transform the preservation of their identity into an absolute end. After that, the end justifies every means needed for reaching the objective. Elements of such ideology formation are now apparent, also in Iraq. If Western countries remain fixed on their own vital interests and absolute ends, then neither side will be able to prevent new, hideous spirals of violence from erupting.

We have sketched three illustrations, but they teach us one lesson: we live in a world that is careening quickly toward an abyss. But entering that abyss is by no means inevitable. It is rather the outcome of choices made by us and by others. It is time to wake up, to regain consciousness before it is too late.

THE RISE OF SOCIAL PARADOXES AND STRUCTURAL VIOLENCE

Our next task is to consider living concretely out of genuine hope in the midst of today's ominous, devastating spirals of terror. But let us first pull together a number of threads in our discussion thus far. Perhaps this will give us, in encapsulated form, a snapshot of today's seemingly insurmountable problems, a summary situating more precisely the obstacles now faced by the hope that awakens life. To that end, we first try to capture in schematic form the range of risky paradoxes afflicting today's society. Next, we offer a map of the degrees, variations, and types of structural violence occurring in present-day international relationships. Finally, we sketch how this structural violence colors and disorients the current process of globalization.

The Rise of Contemporary Societal Paradoxes

In chapter 5 we recognized the rise of unpredicted, seemingly unsolvable socioeconomic paradoxes. We now expand this, in pictorial form, to present a more comprehensive description of these paradoxes. The top portion of the table (reading left to right and downward) shows the ideological sequence that generates today's paradoxes. The bottom portion (reading right to left and upward, beginning from above the bottom line) describes our society's attempt to solve the problems that continue to confound us. That portion of the table also describes how Western society is continuously ordered today.

Contemporary Socioeconomic Paradoxes

————————————— **Ideological Sequence** —————————————→

Human needs and desires	*Ideologically transformed ends*	*Ideologically legitimized means*	*Actual outcome after autonomy of the means*
Happiness	Increased material wealth	Rise of economic productivity	Unemployment, environmental problems, stress
Community	Organized communication	Electronic means of communication (IT)	Over-information, decrease of community
Peace	Guaranteed security	Advanced weapons and control	Overarmament, preventive wars
Love	Satisfaction of affective needs	Commercial supply of sex, porn	Loneliness, alienation
Care (social)	Organized welfare	Higher efficiency, productivity, growth of GDP	Increasing need for care; increasing inability to pay
Health	Longer and better life	Pharmaceutical technology, genetic research	"Prosperity" diseases, overuse of medical means
Less world poverty, income development, aid	Increase of economic produc- tion in the South	Export scenario for poor countries; structural adjustment programs	Loss of home markets, increase of poverty
Expected Outcome	*"Consumption" desired*	*Solution: more production and technology*	**Current problems**

←————————————— **Societal Solution Sequence** —————————————

This table indicates tendencies only, and it is not meant to suggest monocausal relationships. Nevertheless, it graphically illustrates the relationship between the dominant, largely ideological spirituality of the West and the dangerous, highly paradoxical manner in which our society continues to tackle its problems.

Structural Violence in Contemporary International Relations

Earlier we saw that violence is the primary means used by the revolution ideology (as in the violent repression of the French Revolution and the Soviet Union), the identity ideology (as in apartheid, Nazism, the horrific terrorist attacks by Islamism, and the Israeli-Palestinian conflict), and the guaranteed freedom ideology (as in the intrinsic violence driving the seemingly unstoppable development of ever-more-lethal weapons of indiscriminate destruction). But what about the ideology of material progress and prosperity? Is not this ideology distinct from the others in its choice of means? Perhaps it is an example of an ideology using means that are inclusive and even nonviolent.

This question takes on extraordinary importance. If the means its adherents deploy show aspects of coercion, then their use amounts to acceptance of a form of violence. That in turn could indicate a pervasive culture of violence, which would then only make our situation more bleak. Moreover, we could then expect the interaction between ideologies to create even more sinister spirals of destruction. In part 3 we saw that opposing ideologies can generate devastating spirals by embracing similar means, such as violence. In the case of the Palestinian-Israeli conflict, both sides have regularly reacted and counterreacted by using violence, a spiraling that seems only to further rigidify each ideology.

At first glance, the means used by the ideology of material progress and prosperity may appear to have little in common with violence. But a careful examination reveals that, to greater and lesser degrees, they involve brutal enforcement. That is hardly surprising. No ideology can operate without some kind of power base, the use of which the ideology legitimates in advance. The application of that power base can infringe upon the will and the rights of other living beings, animals included, and trample upon their life-sphere and dignity. Let us therefore examine international economic relations today to see if they display aspects of violence emanating from the economic, financial, and political domains.

To set the stage, consider an example from the ancient world concerning the possible misuse of financial power. The Torah explicitly prohibits a creditor from entering the house of his debtor (Deut. 24:10–11). The creditor must not cross the threshold into the debtor's house. Instead, he must wait outside until the debtor brings him the pledge for his debt. The prohibition clearly assumes a historical context in which creditors had the power to get back their money by using any method available. Within the structure of the Old Testament economy, the command calls for an unequivocal act of self-restraint.

Do the various structures of society today always allow for or honor such forms of self-restraint? In our view, the answer is no. To the degree that this is the case, then, we may describe societal structures themselves as intrinsically violent. From this perspective, the poorest and most indebted countries of the world sometimes oppose the imposition of the International Monetary Fund's harsh Structural Adjustment Programs on their economies. In such programs they experience a type of structural violence where the creditor, in a self-appointed way, crosses the threshold and enters the house (the Greek word *oikos*, from which comes the beginning of our word "economy," means "house").

How then are we to assess structural violence? Violence in general occurs in many forms and gradations. On a scale moving from the relatively weak misuse of power to the strong and structural misuse of power, let us isolate some of the progressive stages of violence:

1. Limited but enforced *infringing* on others' ability to exercise rights in their own domain.
2. Systematically manipulating and/or *subjugating* others to one's own rules of control.
3. Creating fear by a *threat to destroy* the life of others.
4. Deliberately effecting *partial destruction* of human life and the environment.
5. *Destroying* life and conditions for life in a sacralized[1] and systematic way.[2]

To what extent do we find evidence of these stages in the present international scene? This question takes on increasing significance because of the emergence of imperial power within current international economic relationships. In their book *Empire*, Michael Hardt and Antonio Negri distinguish not just the power of the bomb and the media as the means of contemporary imperial control, but also the power of money.[3]

To explore this, let us map the mounting interference between military (M), political (P), financial (F), economic (E), and cultural (C) power in current global financial and economic developments. Each kind of interaction creates its own logic, which may even assume the weight of self-evident truth in today's world. Consider active interactions such as these (where > denotes "active influence upon . . . "):

- Excessive protection: the closing of national borders to economic migrants or foreign products (P>E logic). Here the political decision-making process (P) influences the economy (E) to deny migrants and countries access to the ability to meet their basic needs. Governments usually adopt protectionist measures out of fear that the economic interests of both employers and employees will be damaged.

- The doctrine of vital interests: the return of colonial aspirations in the US Space Command's report *Vision for 2020* and in the Project for the New American Century (M>P>E, P>M>E logic). Here the military (M) pressures the political decision-making process (P) to accept more armaments, which in turn has economic impacts (E), with more employment, but usually also higher government deficits. In complementary fashion, political decision-makers (P) insist on more armaments (M), which in turn has the same economic impacts (E).

- The influence of the US Treasury on International Monetary Fund and World Bank national decisions (P>F>E logic). A clear example of this influence is the complete liquidation of Iraq's debt, alongside huge amounts of soft loans granted in recent years to Russia and Turkey. Soft loans are low-interest loans with long amortization periods, or loans with no strict obligation to pay back in a short period of time. By contrast, except for small gestures that are laden with ideological conditions, similar liquidations and loans have been denied to poorer countries in Africa and Latin America.

- The systematic efforts of private transnational corporations (TNCs) to mold international law (E>P>E logic). The TNCs often try to remove restrictions preventing them from buying and owning all kinds of property in other countries. They further pursue for themselves an exclusive regime of patents on agricultural products (seeds, genetically manipulated foods) and on their own manufactured goods and services. Already by 1989, according to Susan Sell, "developing country resistance . . . to incorporate intellectual property rights in trade negotiations . . . had be[en] overcome. In fact, twelve corporations made public law for the world."[4] Since then each government in the South has been obliged to support the protection of the intellectual property rights of each transnational company. Julian Saurin therefore concludes that "transnational corporate capital has been able to simultaneously strengthen immeasurably its own position while dismantling the authority and self-determining capacity of public bodies, including the state."[5]

- The manipulation of information and media to create public acceptance, as became clear in the debate about the lack of political independence television channels like CNN and other media have had in their reporting of the Iraq War (P>E>C logic).[6]

Here we certainly see some concrete evidence of the five progressive steps of violence: elements of infringement, subjugation, threat, partial destruction, and sometimes even sacralized, systematic destruction. The interference between the powers mapped out here complicates every effort to identify the perpetrators of the violence. Nonetheless, without question, to varying degrees structural violence plays a clear role in international relations today, and it regrettably appears to be on the rise.

Globalization, Inclusion, and Exclusion

Let us now connect this analysis to a graphic depicting the globalization dynamics described in chapter 8. There we found elements of both inclusion and exclusion (referred to many times by the churches of the South). In principle, both inclusion and exclusion can be accompanied by forms of compulsion or enforcement. We may classify enforced inclusion as the subjugation of others to one's own rules of control, while the barriers of protection around Western markets form an example of enforced infringement upon the ability of others to exercise rights within their own domain. A number of threats and fears are related to what Michel Foucault describes as the "power of normalization," which by definition is a power of inclusion.[7] Indeed, most violence in modern economic life depends upon the power to both include and exclude, and often in that order. We may even describe the project of globalization as a process of exclusion on the basis of prior inclusion.

Consider some examples of the enforced inclusion of non-Western nations in the present process of globalization:[8]

- Legal inclusion: insisting solely on the use of the (Western) legal system with respect to contract and property rights.
- Monetary inclusion: no international trade is possible other than on the basis of Western currencies, over which the West exercises complete control.
- Military inclusion: the threat of further preventive wars against those who choose to live outside the domain of Western alliances.
- Cultural inclusion: aggressive advertising around the globe (sometimes called McDonaldization).

On the basis of enforced inclusion, elements of exclusion easily enter the picture. Consider, as we saw in chapter 8, the roots of the enrichment and impoverishment cycles that run parallel to each other in today's global economy, especially in the North-South relationship. The cycles are clearly rooted in at least three types of exclusion:

- Exclusion from the creation of international liquidities (monetary exclusion).
- Exclusion from free entry in Western markets (market exclusion).
- Exclusion from the means to alleviate scarcity (scarcity exclusion).

This threefold exclusion simultaneously whirls into motion the cycles of dynamic enrichment and dynamic impoverishment in today's global economy, as the following picture illustrates:

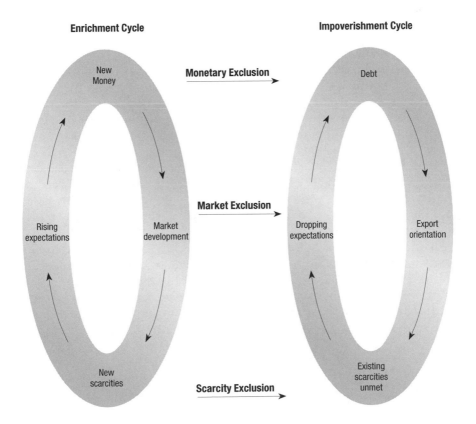

Parallel Cycles of Enrichment and Impoverishment

In a simplified way, this picture illustrates the economic and financial dynamics that emerge in and between countries when the three powers of exclusion are simultaneously applied. Let us begin with the ellipse on the left, which primarily describes the financial dynamics underway within already wealthy countries. We start at the top where Western banks, in concert with Western governments, decide to create more money in the form of their key currencies. The new money is usually disbursed as credits for investments. It circulates largely in the economically protected area of the Western hemisphere (as the downward arrow depicts), and it is used primarily to develop new forms of scarcity through the development of new markets and/or new technologies, such as information technologies (the bottom of the ellipse). If the returns are high enough, they lead to rising expectations in the financial markets (the arrow then goes up). Usually this motivates the banks to issue a new round of credits and money creation. The process of this cycle looks self-evident to us because, in the West, we have become thoroughly accustomed to it.

But let us now examine the ellipse on the right, with the assumption that the three forms of exclusion are fully operational. Here too we begin at the top and face the reality that poor countries have no part in the process of creating international liquidities. That is the monopoly of the rich countries and their banks. So when the poor countries need currency acceptable in the international exchange to pay for the goods and services imports they need, they have no choice but to borrow from Western banks or to undertake a vigorous stimulation of their exports. Given the enormous debts accumulated by the poor countries in the past, a strong export orientation becomes unavoidable (the arrow then goes downward along the right side). That orientation is reinforced by the foreign direct investments they receive, which the foreign investors usually link explicitly to developing the export sector further (by building new export enclaves).

In turn—now at the bottom of the ellipse—the rigid export orientation leads to the remarkable result that in most poor countries almost no capital remains available for further developing their existing markets of products made and sold at home. This is especially the case if transnational companies have already come in and begun their huge acquisition sprees and their advertising campaigns to promote the sale of their own luxury products. New types of consumer needs then emerge, and meeting those needs claims so many resources that the basic subsistence needs of the majority of the population still remain unsatisfied. The new scarcities squeeze out the ability to satisfy the existing scarcities (scarcity exclusion).

One could certainly ask: does not the growth generated by the increase of exports sufficiently compensate for the potential damage? It does not, particularly if export return growth is hampered by the protectionism of Western markets (market exclusion). The export markets of the poor countries usually have a low income and price elasticity. A poor country's effort to increase its return by expanding the volume of its exports may even turn out to be counterproductive: as its export volume goes up, the price per product unit goes down. In that case, the entire effort to reduce one's debt by robustly increasing exports has failed miserably: the country's debt can even increase rather than decrease (the arrow goes up and expectations decline). The economic literature describes this last phenomenon as Triffin's Law: "The more you pay the more you owe." The situation became bitterly real already by the beginning of the 1980s. At that time, many poor countries, confronted with rising interest levels and mounting prices for imported energy, tried to avoid increasing their debt burden by substantially increasing the volumes of their exports. The result was market saturation and such a steep drop in the prices of their products that the amount of their total revenues actually declined. That meant that they had to take on new loans and therefore increase their total debt burden, precisely as a result of following the economic prescription imposed upon them by the West. The upshot is that today, as we saw, the amount of payments by developing countries on their existing debts (for interest and amortization) is higher than the amount of the capital that comes in via foreign direct investments or aid (returning, then, the process to the top of the ellipse).

The impoverishment cycle thus demonstrates that most poor countries have no real chance of escaping from the debt trap, regardless of how hard they try under the adjustment programs partially imposed upon their economies.

The picture here is roughly sketched. But at least three unavoidable conclusions leap to the forefront.

First, it is not enough to describe the huge discrepancies between rich and poor in today's world in static terms or in percentages. Much more fundamentally, today's problem of rich and poor has now become a problem of simultaneous cycles of enrichment and impoverishment that awaken each other. Both rely on forms of ongoing exclusion.

Second, we cannot understand the effort to continuously exclude without grasping the clear ideological impulse behind the exclusion. All these exclusions are driven by a use of power that is fundamentally unjust and that therefore requires some kind of legitimation. They all stem from a prevailing worldview that holds as its supreme objective the improvement or security of one's own individual and national material condition. Functioning as an absolutized goal, that objective makes all the steps of exclusion look like the regrettable but unavoidable consequence of the necessary operation of the current "mechanisms."

Finally, as long as the three types of exclusion are ideologically implemented and sustained by the rich countries in the international arena,
there is virtually no hope that the so-called Millennium Goals (including
reducing world poverty in half by 2015) will be achieved. The globalization process will then remain dominated by the reigning Western project
of globalization, within which further enrichment and impoverishment
between North and South, as well as within the countries of North and
South themselves, will be inescapable.

Where then does the hope lie for undoing the impasses of today's paradoxes and of overcoming today's forms of direct and indirect violence?
This question moves us to part 4.

PART 4

// HOPE AWAKENS LIFE //

/ 9 /

WIDENING WAYS OF ECONOMY, JUSTICE, AND PEACE

Back to the Beginning

The subject matter of this book is hardly uplifting. We have traced vigorous ideologies to which nations and peoples cling. We have discussed the rise of autonomous powers that impose their will on us as gods. And we have spoken of ominous spirals that, like violent whirlpools, pull us in and under. These spirals seem to cast an evil spell on us, a spell reminiscent of the diabolical intent to divide and conquer. At first glance we might be accused of the most depressing variation of fatalistic thinking that one can imagine. It is therefore high time that we return to the beginning, to the question with which we began.

In chapter 1 we expressed amazement at how many recent book titles contain the word "end." The titles indicate the profound uncertainty preoccupying many people today, academics and otherwise. But they also mark out a line in the sand or a watershed moment in time. It is as if the future has struck off on its own path, largely independent of our own hopes and desires. That new sense has encouraged us as citizens to retreat into our own small worlds. Even if our own worlds may also be crumbling, at least many things remain more or less under our own control.

In the chapters that followed we moved, step by step, closer to a possible explanation for this strikingly prevalent sense in the Western world. Clearly there are influences at work, particularly in Western society, which morph into paralyzing and seemingly autonomous powers. By themselves, there is nothing evil about technology, the economy, money, the market, and the exercise of power in the service of justice and reconciliation. But the modern project of creating a malleable society, organized to suit our own goals, has given them an exalted status. Their enthronement process has gone so far that we begin to see these forces as living, self-propelling powers. We then follow them as gods wherever they go, initially because we expect their progress over time to deliver only good things, but later because we find it difficult to escape their almost hypnotic influence. From that point on, we may feel that the ability to chart our own future has been whisked out of our hands. There seems to be no recourse, no ability to withdraw us from where these dynamic powers and forces could ultimately bring us. And then a sense of betrayal and paralysis creeps in.

This hypothesis strikes us as the only reasonable explanation for why so many people today feel that the future is now moving unpredictably, for good or for ill, beyond their control.

The hypothesis sounds quite heavy, and no doubt it is. But if it is true, and the evidence points in that direction, then it also opens up a window onto genuine hope. It means that the so-called end of our history is by no means an inescapable fate. Today's general feeling of insecurity is actually not a sign that the powers now dominating us are beyond our control. On the contrary, it is a sign that we have abdicated our human responsibility. We have off-loaded our responsibility to chart society's course, letting the powers that be handle that task. We are tempted to say, "There is no alternative." And after that perspective has become entrenched, we have no choice but to believe the illusion either that the path history will take us down will be positive, even providential, or that the world really is a malicious, unsafe place from which one had better hide.

But how does this insight actually inspire hope and not despair? As authors, this question requires us to articulate at least in part the very roots of our faith. That need in turn calls to mind the invitation issued in chapter 1. There we identified the aim of this book: to stimulate and contribute to the broadest dialogue possible. And we invited readers to participate in that exchange on the basis of their own deeply held convictions about life. In our experience, genuine dialogue occurs only when each participant, in an environment of safety and mutual respect, lays open their deepest convictions for examination and review by others. From there, the dialogue's participants can often locate areas of common ground and explore genuine partnership around steps for concrete action. All of us live in the same world and share in the human condition.[1] Indeed, it is our hope that people representing various basic beliefs and orientations will find themselves able to embrace and even improve upon much of the concrete guidelines, real-life examples, and policy proposals offered later in this chapter. Together we faithfully seek to contribute to actually turning around the scourges of global poverty, environmental degradation, and war.[2]

The Demonic

In that spirit, let us then begin to drill down deeper into our own convictions. A moment ago we raised the specter of a vicious, unsafe world. In this context we often hear words like "demonic" or "diabolical." Diabolical means literally "thrown back and forth," the very dynamic that sets spirals in motion. *Diabolos*, the Greek word for "devil," means the unrestricted power of evil or of the evil one to pit people against one another and thereby divide and conquer.

But coming from our gospel perspective, let us be as clear as possible about the nature of evil. Without question, the "diabolical" has played a role throughout human history, including recent events (think only of Nazi concentration camps, ethnic cleansing in Rwanda, and the unconscionable attacks of September 11, 2001). But we must use utmost caution here. The Bible is clear that people can be seduced into serving gods other than the living God, with all the devastating consequences that follow. Milton's *Paradise Lost* even suggests that a kind of orchestration of seductions occurs (thus "Beelzebub," described in the New Testament as "the prince of demons," may mean "lord of the house"[3]). Yet at no time does Scripture speak of an independent Kingdom of Evil (with capital letters), which by means of its own power has the capability of pulling our legs out from under us, particularly unexpectedly, in ways that we cannot perceive or understand. That image of evil is intended solely to create fear and make us dependent and helpless. Rather than respect human responsibility, it tries to destroy it. It therefore is an entirely false image, a delusion perpetuated by the horror films and games foisted upon us every day in television broadcasts and computer games. Such so-called entertainment can simultaneously terrorize and fascinate children (perhaps not accidentally, for does not every ideology have its terror phase?).

But the gospel, as good news for the entire inhabited world (literally, *oikoumene*, from which we get the word "ecumenical"), uses entirely different language to describe evil. It states that after Jesus's resurrection, one can speak about evil only as a temporary counterpower, one whose effectiveness depends solely on enticing and seducing people with things like money, power, and the longing to survive. It thus is no wonder that idols in the Bible always bear the names of their specific temptations: "Mammon" for money, for example, "Molech" for power, and "Baal" for "lord of much wealth" (cf. chap. 2).[4] Outside the sphere of seductions such as these, evil is powerless. The spiritual battle in history therefore revolves around the hearts of people, nothing else. The battle is about human choices and responsibilities, individually and collectively. That also means that the battle scene where the decisions are made is the earth. It is not hell or the underworld.

In our view, this simple insight into the fundamentally limited scope of evil throws the door wide open to genuine and living hope. The hope is real because, at its core, it is not a human creation. It attaches itself directly to the faith that God is deeply engaged in all of human history. The God whom we confess has already fundamentally conquered the power of evil through his Son. Jesus is therefore worthy to hold "the whole world [including our future] in his hands."

This is not loose religious prattle. On the contrary, in our view it is directly and specifically oriented to each of the fundamental and gripping problems outlined in the previous chapters.

Addressing today's endemic dilemmas from that deep reality is the task of this chapter. The first section ("Hope in Today's World") sets the stage by describing the contours of living, genuine hope in today's world. Because this hope puts us to work, the next section ("Paving the Way") searches out openings for taking different paths and for locating, along the way, different kinds of solutions, using as a foundation what we have already obtained in the previous chapters. In it we describe three down-to-earth, concrete guidelines—the periscope, minesweeper, and rope ladder—metaphors that are eminently suited to help direct the journey away from ruin and death. Finally, in "The Vision and Its Implications," we propose a vision for a future that is awakened by genuine hope rather than by ideological influences, a hope that deeply engages today's structural problems. In doing so, we revisit the ideologies of material progress and guaranteed freedom. We then conclude with concrete examples at the microlevel and a specific policy proposal at the macrolevel, each of which provides glimpses of the awakening of life that genuine hope brings.

Hope in Today's World

Our sense of the reality of hope in today's world is inspired by three themes: the active presence of the Spirit of God in our time, the sign of the cross as an antidote to the closed circles and spirals of our age, and the concrete implications of the "morning star" as the biblical image of hope.

The Spirit Inscribes Paths in Time

Many people consider making reference to the activity or presence of God in human history as much too hazardous. For some, the spiritual and eternal message of salvation and reconciliation may apply to a far-distant future, but not to the difficult processes of our time. Coming too close to our present realities could even contaminate the purity of the salvation message itself.

This notion, common among Christians, is perhaps the most significant reason why many people tend to misunderstand or even disregard the spiritual dimension of contemporary world events. But then they effectively scratch out or erase perhaps the most decisive element in current events, the intensely active role of God's Spirit in history. The Spirit inscribes paths of grace and judgment throughout time, even through our time.

The French-American philosopher and literary critic René Girard has underscored this biblical theme. Girard is the thinker we referred to earlier who, in a series of books, has so adroitly laid bare the mechanisms of violence and power in the world.[5] In his study *The Scapegoat*, Girard refers to the Gospel of John, where Jesus uses the word "paraclete" to describe the Spirit's work in history (as in 16:7).[6] The Greek word *paracletos* means both "comforter" and "advocate." Though we usually take it to mean "comforter," that is not the meaning intended here. Jesus declares that the Spirit about to come will supply the world with convincing proof of sin, justice, and judgment (John 16:8). Here Jesus names no less than three categories of justice: guilt (sin), justice (as a measure), and sentence (judgment; John 16:8–11). Thus, the Spirit of God is an advocate. Jesus portrays all of history after his ascension as unfolding in a court of justice, the court of world history. In that court, time after time the Spirit of God, as God's great Advocate, in a cogent argument provides convincing proof of where guilt lies and ultimately proof of how judgment must be pronounced. The Spirit always begins the plea by referring to what once took place in history to a man called Jesus: a completely innocent person who—because he was subjected to the religious leaders' judgment that "it is better that one person dies than that we all become lost"—was made a victim of brute violence (John 11:50, adapted). That reference then serves as the grounds for the compelling legal argument that God's Advocate makes over and over again throughout human history. "The Paraclete is called on behalf of the prisoner, the victim, to speak in his place and in his name, to act in his defense. The Paraclete is the universal Advocate, the chief defender of all innocent victims, *the destroyer of every representation of persecution.*"[7]

This insight is tremendously helpful, especially for those who experience the turmoil of ideological powers around and even within them. John 16 accents the highly active form that the work of the Spirit in history takes: "And when he comes, he will convince the world [not just Christians] . . ." (16:8 RSV). Clearly, the future falls under the same judgment pronounced by God's Spirit against all victimizing ideologies. God, through the activity of his Spirit, continues to make his home in our history. When ideologies die after or as a result of their power being usurped, that too is truly the work of the same Spirit. All this means that today's abhorrent, spiraling ideologies have no ability to close off the future. The future is not theirs, but God's.

So with the historical demise of every decaying ideology, the Spirit provides incontrovertible proof that, in the long run, there is no life outside of God's norms for life. For a period of time, people can try to take everything into their own hands, but outside of the life-sustaining ways of God, sooner or later, they run headlong into death.

Does everything then, including the solutions, revolve around "Christians and their God"? This question contains a trap. The phrase "their God" cannot serve as a yardstick. God is no one's possession, certainly not Christendom's. One of Bach's most beautiful chorales is called "Nun komm, der Heiden Heiland" ("Come Now, Savior of the Nations," from Cantata no. 61, referring to the Hebrew Scriptures; lyrics by Martin Luther). God seeks to be the Savior and Redeemer of the whole world and thus of all who long for the coming kingdom of justice. God certainly stands on the side of Christians who walk in God's way. But God stood no less, and perhaps even more, on the side of the millions of Jews who were killed by "Christians" in World War II. God still stands beside oppressed black people and enslaved Muslims and brings judgment upon all those who hinder their lives. God also hears the cries of animals killed needlessly. The whole creation, the whole cosmos, groans with longing for the revelation of the children of God (Rom. 8:18–25).

Groaning with longing is the language of hope. The ways inscribed by the Spirit in history are not confined to punishment and judgment. God's grace also inscribes ways or paths of hope and healing in time. A healing grace remains ever active in creation. By it wounds are healed and the environment, even after massive attacks, revives. After cleanup, even of terribly polluted rivers and lakes (such as the Thames River or Lake Erie), salmon again swim upstream. And as soon as it is given the opportunity, that healing power also works between people and nations.

Was not the great healing miracle of the twentieth century the extraordinary reconciliation that took place, contrary to every expectation, between many blacks and whites in South Africa? When they appeared before the South African Truth and Reconciliation Commission, cold-hearted people who had murdered others as brutes occasionally burst into tears, deeply astonished that they were forgiven, sometimes on the spot, by survivors of their brutal acts.[8]

There are many other signs of the ongoing activity of the Spirit's grace in history. The Spirit moves a remarkable number of people to joyfully commit their lives to assisting victims all around the world, often at great danger to themselves. Others engage in the centuries-old practice of caring for the sick; it is not by accident that in most European hospitals the sick call their aids "sister" or "brother." Moreover, people who have lived under horrific, life-threatening dictators do not forget how, after the fall of these powers, a time of respite often appears (a *Gnadenfrist*, the Germans call it). New chances, new possibilities emerge, often over and above people's original expectations.

Circle and Cross

Sometimes we doubt that much can happen. But the difficulty is not just that our expectations can fall short. Often the images we use to guide our thoughts and actions can also be terribly narrow. Our images can be as closed as an oyster, a reality by which we create room for ideologies to exercise power over us. In his famous book *Orthodoxy*, G. K. Chesterton states that most modern thinkers often strike him as lunatics, as people who have lost the broad sense of things.[9] He finds that many modern, even brilliant academicians suffer from a strange combination of logically constricted, narrow circularity and spiritual poverty. Chesterton may carry this too far. But his contribution is most significant when he juxtaposes the image of the closed circle with the openness of the cross:

> The circle is perfect and infinite in its nature; but it is fixed forever in its size; it can never be larger or smaller. But the cross, though it has at its heart a collision and a contradiction, can extend its four arms forever without altering its shape. Because it has a paradox in its centre it can grow without changing. The circle returns upon itself and is bound. The cross opens its arms to the four winds; it is a support for free travelers.[10]

Symbols have a relative value. But sometimes their truth reaches deep. There is truth in this image for people who in their personal and societal worlds find themselves imprisoned in cramped circles and pinched spirals. The symbol illustrates that the only possible way to break out of the circle is to accept the reality of the cross. The cross represents the only genuinely anti-ideological stance. All efforts to survive and maintain life at any cost must be crucified, following Christ's example.

This is the collision and contradiction to which Chesterton pointed. They take place within our hearts. The cross of Jesus therefore also has a significance reaching much deeper than our individual salvation. The apostle Paul describes the cross even as a victory over the principalities and powers of this world: "On that cross he discarded the cosmic powers and authorities like a garment; he made a public spectacle of them and led them as captives in triumphal procession" (Col. 2:15 NEB).

What powers did Jesus conquer? The answer lies in the nature of his suffering. Jesus died in complete poverty, in the renouncing of all earthly power, and in the abandonment of his divine identity. In dying this death he became stronger than the powers of the kingdom of darkness, which seduce and imprison people and nations in their relentless search for wealth, power, and a sure identity. Despite their assault on the cross, these powers were impotent against Jesus. Defenseless and on display, the Messiah defeated them and triumphed over them publicly. The cross of Christ delivered the mortal blow to all the powers of the abyss, whether they are called Mammon, Molech, or Baal,[11] or whether in our day they are clothed in the disguise of the spectacular gods upon which rest the hopes of revolution, identity, material progress, and guaranteed freedom ideologies.

The Morning Star

Many of us have lost awareness of this kind of hope. Ideological hope comes only by the grace of a few tiny cracks in the wall that throw slivers of light onto our bleak situation. That hope is then extinguished as one by one the cracks disappear and the darkness envelops us. But this is the opposite of Christian hope. Christian hope is a hope of contrast: it revives in the middle of the night, just when the darkness seems to overpower us.

The biblical image of hope is the morning star. The morning star often appears between two and three o'clock at night, when the darkness is complete and the faintest sign of morning is not yet visible. So small that it threatens to vanish, the star seems unable to vanquish the overpowering darkness. Yet when you see the morning star, you know that the night has been defeated. The morning star brings the morning in behind it, just as certainly as Jesus brings the kingdom in behind him. "I am . . . the bright Morning Star" (Rev. 22:16). These were Jesus's last words to his disciples. They appear as words of comfort on the last page of every Bible.

How do we act on this image of hope? The example of Esther can help us here. Friedrich Weinreb, a Jewish scholar, wrote an impressive book on the story of Esther, entitled *Ik die verborgen ben* (I Who Am Hidden).[12] The hidden I is the God of the covenant. His name never appears in the book of Esther. Fate, not God, seems to occupy center stage. The decision to eliminate the people of Israel was written in the unbreakable laws of the Medes and Persians and sealed by the king. God seemed absent. But Esther's name means "morning star." "Who knows," Esther's foster-father Mordecai said to her, "but that you have come to royal position for such a time as this?"[13] So late on Passover morning, with her life in the balance and trembling with fear, Esther went to her husband the king, who raised his scepter to her. At that point, Israel's history began to turn.

Esther's simple walk to the king, while seemingly small and insignificant, was the turning point in Israel's story of sure destruction. Miracles did not save Israel, at least not miracles as we understand them. But as a God who works hiddenly, God linked his saving acts to the act of Esther, who in obedience put her own life in jeopardy. That act God blessed. That was the act that God, the Doer, waited for in hiding. "When Esther appears," writes Weinreb, "when Esther is seen in the darkness of the exile, that is the sign of daybreak. Where God in his hiddenness can be delineated, there is the sign that the defeat of the night has come."[14]

Living out of messianic hope is therefore different from just waiting passively.[15] It requires that we leave our protective shelters behind and put our future, our prosperity, and if necessary our whole lives in jeopardy for the sake of love, truth, and justice. Indeed, growing into God's story implies growing into a living obedience to the risen Lord.[16]

The image of the morning star also means that we ourselves are neither able nor called to dismantle today's demonic spirals and deified powers. Instead, we are called to take first steps, small beginning acts of undistorted justice and unperverted love in the midst of powerful ideologies. Even our smallest acts can sometimes mobilize the forces of God's kingdom in a time of doom, just as Esther's act did centuries ago. Who knows whether the "God who is hidden" is waiting for just that to happen? We do not need to know precisely what the outcome of the spiritual battle will be. "Who knows?" Mordecai said that too. Like him, we do not have a corner on wisdom. But risking first steps is the only option for those who seek to answer to the hope that lives within them.

Paving the Way

What Esther-like steps might make sense in the current environment, concrete first steps that might even help to pave a way out? Remember that the present environment is extremely unstable, even explosive. If beginning steps are actually to grapple with the force field created by today's spirals, then actions motivated by good intentions alone are not enough. In fact, well-meaning steps driven solely by good intentions may even do more harm than good. They could play into the dynamic that opposing ideologies, despite or even because of their contradictions, cross-fertilize, reinforce, and even empower each other. Well-meaning steps could inadvertently contribute to today's perilous escalation dynamic. We think of the increasingly destructive escalation pattern of hurricanes, whose power and range appear to increase as ocean temperatures rise. In our view, therefore, first steps make sense that are specifically geared to engage current systems of differing but mutually interactive causes.

This orientation leads naturally to an initial practical first-step approach, one that focuses on preventing further escalation. It applies at both the micro and macro levels. As individuals, groups, and sectors of society, we ought to begin by taking steps to end or turn back from the activities and measures that, implicitly or explicitly, support the cooperation and cross-fertilization of opposing ideologies. Advancing the collaboration between ideologies is like playing with fire or touching a high-tension power line. Such actions amount to taking steps of despair, not steps of hope. Living out of hope therefore begins by turning away from today's steps of despair.

What do we mean by steps of despair? Consider, as an illustration, what can occur when countries become consumed with their own security and, at the same time, do not under any circumstances tolerate slackening the expansion of their material prosperity. They frequently embrace a desperate, untenable solution: they use increased weapons exports to partially finance the expansion of their own armaments, building them up even to the point of becoming ready to undertake a preventive war. We may call this the "McNamara trap." It was precisely this approach that US Secretary of Defense Robert McNamara adopted in the 1960s to solve his mounting defense budget problems. As John Ralston Saul observes, "McNamara concluded that it would be rational to limit armament costs by producing larger runs of each weapon and selling them abroad. The United States also happened to be running a three-billion-dollar general trade deficit. Foreign arms sales would be a way to balance the situation."[17] The inevitable consequence was that within a few years American soldiers and American allies ended up becoming the targets of American weapons.

As we saw in chapter 7, McNamara's step of despair is not just a thing of the past.[18] Numerous countries today, especially the wealthier ones, engage in a deliberate, systematic attempt to simultaneously expand their weapons arsenals and increase their economic growth by vigorously pursuing arms exports. They act as if weapons are ordinary economic goods available for purchase by others. According to figures provided by the US Congressional Research Service, the five members of the United Nations Security Council (the United States, Russia, Great Britain, France, and China) delivered 86.7 percent of the world's arms exports in 2004, often for reasons more economic than strategic.[19] Add other European nations, and the figure climbs to 93.1 percent.[20] The United States exports more arms than the rest of the world's nations combined.[21] Weapons manufacturing is its most heavily subsidized industry after agriculture.[22] Moreover, the majority of the world's arms exports go to the developing countries. In line with the actions of other G8 nations, in 2003 some 80 percent of the United States' top arms clients in the developing world (20 of 25) were countries that the US State Department had declared either undemocratic or known for poor human rights records.[23] In 1999 the United States supplied arms in 92 percent of the world's conflicts, sometimes to opposing sides.[24] And from 1998 to 2001, the United States, Great Britain, and France earned more income from arms sales to developing countries than they gave in aid.[25]

These foolhardy steps of desperation amount to digging one's own grave. They reflect an ideological insanity on the part of the G8 nations. Also, they drive the global spirals we discussed earlier to their seemingly irreversible, destructive, absolute maximum.

Against this backdrop, consider an example of a concrete, preventive first step that is specifically keyed to redirecting this system of multiple causes. All countries, especially the wealthiest, must dramatically reduce and ultimately discontinue their weapons exports, irrespective of the fierce opposition that such a step will undoubtedly elicit from domestic lobby groups, especially the powerful arms manufacturing industry. Ratifying the International Arms Trade Treaty is a good place to start.[26] It simply cannot be otherwise because the survival of ourselves and of others is at stake.

A second step of despair occurs when absolute identity and absolute economic interests collide. If wealthy countries respond by further linking globalization with empire, they embark down a path of despair. Some powers try to order and manipulate the globalization process in such a way that globalization serves primarily to expand their own economic and political power at the expense of all weaker interests and parties: poor countries, which experience inflexible forms of exclusion; Islamic nations, whose identities become deeply threatened; and in a different sense the vulnerable ecosystem, which has no opportunity to regenerate against the economic onslaught perpetuated against it. The boomerang effect created by these enforced expansions of power is immense and becoming more and more visible. Seen from the perspective of the real interests of the richer nations, is it not insane to incite rising, explosive protests by the poor and the oppressed, while at the same time systematically undermining the very environment that will make life possible for their own children?

Consider a second illustration of a first step designed to begin reversing the deadly mutual stimulation of the material prosperity and identity ideologies. As inhabitants of the rich countries, let us admit that such further steps of despair serve only to intensify global spirals of horrific devastation, much like warmer ocean water increases the awful devastation of hurricanes.

In our view, no other conclusion is possible. The wealthiest nations in particular need to learn to give up their haughtiness and pride, especially in the international arena. Concretely, that means that they need to loosen their inflexible positions of restricting access to their own markets, opening up other economies, and rejecting almost every consensus on environmental protection and climate change. Inflexibility on such issues may seem to be a self-evident necessity, but that stance is extremely short-sighted and fundamentally wrong. It is a blindness inflicted by ideology. To become realistic, we in the wealthier countries require conversion—a turn in the other direction—to permit facts that presently have no opportunity to influence decisions to enter our consciousness.

Three Practical Guidelines on the Way

We have seen two illustrations of steps geared to begin reversing current systems or constellations of differing but mutually interactive causes. They focus on leaving certain activities behind. But what actual positive steps, both small and large, make sense at this particular juncture in history?

Naturally, our positions as people differ. The nature and difficulty of positive first steps will vary according to our situations. Yet in keeping with the first-step directive outlined above, our choices, our steps, will display a certain commonality. They ought to flow in the same stream. To enhance that likelihood, we offer three practical guidelines for taking stock of or measuring the suitability of potential creative steps. These standards, or touchstones, surface spontaneously from the content of the previous chapters. They hint at the rough seas and perils that emerge when battling the churning, hurricane-like spirals set in motion by the ideologies of our time. We therefore describe them by using the language of modern-day seafarers, calling them the periscope, minesweeper, and rope-ladder guidelines.

The Periscope Guideline

To grasp the periscope guideline, recall chapter 1, where no fewer than four case studies illustrated that a number of current approaches do not solve today's problems and sometimes even aggravate them. We thus saw that in spite of intensive development and loan programs for the poorest countries, poverty in those countries has increased, not decreased. In spite of higher military expenditures, insecurity in the world has heightened rather than diminished. In spite of every regulation and accord, the global environmental situation has degenerated. And in spite of the advent of free global financial markets, the monetary tensions in a number of countries have risen, not fallen. Why is that the case?

From the knowledge we have accumulated in the previous chapters, we may now identify the source of the pain more clearly. In each situation, at every turn, political and other decision-makers display an overestimation of faith in the means of progress, such as environmental technology, military technology, modern organizational techniques, the pursuit of maximum economic growth, and financial instruments such as conditional loans and the promotion of free financial markets. Decision-makers defend these instruments and tools to a much higher degree than their successes could ever explain or account for. They often promote them as if they were inherently capable of saving the day, or, following a more prevalent notion, as if they will make us pay if we veer off their promised path of liberation. Decision-makers repeatedly summon us to follow the way of the market or to swear off interfering with the dictates of the economic and technological forces of progress, as if living gods have spoken. So it is that unmasking the gods is utterly necessary today. As soon as we believe in economic growth, technological progress, the free market, and even democracy, we gradually regress into a narrowing of perspective until we fall prey to the illusions already woven into people and nations today.

The situation of the contemporary world is not unlike that of a submarine submerged deep under the water. Small windows onto reality supply only a narrow and limited view of the surroundings, just as the tiny portholes of a submarine reveal only a fraction of the immediate area. Submariners know that a widened view requires a periscope. A periscope would give a comprehensive perspective; it would permit us to scan the whole horizon above, not just part of it. The *Oxford Dictionary* defines "periscope" as "*peri*: roundabout; *scope*: look; a periscope can see things otherwise out of sight." Perhaps a periscope is exactly what our situation today requires. It is the shrunken view of reality, the fixation of our gaze solely upon the interior of our fast-moving ship, that blocks the quest for actual solutions.

How do we locate such a periscope? What constitutes a broad, realistic view of reality today? Remember that ideologies possess a power or force by which they influence our norms and warp our values. With ideologies, values like justice, love, truth, freedom, solidarity, and *oikonomia* (economy) become emptied and then refilled for the sole purpose of legitimating certain ends and justifying the means required to implement them. Ideologies thus cripple the original power of these profound, direction-setting ways. Perhaps then regaining the original meaning of these ways could serve as our periscope. By reclaiming their original breadth, perhaps a broad, unclouded view of reality will have an opportunity to return, not just in the abstract, but particularly in the concrete.

But this approach is only viable to the degree that ways like justice, love, and truth belong to the landscape of reality itself. How is that possible? How can such principles ever be considered part of the reality of life and society?

The claim is not so remarkable, however. It might seem that people and societies can bring to reality their own ends, ideas, and institutions and then regard everything else available as potential means for reaching the ends. But that approach is couched in pure Enlightenment language. It reflects a vision of the world as an empty universe in principle, a universe that one can fabricate entirely according to taste. Yet every religion and every notion of the existence of God run counter to this view. They each acknowledge the existence of at least a few firm norms or commands that are not humanly made, directives that we are called to follow. All the major religions also speak of given paths or ways to walk.[27] Secularized Westerners often think that norms or values are simply the outcome of certain agreements made between people. But the Christians among them know differently. If we believe in a reality consciously created by a living God, then that reality is itself stamped by that loving, caring God. And God is not someone who can lie. The same God who taught humanity good ways in the Torah had already prepared for their possible obedience in the good creation. Ways like justice, love, and care therefore have a reality value. As a result, they possess healing power to this day. People can resist such ways or in arrogance not bother themselves with them, but then they are misled and deceived.

Ideologies, Jacques Ellul once wrote, often recognize the enduring validity of norms much earlier and much better than Christians do. Without exception, all the great ideologies have systematically and vigorously hunted down words like justice, truth, solidarity, and love in order to annex them to serve their own ends. In so doing, ideologists unwittingly acknowledge that their ideologies cannot carry the day without hijacking the inner, convicting power of these ways. Nevertheless, Ellul notes indignantly, they remain a stolen inheritance. For Ellul, such life-giving norms or ways represent nothing less than the fruits of the tree of Christ's crucifixion.[28] They are laws out of which life itself emerges.

Let us then try to apply the periscope guideline to the four problems sketched in chapter 1, while testing its practical value and significance.

- Naturally, it is possible to financially assist impoverished countries. But by itself such intervention does not prevent the deepening of their poverty. Poverty subsides only when *justice* prevails in the interaction between rich and poor countries. The requirement of justice awakens us to the deliberate exclusions described earlier. It exposes the hypocrisy of rich countries' rigid, harsh insistence that poor countries do better at exporting, while at the same time they protect their own markets with high tariffs on imports.[29] Wealthy countries also flout the requirements of justice when they and their banks hoard the creation of international currencies entirely to themselves, resulting in the reality that the poorest countries, if they cannot increase export revenue, must permanently borrow from the rich countries. Their debts therefore keep piling up, and the perpetual net transfer of capital from the South to the North every year is the result.

- Naturally, protection and safety are legitimate personal and national needs. Pursuing them can even be a duty. But on balance, today the national goal of self-protection has become entirely one-dimensional, and it simply cannot bring *peace*. Self-protection, while a valid goal, is not synonymous with peace. *Peace* is primarily a way or path for us to walk down, as a number of responsible peace movements have long understood.[30] On it we fall down and get up again. On it lies the radiance of the Messiah himself: "[He will] guide our feet into the path of peace," sang Zechariah (Luke 1:79). And it is impossible even to arrive at the path of peacebuilding, much less walk down it, by clinging incessantly to ever-expanding arsenals of weapons of lethal destruction.

- Naturally, it makes sense to devote technology to conserving energy and resources and to taking care of the environment. By itself, however, the application of technology falls short of the requirements of *oikonomia*: good stewardship. *Oikonomia* requires that all economies (including our own) comply with the capacity of the earth to sustain life and nourish everyone in the world. Genuine stewardship therefore requires that we be prepared to rein in our consumption desires in such a way that all of the world's inhabitants can have a good life. "Economy" in the biblical sense means first and foremost the "caring administration" of all that has been entrusted to us.[31] If we do not adopt at the beginning of our plans the requirement to care for what has been entrusted to us, then our actions will fail.

- Naturally, there is nothing wrong with financial markets operating on a global scale. Under certain conditions of freedom, they can even be highly beneficial. But how quickly we hear the word *freedom* misused here! *Freedom* in the biblical sense does not mean life without rules. Rather, it involves persons and nations refusing to become enslaved to an alien power. "It is for freedom that Christ has set us free. Stand firm, then, and do not let yourselves be burdened again by a yoke of slavery," wrote the apostle Paul (Gal. 5:1). Consequently, when the entire world increasingly subjects itself to the tyranny and volatility of financial markets, which we have left entirely to their own devices, then we have literally endorsed insanity and relinquished freedom. Such markets are driven by little more than greed and speculation. Markets are to freely serve real economies, not the other way around. We therefore need to reanchor the creation of international currency in the soil of what the world genuinely needs in relation to both consumption and production.[32]

These comments illustrate that we require a concrete, vital sense of life-norms in order to return to a real, expanded societal perspective, one that takes in the whole horizon. An expanded perspective is not closed in upon itself like a circle, but opens out on all sides, like a cross. At the same time, a cross possesses, at its center, an internal tension, one that calls us to pay the price of candid self-criticism.

The Minesweeper Guideline

The identity ideology provides an appropriate context for exploring the minesweeper guideline. Earlier we encountered the ideology's spirals of violence, such as have played out for years in the Middle East between Israel and the Palestinians. Identity conflicts around the world, driven by clashing ideologies bent on preserving cultural identity at all costs, can create horrific spirals of terror. Action provokes reaction: the ideological response most readily available is to reply in a similar way. The ideologically constrained impulse is to pay back in the same currency, whereby revenge counteracts violence, and war becomes the self-evident answer to terror. But conflicts then escalate as if on their own, to the point where mutual intimidation and death threats become tragic and seemingly permanent features of the landscape. The law of self-preservation at all costs replaces the law of love for one's neighbor.

Let us consider the possibility that the brutal, unconscionable attacks of September 11, 2001, provoked a similar ideological response in the West itself, and then explore the minesweeper guideline in perhaps a broader context. In a flash, a nation consumed with its own security was shaken by the reality of terrorism on its own soil. When the attacks occurred, what had been a far-off notion became a fact of life. Understandably, the American people's sense of safety and security became shattered. The response was therefore somewhat predictable: increased airport security, together with the creation and implementation of the USA Patriot Act, the Department of Homeland Security, and a doctrine of war centered on preventive military measures.

As we have observed, the preservation of cultural identity is a legitimate and even essential goal. But when the end justifies the means, an illegitimate prioritization of values takes place that can, in turn, pave the way for a blind acceptance of means. Consider one way in which the response to 9/11 displays such ideological traits.

The attacks reactivated a powerful drive to preserve the identity of the American people, a people now under threat.[33] The US government quickly retreated into a black-and-white, dual vision or paradigm of the world. That vision redefined good and evil, classifying individuals and nations as either allies or adversaries, with its chief adversaries making up the "axis of evil." Against this evil the American people, despite or even because of being under attack, would demonstrate their unshakable resolve to ensure that the rekindled "light" (America) would overcome the new "darkness."[34] The vision permitted no variation on this theme: people were either for us or against us, and they needed to decide immediately which side they were on. The ensuing categorization of various groups of people led to widespread stories of suspicion, harassment, and even detention without cause of US citizens who happened to be of Arabic descent or Muslim belief, spurred on by the Patriot Act, which curtailed civil liberties. Regrettably, some people maligned the way of love: the call to love one's neighbor regardless of race, class, gender, or position. An identity ideology thus flared up in the United States that resembled too closely that of its fierce adversary.

So it is that ideologies set their adherents on the path of mirror-image reactions. But the ways of God hold open the possibility of reacting differently. And this leads us directly to the minesweeper guideline. If an enemy has buried land mines, naturally one can immediately fight back. But another tactic is to call in minesweepers. Minesweepers trace the sea or the land in search of the threat. Then they get rid of the threat by dismantling the mines.

The lesson is simple but far-reaching. The minesweeper guideline suggests that responding differently has the potential to deal with the root of the conflict. The best answer to evil is not evil but good. Terror often first requires psychological, spiritual, diplomatic, intelligence, and police types of combat rather than military attack. Indeed, we approach solutions not by going after the symptoms and destroying them, but rather by discovering the origin of the evil acts and exposing them. Often then we become aware that the instigating action was born out of a deep injury or an unnecessary humiliation. Even Osama bin Laden on numerous occasions has said that his unbridled aggression originates from forms of deep injury to his faith and culture.

The minesweeper guideline may sound entirely practical and therefore not rooted in principle. But that is an illusion. The guideline is anchored deeply in the reality of a world that knows sin and guilt and therefore needs reconciliation. In a conflict, possessing and exercising power exposes the power-holder to a potent inner temptation. One's own guilt in escalating the conflict cannot serve to justify the application of overwhelming force. But assuming that the other is "evil" can manufacture justification. A country that exercises power but does not engage in self-criticism—a country without a sense of its own role in escalating the conflict—does not think it needs reconciliation between people. Power exercised on that basis inevitably poses a grave, deadly danger.

Conflicts rooted in fiercely held identity ideologies rage in various places around the world, such as the Congo, the Sudan, and Palestine. How then does the minesweeper guideline operate in such situations? Consider how deeply it animates those involved in the many courageous peace efforts undertaken jointly by Israelis and Palestinians, such as the Neve Shalom/Wahat al-Salam community and in Peaceful Tomorrows. Neve Shalom/Wahat al-Salam is a living example of the genuine reconciliation that can occur by not responding to the other in kind. Peaceful Tomorrows is an organization of family members victimized by the 9/11 attacks, who actively oppose ideologically based counterreactions to 9/11.[35] These examples illustrate a larger reality that every conflict, no matter how dire, possesses local capacities or impulses toward peace, rooted in the conviction that breaking through powerful ideologies requires not escalation but rather the possibility of truth-telling, admitting, confessing, and forgiving.

As of this writing, recent hopeful signs in the Middle East include the election of Mahmoud Abbas as president of the Palestinian National Authority (Jan. 9, 2005), partial withdrawal of Israeli settlements, an Israeli-Palestinian cease-fire declaration (ending a four-year intifada), the release of nine hundred Palestinian prisoners, and the opening of Israel's Gaza border to Palestinian workers and merchants. Regardless of setbacks, such as the Hezbollah/Israeli conflict, these indicate some experimentation with the minesweeper guideline at the political decision-making levels in both administrations. If these tentative steps take hold, they could, in combination with the room created by local capacities for peace, pave the way for a just political solution. That could, in turn, lead to an opportunity for a desperately needed reconciliation process, a moment similar to the one seized upon by South Africa's Truth and Reconciliation Commission. Acting from within the minesweeper guideline could help to stimulate a reversal in the spiral of violence.

But this possibility anticipates our third marker along the way: the rope-ladder guideline.

The Rope-Ladder Guideline

Consider the rope ladder. A rope ladder, such as a ladder on a ship, requires a different manner of climbing than does a regular ladder. To climb higher, one needs the hands and feet to work in tandem in such a way that while moving one hand up along one rope, the opposite foot follows along the other rope.

What is the purpose of citing the rope-climbers' technique here? And does pathfinding still involve the art of discovering new ways or paths?

Here too we refer to previous chapters, particularly chapter 8, on globalization. At first glance, the treatment of globalization there did not inspire courage or hope. We saw that the prevailing style of globalization displays, as shadow sides or paradoxes, forms of injustice and exclusion that reinforce or deepen each other. One problem evokes the other. The enduring protectionism of Western markets and the growing burden of debt in the South deepen poverty in the South. But they also increase damage to the already terribly threatened global environment. At the same time, deeply entrenched poverty and the ongoing depletion of natural resources propel innumerable streams of people in motion, both within continents and to other continents. More and more migrants knock on the doors of the rich countries, and they sometimes find themselves compelled to climb over the fences. That in turn puts more pressure on the social stability of the rich countries. In response, people then take refuge behind more exclusive or gated arrangements, which only closes the circle again and pulls the spiral down further. Clearly, today's various problems egg each other on. They threaten to plunge the world into the depths, with all of its inhabitants, people and animals.

Many forms of pessimism and helplessness today originate in the unmistakable reality that current problems reinforce each other. Contemporary problems collaborate to create dead-end spirals that seem, step by step, to suck us downward.

But what then remains of so many biblical promises that if we concretely follow the ways of God, life will return, not only personally but also as communities? Are they merely empty words or words meant only for the hereafter?

Dietrich Bonhoeffer, the great Christian martyr who was executed by the Nazis in prison only a few days before the Americans liberated Berlin, believed differently. In his diary he commented on a verse from Psalm 119: "I have seen an end to everything, but your Way is very wide." Bonhoeffer wrote that the courage to take first steps in doing justice and loving others always brings with it the promise of a way that widens, a way that leads, step by step, out of the present entanglement.

Bonhoeffer's reflection generates a simple question. Do spirals only spin downward? Of course not. If problems are related in the sense that they enhance the difficulty and bleakness of each other, then at least a similar dynamic applies to their potential solutions. As we talk about ways out of trouble, a step toward solving one problem will in principle also positively affect the solution of another problem (and possibly even more than one). This process, moving step by step, can launch an upward-moving spiral, one that lifts us from the depths that threaten to engulf us. The hands help the feet, just as the feet in turn help the hands along the rope ladder.

Though it may sound strange, the rope-ladder guideline brings us close to the heart of what the biblical word "blessing" means. Doing good in the sense of taking first (often small) steps along the way of love, justice, and care for the creation has a much greater radiating effect than we often suspect. When that radiating effect returns in a roundabout way, then something of what the Bible calls blessing occurs. When countries make peace, often they receive blessings in other ways. Their war economies also blossom into peace economies over the course of time. And if justice is actually done to poor countries so that the countries of the South can give higher priority to meeting the basic needs of their populations, then the direct consequence can be a restoration of the environment and slackened migration pressure. The International Labour Organization calculated that in the 1980s the continued debt burdens of the South cost the US economy no less than three million jobs. Why not then stimulate a reverse, upward-moving spiral instead, trusting that genuine debt relief could bring blessings for ourselves too?

In a time of violent, downward spirals, let us claim the promise of ways that widen. One step invites the next, and that step in turn makes possible a third step. The rope-ladder guideline suggests that genuinely addressing one problem may well contribute to the solution of others.

The Vision and Its Implications

What happens if we combine the three practical guidelines we just described: the periscope, minesweeper, and rope ladder? Ought we to use them to draft a blueprint for a better society? Under no circumstances will we do that. New blueprints morph all too easily into new absolutized goals. They thus become the cradle for new ideologies, ideologies that would again try to close off the future, imposing perhaps even harsher demands than those foisted upon us by today's ideologies.

But a vision or a way is different than a blueprint. Martin Luther King Jr. spoke of a dream. A blueprint is closed in its goals and its outlook. A vision or a dream, however, opens up ways or paths, and it motivates people to walk down them. "Where there is no vision, the people perish," says the Bible (Prov. 29:18 KJV). In that light, before we provide some concrete illustrations, we place the three guidelines in the context of an alternative vision or dream for the world economy and for global peace and conflict.

Economic Life

In a number of ways, we can compare economic life today to a tunnel. The tunnel economy is not a new image: the renowned economist John Maynard Keynes used it in 1930. During the dark days of the Great Depression, Keynes was asked to write about the economic possibilities for his grandchildren. He wrote these famous words: "Avarice and usury and precaution must be our gods for a little longer still. For only they can lead us out of the tunnel of economic necessity into daylight."[36]

Keynes penned a striking metaphor. The economy is a tunnel, and avarice and usury are required to speed up the flow of traffic in order to reach the light at the end of the tunnel: a rising standard of living for everyone. Avarice and usury accomplish this by functioning as gods, in Keynes's estimation. He recognized that they establish the rules, and he advocated that they continue to do so, at least temporarily.

Quite unexpectedly, the metaphor still describes today's global economy. Perhaps our contemporary economy is even completing the image, with its now-universal drive for maximum productivity, efficiency, and profits. But how astonishing that is! Did not Keynes predict that, once out of the tunnel, the daylight would arrive? Why do we now, even glob-ally, still find ourselves inside the tunnel?

The answer lies in the dynamics of present-day globalization and its largely ideological context. When gods are installed, they do not leave simply of their own accord. They carry on with their regime as long as the purpose that sustains them remains active: the betterment of our material condition by means of untrammeled, unbridled economic growth. The gods and their dynamism then stay in place despite the consequences they bring. They carry on regardless of whether the noise and pollution inside the tunnel increase, or the tunnel operators find that they have to exclude slow traffic from entering the tunnel, or the tunnel propri-etors need to institute priority lanes for fast traffic in order to increase the average speed. Regrettably, certain countries may temporarily fall further back. Sometimes mass layoffs will be necessary. We will need to exclude from the production process people who are deemed unsuit-able for work. Further, we cannot avoid some environmental damage. These sacrifices, while unfortunate, are necessary for us to reach the daylight: rising material prosperity with enough resources to pay for environmental remediation, social assistance, health care, and additional development aid for impoverished countries. We may call this regime a postcare economy, one that engages in the highest possible consumption and production and only afterward tries to mitigate the mounting care needs, often with extremely expensive forms of compensation. Its rigid, extreme fixation on the future, on dynamic material progress, carries on despite horrific consequences, such as the tragic effects of Hurricane Katrina in New Orleans—effects that a precare economy could have largely prevented.[37]

How narrow and false this perspective of the future is! It is devoid of vision. It makes people in today's economy look like fish swimming into a net. The fish want to get out, but they see no alternative to swimming more and more frantically into the net.

Let us therefore turn toward a more positive view of society. Focusing our periscope on a wider vision of economic growth, let us move toward the type of economic growth that our society actually needs. Perhaps the growth of a simple fruit tree serves as our best instructor, because the growth it employs is altogether different from ratcheting up the speed of traffic in the tunnel. Picture a fruit tree in an orchard where a variety of fruit trees of different species, like a variety of cultures, simultaneously flourish and bear fruit.[38]

A fruit tree is bursting with energy. It deploys all its cells, and it does not burden the environment around it. Despite all of that, it bears fruit.

How can a simple tree manage this, while our own most advanced economies cannot manage to create sufficiently meaningful work for all (the
utilization of all cells), satisfy basic needs (bear fruit), and not exhaust
the environment? The answer could not be simpler: no fruit tree is inclined to grow infinitely in height. If it did so, it would have to jettison
all of its inefficient cells. It would have to put greater pressure on the soil
and forgo the production of fruit entirely. Instead, at a certain point a
fruit tree exercises built-in wisdom to redirect its growth energies away
from expansion in height and toward the production of fruit. It reaches
a saturation point and recognizes that point as such. This allows the
tree to create room to build up reserves and then to redirect its growth
energies toward the production of fruit.

At a certain stage, a society, like a fruit tree, needs to establish some
saturation points in order to bear fruit. Invoking the rope-ladder guideline, a society will at a certain point—and for the rich countries that
point is now—utilize restraint in the domain of consumption in order
to create room to build up resources for other forms of growth. Using
these reserves, the rich countries will make room for poorer countries
to adopt their own, culturally specific, and possibly somewhat sluggish
paths of development. And they will create room within their own countries for people to preserve and enhance the human, social, and natural
capital that still exists.

Let us therefore urgently learn to leave behind the infinite material
expansionism of the tunnel and make a substantial economic realloca-
tion toward a global orchard of fruit-bearing economies.[39] Today we
produce and produce in order to maintain and increase our incomes,
protect our consumption abilities, and preserve our material well-being.
But we swim continually into our own self-made net. We squirm hopelessly, when meanwhile—invoking the minesweeper guideline—one
abrupt movement backward would probably return us to the freedom
for which we yearn.

Then why not take one decisive, perhaps painful, but also realistic
step back from the economic goal that hypnotizes us? Why not accept a
threshold in our levels of income and consumption and orient ourselves
to a level of *enough* so that our production process can be liberated from
extreme stress, turn to meeting the needs of the poor, and invest in the
genuine preservation of culture and the environment? Indeed, our businesses, labor unions, political parties, other organizations, and even we
ourselves must urgently turn away from infinite material expansion and
move instead toward genuinely sustainable economies.

Our calling is stewardship, and our faithful acts of stewardship reflect
the image of God. Consider what stewardship could mean today. Our
current economic thinking and social system promote economic growth

as the first priority. Only then do questions arise about what to do with the resulting unemployment, the dehumanization of work, the rape of the environment, and other problems that surface in the paradoxes we described earlier. Our priorities constrain us to use increasingly large-scale technologies and to be involved in the world only insofar as profit is generated. These are obvious signs of our adherence to an ideology of prosperity.

But no shalom awaits those who follow this ideology. It generates a tunnel, postcare economy, one that streamlines everyone and everything according to the demands of maximum productivity and competitiveness. The daylight remains far in the distance, the tunnel has elongated, and the tunnel's walls seem to be closing in upon us.

Let us adopt a different, richer vision of society and of the growth our society requires—a precare economy. A precare economy places care needs first rather than last on its list of priorities and only then addresses the scope of production. Let us take first steps down that viable, realistic path of promise.

Much of our problem today is that we have failed to imagine that the world can operate in any other way. J. Richard Middleton and Brian J. Walsh lament this lack of imagination:

> It is only when we can imagine the world to be different than the way it is that we can be empowered to embody this alternative reality which is God's kingdom and resist this present nightmare of brokenness, disorientation and confusion. . . . A liberated imagination is a prerequisite for facing the future. . . . If we cannot have such a liberated imagination and cannot countenance such radical dreams, then the story remains closed for us and we have no hope.[40]

Building Peace

In chapter 6 we found that, despite the end of the Cold War, the West clung tenaciously to an ideology of guaranteed freedom. As a result, the widely anticipated peace dividend did not materialize. A peace dividend could have helped repair the fundamental structural imbalances that had crept into Western economies, leading to the reality that today, for example, the ratio of military spending to official development assistance for the US government is twenty-five to one. The diversion of 10 percent of current global military expenditures for each year would fund the entire cost of the Millennium Goals, an eleven-year project designed to cut global poverty in half.[41] At that critical moment, a rebalancing—which would have created more flexibility for the wealthier countries to help the impoverished countries meet their basic subsistence needs—could have prevented some later conflicts around the world. Poverty is inherently destabilizing. As Susan Brown reports, almost half the countries on the bottom third of the Human Development Index experienced serious conflict in the 1990s, and low-income countries are fifteen times more likely to experience civil war.[42]

Instead, tragically, we observed the unbelievable momentum driving the further development of means of mass destruction and of small arms and light weapons, a momentum that relentlessly breaks through every conceivable ceiling. We recognized that these means are intrinsically violent and have contributed to the now-pervasive culture of violence in the West. Violence is guaranteed freedom's word become flesh.

How then does a different vision, articulated by using the periscope, minesweeper, and rope-ladder guidelines, engage this frightening, macabre, and powerfully dynamistic reality, to turn it in another direction?

In the area of peace and conflict, the majority of commentators, decision-makers, and citizens suffer from an unwavering attachment to an extraordinarily narrow lens through which they view war and peace. All of us—politicians and citizens—desperately need the widened view that a periscope could offer.

When faced with a specific conflict, the immediate approach is to confront the conflict strictly by asking the question of permission: can we "morally" permit ourselves, as citizens and governments, to take up arms in this conflict or not? We ask whether the particular conflict meets the criteria for a just war. The just-war/pacifist continuum is the lens, the interpretive framework through which most people in Western society approach, understand, and deal with the issues of peace and conflict. When we have answered the permission question for ourselves, then for all practical purposes we behave as if we have exhausted the issue of war and peace. War and peace fades in our awareness until the next noteworthy conflict demands our attention, and then the cycle begins again.

The outcome is that for far too many people today the issue of war and peace comes and goes when a conflict that happens to catch our attention comes and goes. It ebbs and flows, disappears and reappears. Specific wars therefore usually take us more or less by surprise. Wars seem to simply occur, with the result that we react by instinct and exigency rather than principles rooted in established peacebuilding practices.

But what a notoriously narrow perspective this lens produces! It cripples our ability to arrive at genuine solutions. Not surprisingly, then, the just-war/pacifist paradigm has lost its explanatory power.

The just-war position was not designed to address the reality that peace and conflict are structurally rooted in social, economic, spiritual, and cultural realities. Further, it does not grasp the developmental stages of conflict, the fact that each conflict has a beginning, middle, and end, with different approaches required at each stage. In addition, by its own definitions the just-war tradition does not apply to most contemporary conflicts. It was developed primarily to address situations where one government formally declared war on another government, and where trained government soldiers fought opposing trained government soldiers on a battlefield. It was not meant to address today's intra-state conflicts. It was not designed to grasp civilian suicide bombers and the social chaos or criminal activity that gives birth to much war today. Moreover, it is incapable of speaking to today's pervasive culture of violence. And most dangerously, it was not meant to confront the overpowering, comprehensive grip that the ideology of guaranteed freedom holds on people's imaginations today.

As a result, the just-war interpretive framework is silent on the social, economic, and cultural conditions that prevent war and make for a just peace. It therefore systematically overestimates a possible military reaction in distinction from the myriad possibilities of conflict prevention, resolution, and transformation. The just-war tradition cannot comprehend high-tech, supposedly antiseptic, virtual military strikes or the fact that 90 percent of those killed in war today are civilians; hence, it puts forward military approaches that are badly out of sync with the realities of contemporary conflict.[43] Further, because the question of the possible use of military force usually surfaces relatively late in the life of a conflict, the approach altogether bypasses the possibility of implementing specific interventions geared to the specific developmental stages of conflict. It misses the invitations that exist in every conflict, no matter how dire, to implement developmentally, historically, and culturally appropriate approaches to conflict transformation. Finally, rather than engaging society as a whole in transforming conflict, it fixates on formal government agendas.

The just-war lens is perhaps most entrenched in the political world. The permission debate thus raged during the lead-up to the invasion of Iraq, with opposing sides using the same just-war theory to defend their positions either for or against the preemptive invasion. The just-war conditions used to answer the permission question have themselves undergone profound ideological adjustment. Some senior US decision-makers appeal to just-war principles and argue that aspects of the Geneva Convention, itself a product of the just-war tradition, no longer apply. That argument has led to inhumane treatment of prisoners at Guantanamo Bay, treatment that violates the Geneva Convention. The end justifies the means, but the outcome is that the seed of hate is planted. Further, under the influence of the guaranteed security ideology, principles such as balance of power, originally expressly incompatible with just-war principles, are now central tenets of the just-war paradigm. The just-war perspective has actually become an instrument of the ideology itself. Contrary to its own principles, the approach has sometimes served only to rationalize unprecedented, devastating escalations of war and violence. Indeed, just-war theory is an extraordinarily weak policy instrument; its lack of internal rigor has left it unable to mount an adequate defense against the ideological undermining of some of its most basic principles.[44]

Like a tiny porthole on a submarine, this narrow view reveals to us only a tiny fraction of the landscape of war and peace. What then can serve as an adequate periscope, which would give us a broad vision or alternative paradigm, a peacebuilding paradigm? And how might Western governments and their leaders embrace the wider, peacebuilding perspective so desperately needed to overcome the guaranteed freedom ideology?

Perhaps the answer lies in reclaiming the original, broadening, radical meaning of peace and justice. A good beginning would be to genuinely hear how Scripture describes them. The just-war/pacifist polarization has profoundly distorted our view of current events, causing us to isolate peace and conflict from their rootedness in social, economic, and cultural realities. But it has no less profoundly distorted our reading of Scripture. It has led us to divorce the scriptural material related to war and peace from its embeddedness both in the rest of Scripture and in the practice of warfare in the ancient Near East. Indeed, we need to read this material as if for the first time.

At least two themes stand out. First, there are two inseparable impulses at the very center of Scripture. If God's people would practice Jubilee justice and righteousness (genuine social, environmental, and economic justice, where periodically debts are canceled, slaves set free, and land returned to its original owners) and *at the same time* refuse to adopt the military conventions of the day, then God would bless the land with peace and prosperity.[45] The prophets continually call God's people back to God's ways, based on this twin, integrated emphasis.

Second, God prohibited God's people from acquiring and using the most advanced weapon system of the day: the horse and chariot. The horse and chariot gave an army a huge military advantage, and enemies used them by the thousands against God's people. Militarily speaking, it would have been ludicrous not to have them. Later, the prophet Micah called the eventual militarization of God's people by means of the horse and chariot as nothing less than "the beginning of sin" of God's people.[46]

Jesus then explicitly vindicates both inseparable themes. In his inaugural sermon, he declares that he has come to proclaim the Year of Jubilee (Luke 4:16–30). And in his triumphal entry into Jerusalem, marking the beginning of his passion, Jesus uses the ancient Near Eastern form of a victorious king returning home to his capital city from battle. The people of the city come outside of the city walls to greet the king and usher him in as he processes on his impressive horse and chariot. But contrary to every expectation, Jesus rides into Jerusalem on a donkey instead of a horse and chariot (Luke 19:28–38). The allusion to the Old Testament prophecy is clear: "See, your king comes to you, . . . gentle and riding on a donkey. . . . I will take away the chariots from Ephraim and the war-horses from Jerusalem" (Zech. 9:9–10).

The military thrust of the triumphal entry is not somehow just an interesting element in the story. It *is* the story.[47] It is the vindication of the entire Old Testament material about shalom. One cannot underestimate either the drama of the event or its clarity to the people of the time. It would have been something akin to meeting a squadron of F16s in a hot-air balloon. This was how this king would approach the palpable militarist oppression of the Jews by the Roman Empire.

So it is that Jesus, in his inaugural sermon and at the entrance to his passion, indicates the fundamental nature of his kingship. He makes unequivocally clear the specific justice (Jubilee) and peace (refusal to adopt the military conventions of his day) that his servants, those who are in authority (Rom. 13:1–7), should use to serve others. This is the same fundamental expectation of justice and peace placed earlier on the kings of God's people.[48]

But what can ancient stories teach us today? Clearly, we cannot somehow simply apply them to today's situation nor should we try.[49] Nevertheless, these peacebuilding stories—indeed, all of Scripture—contain a clear direction, a grain as unmistakable as the wood grain of oak or cherry. That direction urgently calls all of us—citizens, governments, decision-makers—to embrace a life-sustaining peacebuilding vision or paradigm. It suggests a peacebuilding paradigm that, grounded in the multiple roots and developmental stages of specific conflicts, carefully integrates military de-escalation and even vulnerability with economic, social, and cultural justice. It serves to integrate development and peace initiatives and agendas at both policy and practice levels.

But how can this integration develop? What might the first possible steps be, steps that, while they may seem risky, may well pose far fewer actual risks than the present strategies?

Invoking the minesweeper guideline, a new peacebuilding vision urges all of us—citizens and government leaders alike—to de-escalate by beginning with refusal. We can refuse to participate in the relentless development of arsenals of lethal destruction, including new chemical, biological, nuclear, and other weapons and defense systems, such as the Anti-Ballistic Missile Shield, which are patently destabilizing. The peacebuilding vision compels NATO to renounce nuclear deterrence as a component of its overall strategy.[50] And it urges us to reject preventive war-making as unjust by definition. A peacebuilding vision therefore moves us to opt out of ideological counterreaction. In a conflict situation, a comprehensive peacebuilding paradigm urges us, concerned citizens and government leaders, to support and enhance local capacities for peace rather than militarist power-holders. It focuses our attention on converting military capabilities to police and peacekeeping-force capabilities, deployed under the auspices of internationally acceptable frameworks designed to enhance human security.

With reference to the rope-ladder guideline, a new peacebuilding paradigm then brings us to understand that justice without peace is a hobbled justice, while peace without justice is no peace at all. By it we recognize that aid and development assistance are never neutral with respect to conflict. As more and more nongovernmental organizations (NGOs) are learning, in principle each aid or development initiative, to be successful, ought to be accompanied by complementary, integrated conflict resolution initiatives. One without the other will not reverse the horrific spiral of impoverishment and conflict in a region, but together they could create an upward-moving spiral of both reconciliation and greater economic self-sufficiency. By the same token, a security agenda may never trump the need for genuine, life-sustaining development.

A peacebuilding vision therefore calls us at some level to reallocate resources freed by refusal to continue developing weapons and use them to deliver the long overdue, desperately needed peace dividend—much as a fruit tree redirects its growth energies away from infinite expansion and toward the production of fruit instead. As the rope-ladder guideline has taught us, investing in the fight against poverty and against the destruction of the environment, done if possible in a coordinated fashion, could also gradually remove the seeds of violence. When the hand moves so that the foot can follow, peace can become genuinely sustainable over the long term.

At a bilateral level, a peacebuilding vision calls us to join together the disciplines of international relations and conflict transformation, paying specific attention to all sectors of society (the street-level or NGO sector, the middle range of senior decision-makers across sectors, and high-level government leaders) and to what interventions are effective at what developmental stages of conflict.[51]

Thankfully, a great deal of activity now underway already finds its home within such a vision and is bringing results.[52] Dogged disarmament efforts, such as the Convention to Ban Land Mines, Small Arms and Light Weapons (SALW) initiatives, the effort to eliminate child soldiering, and specific initiatives to safely scrap nuclear warheads—all these are showing tangible results, though much more needs to be done. The work of John Paul Lederach, Mary B. Anderson, and many others over the past twenty-five years has brought impressive maturity to the field of conflict transformation.[53] Militarily, the Center for Defense Information and Foreign Policy in Focus rebalanced the Bush Administration's 2005 defense budget without increasing or decreasing it. Altering the current seven-to-one ratio of military to nonmilitary security tools to a three-to-one ratio, the report argued that this improved balance would have a better impact on American long-term security needs.[54]

In a similar vein, the Responsibility to Protect movement is a significant joint international effort to redefine international responsibilities in the wake of the armed conflicts in Somalia, Bosnia, Kosovo, and Rwanda. With the support of several countries and assisted by the active involvement of Canada, the International Commission on Intervention and State Sovereignty was appointed to advance the concept of human security.[55] The human security concept approaches conflict of any kind, whether between states or within them, from the perspective of the people needing protection, rather than from the point of view of the aggressor parties. It puts the focus on responsibilities and mutual accountability under universal norms through international institutions, rather than on power and control through political alliances. It reorients notions of national sovereignty to address the reality of weak states and superpowers, and it takes conflict prevention seriously. The commission's conclusion is that "where a population is suffering serious harm, as a result of internal war, insurgency, repression or state failure, and the state in question is unwilling or unable to halt or avert it, the principle of non-intervention yields to the international responsibility to protect."[56]

At the United Nations Summit held in September 2005, member states adopted the Responsibility to Protect framework. Later, as a follow-up to that summit, the United Nations established the long overdue United Nations Peacebuilding Commission, a collaborative effort whose aim is to assist countries coming out of conflict to achieve sustainable peace. Recognizing that about half the countries emerging from war lapse back into violence within five years, the commission plans to "marshal resources at the disposal of the international community to advise and propose integrated strategies for postconflict recovery, focusing attention on reconstruction, institution-building, and sustainable development."[57] Regrettably, however, the present method of resourcing the commission appears to be inadequate; if the commission's work is to succeed, member states must give their commitment high priority.

Finally, the widely respected organization Project Ploughshares published an authoritative report called "Reshaping the Security Envelope."[58] Using the human security concept as its touchstone, the report builds on what it calls the "five Ds of a comprehensive security envelope": development, democracy, disarmament, diplomacy, and defense. It calls for alternative military models, a comprehensive security policy, and a more effective multilateral institutional framework and decision-making mechanism.

All these are creative, courageous attempts to move away from the destruction and ruin spread indiscriminately by the ideology of guaranteed freedom and to risk first steps down the path of peace. They reflect the truth behind the statement made by Desmond Tutu in his deeply eloquent foreword to this book, namely that peace is not a goal to be achieved but a way of life to be lived.

Concrete Examples

With these reflections we already find ourselves at the level of describing current, concrete examples of living out a vision of fruit-bearing economies and genuine, sustainable peacebuilding.

The Microlevel: Community-Based Examples

At first glance, our own personal lives may seem inconsequential, if not irrelevant to the daunting problems and overpowering ideologies we have discussed. We certainly recognize how they influence our lives. But the possibility that we ourselves could influence what happens in the larger world may seem like a far-off daydream, not unlike the dreaming of Esther in the Bible or Frodo in the *Lord of the Rings*.

Yet the comparison to Esther or Frodo may be legitimate. Our personal lives are already connected to the vast problems and the great ideologies of our time in at least in three ways. First, we interact with them as consumers. We take part in today's cycles of production and consumption. We use a small part of the world's resources and add something positive and/or negative to the environment. Second, we interact with them as citizens, possibly as voting citizens. We may feel compassion for the poor and want to translate that into votes that support additional development assistance. Or we may feel threatened and want to express that by voting for an increase of military expenditures in pursuit of maximum protection. Third, whether we like it or not, all of us are community members: members of a family, a firm, a school, perhaps a church, and other communities. Community membership stamps our sense of identity. Community membership also influences today's world, whether for good or for ill.

So it is that we are interconnected with our present world in many ways. We are therefore called by God to live and act responsibly within it. We are called to use our creativity to contribute to solutions, to open ways that might help others to escape from their present paralysis and open themselves up to a new vision.

In this section we could cite many inspiring initiatives at a personal and community level that serve as concrete examples of the alternative visions of economic fruit-bearing and peacebuilding. A remarkable number of efforts are underway in environmental and social entrepreneurship, where those involved place care needs first on their list of concerns and only then address the scope of production and consumption. Some of these are documented in books like *Good News for a Change: Hope for a Troubled Planet*.[59] Here too we think of the extraordinary efforts of Habitat for Humanity and its thousands of volunteers, where those who purchase housing are themselves full partners in alleviating housing poverty around the world, as well as the Carter Center's cutting-edge peacebuilding, community-building, and economy-building work in impoverished and war-torn areas around the world. Innumerable responsible global civil movements focus on the environment, corporate responsibility, human rights, poverty, and peacebuilding. They are helping to initiate the step-by-step change process of the rope ladder principle. These alternative globalization movements are signs of hope, and they illustrate the rising awareness among so many young people of the need to return to paths of justice and care.

The drive toward alternatives is perhaps most active in the South. Some of the most successful, advanced activity in peacebuilding has occurred in some of the most ethnically riven, war-ravaged areas of the South. Similarly, with microcredit support (provided by organizations such as Oikocredit, once called "the poor man's World Bank"), the South has provided outstanding community economic development success stories in the midst of untold deprivation.[60] The awarding of the 2006 Nobel Peace Prize to Muhammad Yunus and the Grameen Bank "for their efforts to create economic and social development from below" is an affirmation of the success of microcredit.[61] Indeed, the amount of activity worldwide demonstrates a clear truth: "there are thousands of alternatives" (TATA) to an ideologically devastated future.

In this section we outline two specific examples that have inspired us, particularly because they contain living models of the three guidelines at work. Each initiative began with a widened horizon. Each responded to challenges in new, creative ways. And each has traveled a path step by step, as if climbing a rope ladder with hands and feet in coordination.

The John Perkins Initiative

In 1960 a pastor named John Perkins and his wife moved from California to Mississippi. His friends declared that he was mad: why would he go from relative luxury to misery? Perkins's reply was, "We must be attentive to the needs of people, to their physical and emotional needs no less than their spiritual needs." The area to which he relocated in Mississippi lacked adequate nutrition, health, and employment, and it suffered from racial discrimination. John Perkins therefore asked himself how he could contribute to a "whole-person ministry" (here we already see a widening of the horizon). First, he asked the people to take sharing seriously, not just in goods but also in time, by using their labor and service to carry out acts of true cooperation.

In his biography *A Time to Heal*, Perkins describes "trying out various models of community life."[62] An outcome was that a day-care center was created, as well as a preschool and a number of food and housing cooperatives. Each of these steps mutually strengthened the other: more care and better food further encouraged people to help others, and in turn the people helped were inspired to spend some of their time and money on behalf of the community (the rope-ladder guideline). Perkins invested in people: "I consider myself primarily a businessman; these enterprises just developed around me." He expanded his work to the inner city in 1972, and in 1982 he chose to live and work in Pasadena, California, a city full of crime. Moving step by step, Perkins took inspiration from the vision of a restored economy that flourishes and bears fruit for all.[63]

The Focolare Movement

In northern Italy in 1943, the Focolare Movement began during heavy Nazi bombing of Trento (= Trente). Some young women, among them Clara Lubich, lived day after day under the continuing barrage of terror. Driven by the love of Christ, they decided not to flee the city but rather to open up their house for the collection and free distribution of food and as a center of help. Their action motivated others to contribute some of their food, leading to what they called "the economy of communion." At its heart was a culture of giving and sharing. Later the participants added the sharing of productive labor. The effort gave rise to a number of largely new corporations wholeheartedly joining the movement. They often worked together in new local centers or in regional settings.

The Focolare Movement is now active in about 180 countries. Millions of Catholics and thousands of Protestant, Anglican, and Orthodox Christians have found a new impetus in the Focolare Movement's "Spirituality of Unity" for living lives based on the gospel. Now a nongovernmental organization (NGO) recognized by the United Nations, it is actively engaged in numerous large and small social initiatives. A number of companies (764 in 2001, with 478 located in Europe) participate in the Economy of Communion project. Member companies keep one-third of their profits, allocate one-third toward meeting the immediate needs of the poor, and earmark the final third to support the formation of people in "the culture of giving." The companies operate within the market economy.

Sixty years of experience undergird them in living out the gospel practically in ways that make one think of the lives of the first Christians as Acts 4:32 describes them: "All the believers were one in heart and mind. No one claimed that any of his possessions was his own, but they shared everything they had." The companies belonging to the Economy of Communion put people at the center, not money. That pre-care approach has far-reaching consequences for management and also for relationships with customers, suppliers, creditors, the environment, and internal working conditions. The Focolare Movement has created nothing less than a new, sustainable business culture almost altogether unaffected by recent economic crises.

These two living examples display the three guidelines or markers in action. Animated by an inspiring vision, they both exhibit the following:

- The courage to begin by listening concretely to authentic ways of love and stewardship and to express them in styles of cooperation and communion.
- A reversal of the ideological order: the willingness to give and share comes first, not the desire to receive, resulting in new types of responsible economic growth.
- The willingness to proceed step by step. In the search for expanding new forms of mutual help and cooperation, the hand prepares for the feet.

The Macrolevel: A Policy Proposal

In chapter 8 we saw that the present style of globalization is oriented so much toward the self-interest of the rich and so little toward the life-interests of the poor and the preservation of God's creation. We sought to understand this more precisely in terms of how the underlying ideologies express themselves in a number of exclusions (the monetary, market, and scarcity exclusions). We also saw that the simultaneously generated dynamics of enrichment and impoverishment begin with a primary exclusion: the rich countries refuse the poor countries any kind of direct entry into the creation of new international liquidities. International currency creation is and has remained the monopoly of the rich countries and their banks. Because of this, efforts to reduce the debts of the poorest countries usually do not have a lasting effect. Sooner or later the economies of most such countries fall back into the trap of mounting indebtedness. Meanwhile, the hold on money creation allows the rich countries, already experiencing unprecedented wealth, to perpetuate their sacrificial tunnel economies and expand their military reach, even if doing so comes at the cost of a partial breakdown of their own social security nets.

How then do we escape this utterly narrow dynamic? How do we end this double downward spiral?

Perhaps, again, the concrete and widened vision we need here emerges by rereading sections from the early parts of the Bible. Though situated in an entirely different time and context, they say something enormously valuable about God's appreciation of human economies. God's rules for Israel's economy do not contain a complete blueprint for an alternative economic order. They reflect a basically sober assessment of human nature and seem to acknowledge, as a grave reality, the enduring wickedness of human beings. But it is precisely to this reality that God addresses the economic laws of the nation. When economic distortions multiply and the poor suffer, the God of Israel comes down to observe and to restore. The beautiful Hebrew word for that is *Jeshina* (from a word meaning "he will deliver us"), the appearance of the living God within our sinful reality and economy.

The Torah institutionalizes this restoration in two ways. Every seven years the people were to cancel the debts of the poor and to set their slaves free. Human economies lead to debt, and they always try to enslave. But a second intervention by God leads to an even deeper restoration of the economy: the Year of Jubilee (Lev. 25). Under the protection of the Torah, the poor receive back the economic sources of their well-being. Their original land is restored to them, and on it they may begin to live and work again debt free, with food that the previous owners must give them in advance. It is not an accident, then, that the Year of Jubilee begins with the Day of Atonement ("atonement" means "reconciliation" or "making reparation"). And this day is not just one of personal reconciliation. It is also the day of economic forgiveness and a new beginning for a sinful economy.

In our time too, the desire of many poor people is to have their land returned so that it can serve as a basis for meeting their basic needs and supporting their own growth. Redistributing land would indeed combat the pressure to continually substitute new scarcities for existing and far more basic scarcities. But by itself it would not address the deep needs of the poor and poor countries to see their monetary exclusion come to an end. In addition to land, capital is among the first resources required by a young, growing economy. Poor countries need access to capital: they want to participate in the benefits offered by the privilege of creating international currency. Indeed, giving them a real share in that privilege enjoyed by the rich is the only way to stop their perpetual indebtedness. Only such a share can serve as a really new beginning, a Jubilee.

This step is certainly possible. For years already, written into the constitution of the International Monetary Fund (IMF), the legal possibility has existed to issue a different type of international currency and, in principle, to distribute it among all the countries of the world. That different but real international money is called Special Drawing Rights (SDRs). In the past, the IMF occasionally issued and distributed a round of SDRs. But that was a long time ago, for why would the world need extra international currency now, when the rich countries already issue international currency in huge amounts? The creation of SDRs would then lead only to more inflation. Moreover, the IMF has arranged the distribution of SDRs in such a way that almost all of it must be given to the rich countries.

But times are changing. In addition to the destabilization caused by debt in the South, the wealthy countries in the North have a pressing internal need to regain their financial stability. They badly need to curtail the highly volatile financial markets and the entirely free, unrestricted, and excessive discharge of key currencies across the world by banks. Why not arrange a possible solution to this in such a way that, through modestly restricting the issuing of new money by the rich countries, the way is freed up for the creation of a separate round of SDRs specifically designed for the relief of the poor and most indebted countries?

Opposition to this proposal may be strong. But in the long run there is real merit to taking this step toward justice and stewardship. The poor nations need deeper and more structural debt relief than what currently acceptable forms of debt cancellation offer. And the rich nations? They simply need to come to their senses. Their present uninhibited material expansion openly tramples upon the limits of what the environment can sustain and people can endure. Further, without some kind of self-restraint, the rich countries will simply go on to secure, militarily and otherwise, access to the resources they think they need for their future expansion. And both rich and poor nations will become increasingly victimized by the torrent of uncontrolled and uncoordinated capital movements across the world.

We do not have much time to come to our senses.
But it is not too late.
An upward spiral is still possible!

Just think about what might happen if the poor countries were granted their right to a modern Jubilee, whereby the use of at least portions of the new SDRs would be linked to reducing debt load and developing home markets. Depending on the amount of new money, poor countries could also raise their investment level in education, health, and the environment. Requiring such allocations as a condition of the new emission (issue) of international currency would not be out of the question. A result would be that employment would naturally increase. Further, such a step would bless not just the poor nations but also the global environment and therefore even the wealthy nations. Indeed, our own well-being may lie in the growth and the well-being of the poor countries. In keeping with the rope-ladder guideline, issuing a special round of SDRs in such a way supports an upward-moving spiral because it slackens the pressure of forced migration, diminishes the motivation to go to war, and reduces military expenditures. Possibilities of true cooperation between nations would return.

Further, it provides the rich countries with the opportunity to begin to turn their tunnel economies toward fruit-bearing economies oriented more toward care and meaningful labor for all than to expanding the tunnel. By this step the rich nations could begin an *economic conversion*, fulfilling to some degree Isaiah's prophecy that nations "will beat their swords into plowshares and their spears into pruning hooks."[64]

Conversions like these are possible. But they assume that people within the rich countries begin to see that in the end their selfish income demands lead only to the destruction of their own minds and bodies. And with this, we seemingly small and inconsequential people reappear in the picture, even decisively. As citizens, consumers, and members of communities, we are called to pattern our lives in such a way that we joyfully convince others to choose life instead of death and to prepare for an economy of care, a fruit-bearing economy that recognizes saturation points and the meaning of enough.[65]

Viewed through the lens of Scripture, the widening ways of God—justice, peace, stewardship, love, truth, freedom—challenge us with a desperately needed, life-awakening appeal today. They urge us to do genuine justice to the poor; to integrate a living practice of peacebuilding into our acts of justice, stewardship, and mercy; and to build an economy of care, an economy of enough. Will our governments, labor unions, businesses, other organizations, and we ourselves listen to this appeal? And will we inscribe it into a personal and national economic program?

It is time to put such a program in place, not because the program itself can help us, but because its implementation will be a sign of our willingness to repent, to turn our ways to the only One who can and who will help us. Perhaps this is the act of Esther today.

NOTES

1. In the Shadows of Progress

1. Ronald Wright, *A Short History of Progress* (Toronto: House of Anansi, 2004), 61. The Easter Island story is written up here and in Jared Diamond, *Collapse: How Societies Choose to Fail or Succeed* (New York: Penguin, 2005), 79–119. Diamond reports that 397 stone statues are still standing today, "mostly 15 to 20 feet tall, but the largest of them 70 feet tall (taller than the average modern 5-story building), and weighing from 10 up to 270 tons" (79). "Jo Anne Van Tilburg has inventoried a total of 887 carved" statues (96). Diamond includes an annotated list of the careful archaeological, scientific, anthropological, and cultural work that has been done on Easter Island in the last 20 years.

2. The report and subsidiary and subsequent reports are available at http://www.millenniumassessment.org.

3. Statement from the board of the Millennium Ecosystem Assessment, "Living beyond Our Means: Natural Assets and Human Well-Being" (Board of MEA, 2005; available via World Resources Institute, Washington, DC), 23.

4. Ibid., 23, 21.

5. This is the British title (London: Arrow Books, 2004). The book is published in North America as Martin Rees, *Our Final Hour: A Scientist's Warning; How Terror, Error, and Environmental Disaster Threaten Humankind's Future in This Century on Earth and Beyond* (New York: Basic Books, 2003; repr., 2004).

6. Ibid., vii, 188.

7. Jeffrey D. Sachs, *The End of Poverty: Economic Possibilities for Our Time*, foreword by Bono (New York: Penguin Books, 2005).

8. For a compelling view of the lack of progress in achieving the Millennium Development Goals (MDGs), particularly in relation to how the tragic HIV/AIDS pandemic interacts with extreme poverty, see Stephen Lewis, *Race against Time* (Toronto: House of Anansi, 2005). Lewis served as the UN secretary-general's special envoy for HIV/AIDS in Africa.

9. For more on this theme, particularly on the interrelationship between the practice of international money creation by the West, the oil crisis of 1973, and the simultaneous quantum rise in the burden of debt in the South, see Bob Goudzwaard and Harry de Lange, *Beyond Poverty and Affluence: Towards a Canadian Economy of Care*, trans. and ed. Mark Vander Vennen, with foreword by Maurice F. Strong (Toronto: University of Toronto Press,

1994), 85–87. A separate edition, entitled *Beyond Poverty and Affluence: Toward an Economy of Care*, was published in 1995 by Wm. B. Eerdmans and WCC Publications.

10. Francis Fukuyama, *The End of History and the Last Man* (Toronto: HarperCollins Canada, 1993); Daniel Bell, *The End of Ideology* (Cambridge, MA: Harvard University Press, 2000); Sam Harris, *The End of Faith* (New York: Penguin Books, 2005); Bill McKibbon, *The End of Nature* (New York: Anchor Books, 1997); John Horgan, *The End of Science* (Toronto: HarperCollins Canada, 1998).

11. The figures come from the United Nations Development Program (UNDP). See Goudzwaard and de Lange, *Beyond Poverty and Affluence*, 14, 154.

12. Quoted in *Time*, March 14, 2005, 35.

13. The data come from the Institute of International Finance, Inc. and various reports of the United Nations Development Program (UNDP). The Institute's September 15, 2006, report "Capital Flows to Emerging Market Economies," reported this negative net balance for the year 2005 to be 56.1 billion dollars (1, http://www.iif.com/press/press+13.php). For more on the reverse net transfer, see Goudzwaard and de Lange, *Beyond Poverty and Affluence*, 15–17, 85–87.

14. See table on p. 149. Similarly, some time ago the European Commission highlighted the "nontransfer of technology" to the South, due to the North having left largely untouched its huge amount of protective duties and patents.

15. According to data from the United Nations' Human Development Program's *Human Development Report 2003*, 2, the number of hungry people in the world did not drop but actually increased in the 1990s. Some 54 countries are now poorer than they were in 1990.

16. As reported by the Comité pour l'annulation de la dette du Tiers Monde (Committee for the Cancellation of the Third World Debt), "CADTM Outraged at the G8's Meanness over the Debt," press release, June 13, 2005, http://www.cadtm.org/imprimer .php3?id_article=1448. The press release further states: "If the measure is extended to all 42 HIPCs [Heavily Indebted Poor Countries] in the coming years, this would still only affect 11% of those inhabitants. Most really poor people live in other developing countries (there are 165 of them altogether)." The cancellation agreement affects 18 countries, but the wealthy countries involved have the option to deduct their contribution from their official development assistance.

17. The world military expenditure figures come from the Stockholm International Peace Research Institute's *SIPRI Yearbook 2005*, chap. 8. The figure for terrorism incidents is cited by Linda McQuaig in "Linda McQuaig Says the War on Terror Has Done Absolutely Nothing to Get to the Root of the Problem," *Toronto Star*, July 10, 2005.

18. These data come from the natural scientist Johan van Klinken, organizer of the Pugwash Conference "Sharing the Planet," Groningen, 2004. In his book *Het derde punt: Een bijdrage tot het conciliair proces met natuurwetenschappelijke achtergronden* (The Third Point: A Contribution to the Conciliar Process against a Scientific Backdrop) (Kampen: Kok, 1989), van Klinken writes: "Between 1500 and 1850 one species disappeared every ten years; between 1850 and 1950 one species disappeared each year; around 1989 one species disappeared every day; around 2000 one species disappeared each hour" (74). Further, "between 1975 and 2000 15 to 20 percent of the world's species disappeared" (74). See also the booklet by Johan van Klinken, Bob Goudzwaard, and Edy Korthals Altes, *Oproep tot Consuminderen en Respect voor de Schepping* (Call to Reduce Consumption and Respect Creation) (Utrecht: Kerk en Vrede, Landelijk Missionair Collectief, 2003).

19. As reported by John A. Coleman in *Globalization and Catholic Social Thought*, ed. John A. Coleman and William F. Ryan (Maryknoll, NY: Orbis Books, 2005), 12.

20. George Soros, *The Crisis of Global Capitalism: Open Society Endangered* (New York: PublicAffairs, 1998), xix–xx.

21. TINA has become a political slogan and even the motto of Shell Oil.

22. See Bob Goudzwaard, *Capitalism and Progress: A Diagnosis of Western Society*, trans. and ed. Josina Van Nuis Zylstra (Grand Rapids: Eerdmans), 185.

23. Karl Löwith, *Nature, History, and Existentialism* (Evanston, IL: Northwestern University Press, 1966), 159–60.

24. The suggestion that contemporary events necessarily possess a spiritual dimension is a bold claim, and some might call it odd. Yet it is not hard to defend. Naturally, the development of a society involves far more than a measurable, material succession of events. By its very nature society's development is as intimately related to the spiritual domain—where feelings such as uncertainty, fear, and longing reside—as it is to the material domain. Just as human beings do not consist of bodies only but also of souls and spirits, so too societies invariably consist of both material and spiritual impulses.

25. Goudzwaard and de Lange, *Beyond Poverty and Affluence*, 33.

26. Goudzwaard, *Capitalism and Progress*, 137.

27. Both the Jewish commentator Martin Buber and the Christian martyr Dietrich Bonhoeffer, in their comments on Ps. 119, make this point, highlighting the verse "I have seen an end to everything, but your Way is very wide" (cf. Hebrew and other versions of 119:96).

2. Myth, Ideology, and Idolatry

1. Jean Baudrillard, *Fatal Strategies*, ed. Jim Fleming, trans. Philip Beitchman and W. G. J. Niesluchowski (New York: Semiotext[e], 1990), 7.

2. An excellent overview of de Tracy's life and thought appears in Emmet Kennedy, *A Philosophe in the Age of Revolution: Destutt de Tracy and the Origins of Ideology* (Philadelphia: American Philosophical Society, 1978).

3. Ibid., 49.

4. Ibid., 64.

5. The philosopher Theodor W. Adorno once wrote that *"ideology is justification"* (emphasis his) (in "Ideology," in *Aspects of Sociology*, by the Frankfurt Institute for Social Research, with a preface by Max Horkheimer and Theodor W. Adorno, translated by John Viertel [Boston: Beacon Press, 1972], 189. The essay originally appeared in Theodor W. Adorno, *Gesammelte Schriften*, vol. 8 [Frankfurt am Main: Suhrkamp Verlag, 1972], 465). The German word translated here as justification, "Rechtfertigung," can also be translated as "legitimation."

6. This ambivalence is also the main theme of Simon Schama's seminal work on the French Revolution, *Citizens: A Chronicle of the French Revolution* (New York: Knopf, 1989).

7. Marquis de Condorcet, "A Sketch for a Historical Picture of the Progress of the Human Mind," reprinted in *The Past as Prologue*, ed. Everett U. Crosby and Charles R. Webb Jr., 2 vols. (New York: Appleton-Century-Crofts, 1973), 2:77–123.

8. John Ralston Saul, *Voltaire's Bastards: The Dictatorship of Reason in the West* (New York: Vintage Books, 1993), 19.

9. An outstanding study of this theme is K. H. Miskotte, *Edda en Thora*, in *Collected Works*, vol. 7, 3rd ed. (Kampen: Kok, 1983), which, regrettably, has not been translated into English.

10. Cited in Crosby and Webb, *The Past as Prologue*, 2:92.

11. Ronald Wright, *A Short History of Progress* (Toronto: House of Anansi, 2004), 4.

12. A clear illustration of this comes from Mao's principle "from the people, to the people" in Communist China. The current values and interpretations held by the people were taken from them in order to be "articulated" and "refilled." They were then placed back in society, and after a period of partial adoption they were picked up again, rearticulated, remolded, and placed back again into the hearts and minds of the people. The so-called *Little Red Book* of Mao's quotations served as the decisive guide for this dialectical process.

13. The German title of Nietzsche's book is *Die fröhliche Wissenschaft* (1882). All quotations in this section are from Friedrich Nietzsche, *The Gay Science*, trans. Walter Kaufmann (New York: Random House Vintage Books, 1974), 181–82.

14. Enlightenment philosophers wanted to rationally reconstruct society in its entirety, using the smallest possible element, called the "individual" ("individual" literally means "indivisible," the final indivisible building block of every society).

15. On this point, see the description once given by Carl L. Becker of the "articles of faith" of the new modern philosophy of the eighteenth century in his *The Heavenly City of the Eighteenth Century Philosophers* (New Haven: Yale University Press, 1932); summarized in Bob Goudzwaard, *Capitalism and Progress: A Diagnosis of Western Society*, trans. and ed. Josina Van Nuis Zylstra (Grand Rapids: Eerdmans), 44. Compare also the title of vol. 1, *The Rise of Modern Paganism*, of Peter Gay's brilliant study of the Enlightenment, *The Enlightenment: An Interpretation*, 2 vols. (New York: Knopf, 1967–69).

16. Francis Fukuyama, *The End of Ideology and the Last Man* (Toronto: HarperCollins Canada, 1993).

17. For a contemporary example, consider the role that images of the gods play in Hinduism. The Bhagavad Gita forms the mythical background. It describes the roles of the great gods Brahma, Vishnu, and Shiva as creator, sustainer, and transformer of the world, respectively. In these myths Krishna, as the incarnation of Vishnu, teaches his student Ardjoena the various ways of salvation, of which the Bhakta-yoga (the way of adoration) is the most important. Following this way, one offers one's heart and brings sacrifices to one's favorite deities (Ishta), gods that are mutually related according to what people most deeply desire (for example, Krishna is oriented to love and affection, Laksmi to beauty, and Hanuman to safety and trust). The adoration of the images or representations undergoes a number of phases: it begins with submission as a servant to one's lord, but it ultimately leads to the person and one's god unifying or becoming one, like lovers. Hinduism therefore explicitly envisions the transformation of a person into the likeness of one's god.

18. Jacques Ellul, *The Technological System*, trans. of *Le système technicien* (1977) by Joachim Neugroschel (New York: Continuum, 1980), 337n16; and see 145:

> We would like to dwell on a further aspect of that autonomy [of technology] from values and ethics. Man in his hubris—above all intellectual—still believes that his mind controls technology, that he can impose any value, any meaning on it. . . . The finest philosophies on the importance of technology, even the materialist philosophies, fall back upon the preeminence of man. But this grand pretension is purely ideological.

19. In this connection, see Bob Goudzwaard and Harry de Lange, *Beyond Poverty and Affluence: Towards a Canadian Economy of Care*, trans. and ed. Mark Vander Vennen, with foreword by Maurice F. Strong (Toronto: University of Toronto Press, 1994), 106: "Today both Christians and non-Christians interact with the forces of scientific, technological and economic progress in the same manner that people interact with idols. Just as ancient ideologies or religions, caught up in the pursuit of prosperity and security, summoned forth their own gods (represented by the forces of nature, for example), so too today, caught up in the pursuit of prosperity and security, our ideology of material prosperity has evoked its own gods (the forces of modernization—economic growth, technological development, scientific advancement, and unrestricted expansion of the market or the state). But our gods have betrayed us. They require sacrifices in exchange for providing us with material prosperity—mounting poverty, destruction of health and the environment, relentless elimination of jobs and reduction of the quality of work, and the perpetual return of the threat of war. Yet time after time we are told in tones borne up by the weight of 'self-evidence' that these sacrifices are necessary, if not 'pre-ordained.'"

3. Ideologies That Spearhead Radical Change

1. For example, organized resistance claims thousands of lives each year in the Andes Mountains of Colombia and Peru. The Colombian Revolutionary Armed Front (FARC, as known by its Spanish acronym) has killed many hundreds of its enemies and innocents alike in pursuit of its absolute, revolutionist goals. Meanwhile, the elected government of Colombia, its armies, and paramilitary enforcement groups are also regularly guilty of egregious human rights violations in their desperate attempts to respond to the decades-old FARC insurgency. Tragically, at present there is no end in sight.

2. Leszek Kolakowski wrote *Main Currents of Marxism*, trans. P. S. Falla (Oxford: Clarendon, 1978); *Toward a Marxist Humanism*, trans. Jane Zielonko Peel (New York: Grove, 1968); and *Der Mensch ohne Alternative: Von der Möglichkeit und Unmöglichkeit, Marxist zu sein* (Man without an Alternative: On the Possibility and Impossibility of Being a Marxist) (Munich: Piper, 1961).

Milovan Djilas's many books include *The Stone and the Violets*, trans. Lovett F. Edwards (New York: Harcourt Brace Jovanovich, 1972); *Conversations with Stalin*, trans. Michael B. Petrovich (New York: Harcourt, Brace & World, 1962); *Land without Justice*, intro. and notes by William Jovanovich (New York: Harcourt, Brace, 1958); and *The New Class: An Analysis of the Communist System* (New York: Praeger, 1957).

Rudolf Bahro's works include *Elemente einer neuen Politik: Zum Verhältnis von Ökologie und Socialismus* (Elements of a New Politics: Toward a Relation between Ecology and Socialism) (Berlin: Olle & Wolter, 1980); *Plädoyer für schöpferische Initiative: Zur Kritik von Arbeitsbedingungen im real existierenden Socialismus* (Plea for Creative Initiative: Toward a Critique of Labor Conditions in Actually Existing Socialism) (Cologne: Bund-Verlag, 1980); and *The Alternative in Eastern Europe*, trans. David Fernbach (Manchester & London: NLB, 1978).

3. V. I. Lenin, "The Tasks of the Youth Leagues," *Selected Works*, 3 vols. (Moscow: Foreign Languages Publishing House, 1961), 3:512.

4. Quoted in David Shub, *Lenin: A Biography* (Garden City, NY: Doubleday, 1951), 355. The selection is from Lenin's speech in 1920, "Left Wing Communism: An Infantile Disorder," repr. in V. I. Lenin, *Selected Works*, vol. 3.

5. Fyodor Dostoyevsky, *Crime and Punishment*, trans., intro. by David Magarshack (Baltimore: Penguin Books, 1964), 277.

6. Nikita Khrushchev, "On Peaceful Coexistence," *Foreign Affairs* 38 (October 1959): 5.

7. Quoted by Nikita Khrushchev, "On the Communist Program," Khrushchev's report on the Communist Party Program to the 22nd Congress of the Party (Moscow: Foreign Languages Publishing House, 1961), 27.

8. Rudolf Bahro, *The Alternative in Eastern Europe*, 176.

9. Ibid., 20.

10. Ibid.

11. To some extent, China's Chairman Mao went even further than Lenin. Mao assumed full control of the mentality of the masses in China. He used his infamous *Little Red Book*, the constant indoctrination in which was an ongoing requirement, as the primary instrument for prescribing his internal and external policies. In some respects Mao was therefore closer to the French Revolution than the Russian Revolution. But Mao's empire also dissolved under the tension of the forces that he had chosen as tools, which turned against him. Though Mao created the Cultural Revolution, it proved in the end to be the undoing of his ultimate objective.

12. He did this in distinction from Marx and Engels. See Leszek Kolakowski, *Main Currents of Marxism*, 383.

13. Ideologies never appear arbitrarily. Instead, they are always rooted in the reality or the sense of oppression and devastation. Situations of almost indescribable cruelty,

enslavement, and bloodshed dominated the French countryside around 1750 and rural Russia around 1900. The emergence of Nazism was somewhat different, but one ought not to underestimate the disastrous impact of Germany's obligatory, degrading war payments to France and England in 1918–1920.

14. Václav Havel, *Václav Havel, or, Living in Truth* (London: Faber & Faber, 1987).

15. Thus 2 Thess. 2:10–11 speaks about God sending "a powerful delusion so that" "those who are perishing" "will believe the lie." The wording in the Greek text is "sends an energy [*energeian*] of error."

4. Identity Unleashed

1. In their important study, Ian Buruma and Avishai Margalit similarly suggest that the roots of Occidentalism can be compared with the German awareness of deep humiliation, which turned inward. Occidentalism is the product of wounded national sensibility and enormous humiliation, says Margalit in a recent interview (NRC, June 13, 2004). See Ian Buruma and Avishai Margalit, *Occidentalism: The West in the Eyes of Its Enemies* (New York: Penguin, 2004).

2. See James Michener's historical novel *The Covenant* (New York: Random House, 1980).

3. For more on the Afrikaner identity ideology and its history in South Africa, see Bob Goudzwaard, *Idols of Our Time* (Downers Grove, IL: InterVarsity, 1984; repr., Sioux Center, IA: Dordt Press, 1989), chap. 4.

4. Other forms of Fascism, such as German and Italian Fascism, display a similar inferiority of the self in comparison to the supremacy of the race or nation. But this disappearance of self and of one's own independent convictions into the agenda of the people suggests that the ideology may not be as far from us as we might think. A strain of it may even be present within some of the extreme expressions of patriotism in the United States today.

5. The term "identity conflict" comes from a number of commentators, including John Paul Lederach, who writes: "In the popular press [current] wars are often called 'ethnic conflicts,' given that what is at issue are group and community rights and not just individual human rights. It is more accurate, therefore, as Mats Friberg has underscored, to name these 'identity conflicts' rather than ethnic conflicts, given that there is nothing innately ethnic about them. Rather, it is often the failure of governing structures to address fundamental needs, provide space for participation in decisions, and ensure an equitable distribution of resources and benefits that makes identification with a group so attractive and salient in a given setting" (John Paul Lederach, *Building Peace: Sustainable Reconciliation in Divided Societies* [Washington, DC: United States Institute of Peace Press, 1997], 8).

6. Quoted in ibid.

7. These data come from the highly reputable *Armed Conflicts Report 2005* by Project Ploughshares, as reported in "The 2005 *Armed Conflicts Report*—Preview," *The Ploughshares Monitor*, 26, no. 2 (Summer 2005): 14. The article states: "Although the world endured 32 armed conflicts during 2004, the total was the lowest since Project Ploughshares began monitoring armed conflicts in 1987. . . . There were four fewer armed conflicts and two fewer states involved in war than in 2003" (14).

The article further reports: "The latest drop in both the number of armed conflicts and the number of states at war is the fifth consecutive decline in annual conflict totals and follows a turbulent post–Cold War period that saw the total number of armed conflicts peak at 44 in 1995. Although extrapolation remains speculative, the general downward trend in armed conflicts since 1987 supports the value of increased multilateral efforts at peacemaking, peacekeeping, and especially peacebuilding to prevent the reemergence of violent conflict. Despite the persistence of political, communal, and criminal violence across the globe, there is evidence that international efforts to reduce, end, and prevent armed conflicts are bearing fruit" (14).

Project Ploughshares defines an armed conflict "as a political conflict in which armed combat involves the armed forces of at least one state (or one or more armed factions seeking to gain control of all or part of the state), and in which at least 1,000 people have been killed by the fighting during the course of the conflict. . . . The definition of 'political conflict' becomes more difficult as the trend in current intrastate armed conflicts increasingly obscures the distinction between political and criminal violence. . . . Thus, in some circumstances, while the disintegrating order reflects the social chaos resulting from state failure, the resulting violence or armed combat is not necessarily guided by a political program or a set of politically motivated or defined military objectives. However, these trends are part of the changing character of war, and conflicts characterized more by social chaos than political/military competition are thus included in the tabulation of current armed conflicts" (14).

8. Consider, for example, Samuel Huntington, Robert Kaplan, and Amy Chua.

Harvard Professor Samuel Huntington predicts that the twenty-first century will be dominated by civilizational battles of collective identity: "The most important conflicts of the future will occur along the cultural fault lines separating these civilizations from one another." After all, he argues, "Over the centuries . . . differences among civilizations have generated the most prolonged and the most violent conflicts. . . . As people define their identity in ethnic and religious terms, they are likely to see an 'us' versus 'them' relation existing between themselves and people of different ethnicity or religion." He concludes, "Governments and groups will increasingly attempt to mobilize and support by appealing to common religion and civilization identity" (Samuel Huntington, "The Clash of Civilizations," *Foreign Affairs* 72, no. 3 [Summer 1993]: 22–28).

Journalist Robert Kaplan sees the chaos and disintegration of West Africa as a microcosm of the world in the twenty-first century. "West Africa is becoming *the* symbol of worldwide demographic, environmental, and societal stress, in which criminal anarchy emerges as the real 'strategic' danger." In a world characterized by the withering of central governments, the unchecked spread of disease, and the growing pervasiveness of war, identity groups rise up to claim power or fight amid the vacuum of power. Kaplan writes:

> While a minority of the human population will be, as Francis Fukuyama would put it, sufficiently sheltered so as to enter a "post-historical" realm, living in cities and suburbs in which the environment has been mastered and ethnic animosities have been quelled by bourgeois prosperity, an increasingly large number of people will be stuck in history, living in shantytowns where attempts to rise above poverty, cultural dysfunction, and ethnic strife will be doomed by a lack of water to drink, soil to till, and space to survive in.

Kaplan too concludes that the chaos of our new century will be between identity groups struggling to survive amid the coming anarchy: "Future wars will be those of communal survival, aggravated or, in many cases, caused by environmental scarcity. These wars will be subnational." Elsewhere he writes, "Everywhere in the developing world at the turn of the twenty-first century, these new men and women, rushing into the cities, are remaking civilizations and redefining their identities in terms of religion and tribal ethnicity which do not coincide with the borders of existing states" (Robert Kaplan, "The Coming Anarchy," *Atlantic Monthly*, February 1994, 59, 66, 74).

In a fascinating recent study, *World on Fire*, Amy Chua argues that the ethnic conflicts of the post–Cold War world have resulted from the explosive combination of free markets, which concentrate wealth into the hands of the few, and democracy, which empowers the economically disadvantaged majority. Ethnic conflict ensues. She writes:

The global spread of markets and democracy is a principal, aggravating cause of group hatred and ethnic violence throughout the non-Western world. In the numerous societies around the world that have a market-dominant minority, markets and democracy are not mutually reinforcing. Because markets and democracy benefit different ethnic groups in such societies, the pursuit of free market democracy produces highly unstable and combustible conditions. Markets concentrate enormous wealth in the hands of an "outsider" minority, fomenting ethnic envy and hatred among often chronically poor majorities. In absolute terms the majority may or may not be better off—a dispute that much of the globalization debate fixates on—but any sense of improvement is overwhelmed by their continuing poverty and the hated minority's extraordinary economic success. More humiliating still, market-dominant minorities, along with their foreign-investor partners, invariably come to control the crown jewels of the economy, often symbolic of the nation's patrimony and identity—oil in Russia and Venezuela, diamonds in South Africa, silver and tin in Bolivia, jade, teak, and rubies in Burma.

Chua observes that the tensions between the democratically empowered majority and the economically benefiting minority become explosive:

In the numerous countries around the world that have pervasive poverty and a market-dominant minority, democracy and markets—at least in the form in which they are currently being promoted—can proceed only in deep tension with each other. In such conditions, the combined pursuit of free markets and democratization has repeatedly catalyzed ethnic conflict in highly predictable ways, with catastrophic consequences, including genocidal violence and the subversion of markets and democracy themselves. This has been the sobering lesson of globalization over the last twenty years.

Elsewhere she concludes, "Rather than reinforcing the market's liberalizing wealth-producing effects, the sudden political empowerment of a poor, frustrated 'indigenous' majority often leads to powerful ethnonationalist, anti-market pressures. And these pressures, as Rwanda, Indonesia, and the former Yugoslavia vividly show, are more likely to lead to confiscation and ethnic killing than to the widespread peace and prosperity that proponents of free market democracy envision" (Amy Chua, *World on Fire: How Exporting Free Market and Democracy Breeds Ethnic Hatred and Global Instability* [New York: Anchor Books, 2003], 9, 10, 16, 261).

9. Edward W. Said, *Orientalism* (New York: Random House Vintage Books, 1978).

10. "*Orientalism* is the generic term that I have been employing to describe the Western approach to the Orient; Orientalism is the discipline by which the Orient was (and is) approached systematically, as a topic of learning, discovery, and practice. But in addition I have been using the word to designate that collection of dreams, images, and vocabularies available to anyone who has tried to talk about what lies east of the dividing line. These two aspects of Orientalism are not incongruent, since by use of them both, Europe could advance securely and unmetaphorically upon the Orient" (ibid., 73).

11. Ibid., 8. Said challenges his readers to oppose the "terrible reductive conflicts," which "cannot remain as potent as they are," and that these distortions "must be opposed." But although the distortions must be opposed, Said's remedy is not to deny all differences but rather to point out that differences do not necessarily have to lead to hostilities. Said writes:

My aim, as I said earlier, was not so much to dissipate difference itself—for who can deny the constitutive role of national as well as cultural differences in the relations between human beings—but to challenge the notion that difference implies hostility, a frozen reified set of opposed essences, and a whole adversarial knowledge built out of those things. What I called for in *Orientalism* was a new way of conceiving the separations and conflicts that had stimulated generations of hostility, war, and imperial control. (ibid., 350)

In the afterword to his book fifteen years later, Said expressed hope that the degree of ideological distortion was at least beginning to dissipate: "There is now at least a general acceptance that these represent not an eternal order but a historical experience whose end, or at least partial abatement, may be at hand" (ibid. [1994], 352).

In the new preface to the twenty-five year anniversary of the book, he writes, "There is, after all, a profound difference between the will to understand for purposes of co-existence and humanistic enlargement of horizons, and the will to dominate for the purposes of control and external enlargement of horizons, and the will to dominate for the purposes of control and external dominion" (ibid. [London: Penguin, 2003], xix).

12. Buruma and Margalit, *Occidentalism*.

13. Ibid., 5, 8. They describe Occidentalism as an inverted Orientalism:

Occidentalism is at least as reductive; its bigotry simply turns the Orientalist view upside down. To diminish an entire society or a civilization to a mass of soulless, decadent, money-grubbing, rootless, faithless, unfeeling parasites is a form of intel-lectual destruction. Once again, if this were merely a matter of distaste or prejudice, it would not be of great interest. Prejudices are part of the human condition. But when the idea that others are less than human gathers revolutionary force, it leads to the destruction of human beings. (ibid., 10–11)

Elsewhere they describe the essence of Occidentalism as "blinkered faith in eco-nomic progress; trust in social engineering by the state; a fetishistic taste for power plants and big dams. Here is the Dead Sea, with 'mighty iron tubes' jutting from the rocks, 'set vertically upon the turbine sheds, resembling fantastic chimneys. The roaring from the tubes and the white foam on the outflowing waters bore witness to a mighty work'" (ibid., 140–41).

14. Frequently, hostility results from this misperception of the West, as the authors explain:

These strands are linked, of course, to form a chain of hostility—hostility to the City, with its image of rootless, arrogant, greedy, decadent, frivolous cosmopolitanism; to the mind of the West, manifested in science and reason; to the settled bourgeois, whose existence is the antithesis of the self-sacrificing hero; to the infidel, who must be crushed to make way for a world of pure faith. (ibid., 11)

15. Buruma and Margalit sum it up nicely, "On the contrary, it is a tale of cross-contamination, the spread of bad ideas" (ibid., 149).

16. Ziauddin Sardar, "Islam: Resistance and Reform," *New Internationalist*, no. 345 (May 2002): 9. Sardar is a noted Middle East scholar and author with numerous books and articles to his credit.

17. In his 1996 Fatwa "Declaration of War against the Americans Occupying the Land of the Two Holy Places" (redistributed in 1998). In the early twenty-first century, we confront again the conundrum that perplexed Reinhold Niebuhr: the "capacity of man's inhumanity to his fellow man."

18. We are sensitive to some of these, particularly the argument that economic injustice is a factor. However, we see that the economic dimension comes into play more indirectly as an expression of modernism spread via globalization (see chap. 8).

19. When, for example, modern-day mathematicians make algebraic equations, they commemorate the contributions of ninth-century Muslim mathematician Al-Khwarizmi, who gave us the word "algebra" and from whose name the word "algorithm" is derived. As reported by Amartya Sen in "What Clash of Civilizations? Why Religious Identity Isn't

Destiny," *Slate*, March 29, 2006, 1, http://www.slate.com/id/2138731. This essay is adapted from Sen's book *Identity and Violence* (New York: Norton, 2006). According to Sen, the word "algebra" is derived from Al-Khwarizmi's Arabic mathematical treatise entitled *Al Jabr wa-al-Muqabilah* ("What Clash?" 1).

20. Quoted in Javed Akbar's "Why the West Has Lost Goodwill with the Muslims," *Toronto Star*, July 29, 2005. See Karen Armstrong's books on the topic: *Muhammad: A Biography of the Prophet* (San Francisco: HarperCollins, 1993); *A History of God: The 4,000 Year Quest of Judaism, Christianity, and Islam* (New York: Ballantine Books, 1994); and *The Battle for God* (New York: Knopf Ballantine Books, 2001).

21. Quoted in Paul Marshall, Roberta Green, and Lela Gilbert, *Islam at the Crossroads* (Grand Rapids: Baker Books, 2002), 87.

22. Indeed, a crisis of Islamic identity was brought on by its collision with modernity. Robert Kaplan explains, "As Iran has shown, Islamic extremism is the psychological defense mechanism of many urbanized peasants threatened with the loss of traditions in pseudo-modern cities where their values are under attack" ("The Coming Anarchy," 66).

23. Bassam Tibi, *The Challenge of Fundamentalism: Political Islam and the New World Disorder* (Berkeley: University of California Press, 1998), emphasis added; quoted from Daniel Pipes's review of the book in *Middle East Quarterly* 7, no. 1 (March 2000): 1, http://www.danielpipes.org/pf.php?id=826.

24. Pipes's review of *The Challenge of Fundamentalism*, 1.

25. Cited in Ian S. Lustick, "American's War and Osama's Script," in "Forum on The 2003 War on/in Iraq," *Arab World Geographer* 6, no 1 (April 2003): 2, http://users.fmg.uva.nl/vmamadouh/awg/forum3/lustick.html.

26. Quoted in Paul Marshall, "This War We're In: Taking Extremist Islam Seriously," *National Review Online*, November 26, 2002, http://www.nationalreview.com/comment/comment-marshall112602.asp.

27. Quoted in Lustick, "American's War and Osama's Script," 2.

28. Quoted in "Text of Osama bin Laden's Statement," *USA Today*, 09/24/2001, http://www.usatoday.com/news/nation/2001/09/24/binladen-text.htm.

29. Transcript of Al-Jazeera TV, December 1998 interview with Osama bin Laden. See Daniel Pinéu, "Al-Jazirah TV Broadcasts Usama Bin Ladin's 1998 Interview," September 26, 2001, http://wsarch.ucr.edu/wsnmail/2001/msg01462.html.

30. Dilip Hiro writes: "Until the late 1990s popular belief in the West associated Islamic fundamentalism with . . . a movement of fanatic mullahs bent on harming Western interests. Yet Saudi Arabia, the oldest Islamic fundamentalist state of our times, . . . has always been firmly allied with the West." Dilip Hiro, *War without End* (New York: Routledge, 2002), xxx.

31. From an interview with bin Laden by *Time*, "Wrath of God: Osama bin Laden Lashes Out against the West," 153, no. 1 (January 11, 1999): 2, http://www.time.com/time/asia/asia/magazine/1999/990111/osama2.html. Also quoted in Marshall et al., *Islam at the Crossroads*, 89.

32. Buruma and Margalit, *Occidentalism*, 144.

33. John Gray, *Al Qaeda and What It Means to Be Modern* (New York: New Press, 2003), 3. Yet Westerners overwhelmingly tend to think of "Islam" in terms like "backward," "uncivilized," and generally "inferior." Images of repressive dictators and poverty-stricken masses, veiled women who are forbidden to drive cars, and *their* terrorists who fly *our* airliners into *our* buildings, along with the daily news stories from Israel-Palestine about the latest suicide bombing—all inform a less than flattering view of the Muslim world. Perhaps nowhere has the Western superiority complex in regard to the Muslim world and the East in general been more powerfully described than by Edward Said in *Orientalism*; Said, as we have mentioned, calls the Western attitude toward Islam a colossal intellectual

and consequentially societal arrogance of historic proportions, one that has motivated and justified the West's hundred years of actual political and economic domination of the Middle East.

Said's more academic concerns aside, one may still argue that present-day realities legitimate those "misconceptions." The Middle East, after all, really has been dominated by dictators, who rule restless masses. Saddam Hussein's attacks on the Kurds, the late President Assad's destruction of Hamas, the Taliban in Afghanistan, and even the more benign but still repressive regimes of Egypt and Saudi Arabia are all legitimately used as examples of an Islamic world that seems to justify our rather negative attitudes toward the religion that in many ways defines the region. The key to understanding all this, as we have argued, is the influence of modern ideology.

34. John Gray, interview in *Trouw*, October 25, 2003.

35. Muslims and Jews both look to Abraham as their father. Father Elias Chacour, a Palestinian Christian who witnessed the violent taking of his father's land as a child, has worked for peace between the Israelis and Palestinians for decades. Chacour has written two books on the Palestinian-Israeli question, one entitled *Blood Brothers* (Grand Rapids: Chosen Books, 1984). When he refers to blood brothers for the first time in the text, he tells the story of what his father said when his brother Rudah brought home a gun:

> Slipping his arm around Rudah's shoulders, Father replied, "For centuries our Jewish brothers have been exiles in foreign lands. They were hunted and tormented—even by Christians. They have lived in poverty and sadness. They have been made to fear, and sometimes when people are afraid, they feel that they have to carry guns. Their souls are weak because they have lost peace within." "But how do we know the soldiers won't harm us?" Rudah pressed him. Father smiled, and all the tension seemed to relax. "Because," he said, "the Jews and Palestinians are brothers—blood brothers. We share the same father, Abraham, and the same God. We must never forget that. Now we get rid of the gun." (34)

36. The six are the following: (1) the war over the birth of Israel in 1948; (2) the war over the Israeli invasion of the Sinai Peninsula in 1956; (3) the Six-Day War from June 5 to June 11, 1967; (4) the Yom Kippur War in October 1973; (5) the Intifada I, 1987–89; and (6) the current Intifada II, September 2000–.

37. *The New Encyclopaedia Britannica*, 15th ed. (Chicago: Encyclopaedia Britannica, 1990), 12:922; quoted by Mohd Elfie Nieshaem Juferi, "Confronting and Exposing Zionism," *Double Standards* (n.d.), 1, http://www.doublestandards.org/juferi1.html.

38. Quoted in Ann M. Lesch, "Zionism and Its Impact," *Washington Report on Middle East Affairs* (n.d.), 3, http://www.wrmea.com/html/focus.htm; from her article in *The Encyclopedia of the Palestinians*, ed. Philip Mattar (New York: Facts on File, 2000; rev. ed., 2005).

39. David Berlin, "Israel's Divided Soul: Can Democracy Survive Religion in the Holy Land?" *The Walrus* 3, no. 3 (April 2006): 46–57, with quote from 53.

40. Lesch, "Zionism and Its Impact," 8.

41. Ibid.

42. Israel Eldad, *The Jewish Revolution: Jewish Statehood*, trans. from Hebrew by Hannah Schmorak (New York: Shengold Books, 1971), 119; quoted in Juferi, "Confronting and Exposing Zionism," 8.

43. Some rabbis certainly have rejected the idea of a secular Jewish state. Today too, in the wake of the Gaza pullout, David Berlin reports that "there are religious Zionists who want nothing more to do with the state of Israel, but who will pursue their dreams at all costs. This group includes many young people who insist that they will not serve in the armed forces, will not vote, and will no longer pray for the state or the army. This group includes young men . . . who no longer think of themselves as mere Zionists but rather as 'saviours' of the Jews and of Judaism itself" ("Israel's Divided Soul," 56).

44. Ibid., 53. David Berlin, who describes himself as a "secular Israeli" (49), relays a recent interview with Dov Lior, the chief rabbi of Kiryat Arba:

When Rabbi Lior spoke directly about *geula* (redemption) his eyes lit up, communicating a sense of excitement that was palpable and intoxicating. He seemed to feel that we would all be better off if we could only believe that the simple, physical act of settling Israel is the expression of a preternatural process that will end with the rising of the dead and peace on earth. If one could only let this idea serve as the marrow from which meaning flowed, then the problem of leading a meaningful life would be solved. The symbols and mythical elements that constitute the language of redemption—through which religious Zionists extend ancient mythology into the present—prop up such a belief. And without the seminal idea of Greater Israel, it is doubtful that Zionism itself would have the mass appeal that it does. The pillar of fire may not have arrived, but the pillar of Israel is Greater Israel itself. (ibid., 54)

45. Theodor Herzl, quoted in Juferi, "Confronting and Exposing Zionism," 3. Consider what Vladimir Dubnow, another early Zionist, wrote in 1882: "The ultimate goal . . . is, in time, to take over the land of Israel and to restore to the Jews the political independence they have been deprived of for these two thousand years. . . . The Jews will yet arise, and, arms in hand (if need be), declare that they are the master of their ancient homeland" (Benny Morris, *Righteous Victims: A History of the Zionist-Arab Conflict, 1881–1999* [New York: Random House, 1999], 49). That same year, another early Zionist wrote, "There are only now five hundred [thousand] Arabs, who are not very strong, and from whom we shall easily take away the country if only we do it through stratagems [and] without drawing upon us their hostility before we become the strong and populous ones" (ibid.).

46. Quoted in ibid., 144.

47. Quoted in Juferi, "Confronting and Exposing Zionism," 8.

48. In Theodor Herzl, *A Jewish State: An Attempt at a Modern Solution of the Jewish Question*, trans. of *Der Judenstaat* (1896) by Sylvie D'Avigdor (London: D. Nutt, 1896); quoted in Lesch, "Zionism and Its Impact," 4.

49. Islamic organizations such as Hamas find many of their supporters in the most destitute and oppressed areas of the Occupied Territories. It is no accident that the power base of militant Islam lies in the Gaza Strip, a sliver of land that acts as more of a holding pen for livestock than a supposed autonomous territory.

50. The injustice prompts a desire for resistance and action. It comes without surprise that Palestinians long for the ability to live in freedom, no longer under the daily humiliations and desperation of occupation. In a region where Islam is the dominant religion, it is not surprising that many Palestinians turn to it for solutions and answers. Though several Palestinian resistance organizations are secular, a significant portion of them include the re-Islamization of Palestinian society within their operational framework.

51. However, a significant portion of Hamas's membership can also be found among the professional class. This diversity in membership speaks to the religious as well as economic pull of being militant.

52. Within the various factions of Hamas, members fiercely debated appropriate engagement in the post-Oslo climate. The military wing urged the continuation of armed struggle, while the political wing considered various levels of involvement with the PNA (Palestinian National Authority). See John Esposito, *The Islamic Threat: Myth or Reality?* (New York: Oxford University Press, 1999), 283.

53. The geographical area of Israel-Palestine is divided into the Occupied Territories (the Gaza Strip, the West Bank, and the Golan Heights) taken by Israel in the 1967 war and administered under the Israeli military (though some areas have become "autono-

mous"), and Green Line Israel, essentially the official borders established by Israel in the 1948 war.

54. Esposito, *The Islamic Threat*, 282. On February 25, 1994, Baruch Goldstein, a Jewish settler, entered the Hebron Mosque of the Patriarch during Friday prayer and opened fire, killing 29 worshippers.

55. Ibid., 199.

56. Quoted in ibid. Esposito further explains these actions of radical movements and comments that militants use two main justifications for taking leave of societal norms:

> They assume that Islam and the West are locked in an ongoing battle, dating back to the early days of Islam, which is heavily influenced by the legacy of the Crusades and European colonialism, and which today is the product of a Judeo-Christian conspiracy. This conspiracy is the result of the superpower neocolonialism and the power of Zionism. The West (Britain, France, and especially the United States) is blamed for its support of un-Islamic or unjust regimes (Egypt, Iran, Lebanon) and also for its biased support for Israel in the face of Palestinian displacement. Violence against such governments and their representatives as well as Western multinationals is legitimate self-defense. . . . Second, these radical movements assume that Islam is not simply an ideological alternative for Muslim societies but [also] a theological and political imperative. Since Islam is God's command, implementation must be immediate, not gradual, and the obligation to do so is incumbent on all true Muslims. Therefore individuals and governments who hesitate, remain apolitical, or resist are no longer to be regarded as Muslim. They are atheists or unbelievers, enemies of God against whom all true Muslims must wage jihad (holy war). (ibid., 17)

57. In the case of Hamas, these justifications clearly allow for the subversion of what would otherwise be guiding principles for moral conduct and call for the sacrifice of believers. It also turns lukewarm Muslims into enemies of Hamas.

58. Therefore, the authority of militant Islam clouds the lines of distinction between a nation's political and military leaders and innocent civilians. Instead of limiting aggression to the perpetrators of injustice, in and of itself an action of questionable justification for Muslims, aggression is extended to those who are not directly responsible—innocent Israelis. These are indeed false enemies, and their eradication will not aid in the creation of a truly free Palestinian state. The consequences of a dynamic full-blown ideology have tragically become evident.

59. This important distinction was recognized by the Dutch philosopher R. F. Beerling in his "Ideologie," *Wijsgerig-sociologische verkenningen II* (Arnhem: W. de Haan/van Loghum Slaterus, 1965), 7–63.

60. Westerners outside of Palestine experience the idol in the form of cynicism that the fighting in Palestine will never cease—a cynicism that picks up precisely on the power of the idol. Within the world of the Israeli-Palestinian conflict itself, those engaged in violence take on special respect. Israeli military war figures like Ariel Sharon become popular political figures, even to the point of being elected prime minister. Palestinian suicide bombers, who give their young lives for the cause of liberation, garner love and respect for fighting the evil of the Israelis.

61. The god of violence requires bloody sacrifices, even human sacrifice, as if the old god Molech has come to life. Molech demanded and received child sacrifice (e.g., Lev. 18:21; 2 Kings 23:10).

62. Berlin, "Israel's Divided Soul," 46; see 49 for the estimate of religious Zionists in the Israeli population.

63. The phrase comes from Berlin, ibid., 46.

64. Ibid., 49. Nissan Slomiansky, a member of the Knesset, lamented: "During the disengagement, the prime minister [Ariel Sharon] raped us. He forces us to choose between the three things we loved equally [*Eretz Yisrael*, *Torat Yisrael*, and *Am Yisrael*; the land, the holy books, and the people of Israel]. It was a black day, but we finally chose *Am Yisrael*, the nation, which is why there was no undue violence during the disengagement. But we must also admit to ourselves that the battle over *Eretz Yisrael*, the land of Israel, was lost in August of 2005" (ibid., 54).

About Zionism, David Berlin further states:

> Because Zionism is a commitment common to both religious and secular Jews, it is not something any politician tampers with easily. Both groups subscribe to the notion of Zionism as grounded in the right-of-return for all Jews. Secular Jews cleave to historical rights, religious Jews to entitlements derived from biblical scripture. As a result, there is a wholly fluid movement between religious and secular Zionism, so much so that it is impossible to change one without seriously altering the other. (53)

65. Quoted in Middle East Dialogue Network, Inc., "Neve Shalom" (1999–2006), 1, http://mpdn.org/neve_shalom.htm.

66. See the "Courage to Refuse" (2002), http://www.seruv.org.il/english.

67. As reported by Mitch Potter, "Arab Lawyer Pays Tribute to Jewish Trauma," *Toronto Star*, June 4, 2005, A1, A12. Says Mahameed: "But there is no question for me; the Holocaust is central to this conflict. It affects everything that happens. They paid the price, and the Palestinians paid for it as well" (ibid., A12).

68. James W. Skillen, *International Politics and the Demand for Global Justice* (Sioux Center, IA: Dordt College Press, 1981), 36, states: "We see, then, that the goal of 'America first' or 'keeping the United States number one' cannot function as a meaningful goal of foreign policy." A highly recommended, anti-ideological book.

69. Some examples of this can be found in Bertram Gross, *Friendly Fascism: The New Face of Power in America* (New York: M. Evans, 1980).

70. President Bush, speech, September 2002. Similarly, on the day after September 11, 2001, Bush declared that there would be a monumental struggle of good versus evil, but good would prevail.

71. See James Tillman and Mary N. Tillman, *Why America Needs Racism and Poverty* (New York: Four Winds, 1973).

5. Material Progress and Prosperity Unshackled

1. These and other statistics are available at http://www.bread.org/hungerbasics/domestic.html (March 1, 2006).

2. Friends Committee on National Legislation, *Washington Newsletter*, no. 695 (March 2005): 8.

3. Ibid.

4. Juliet Schor, *The Overworked American: The Unexpected Decline of Leisure* (New York: Basic Books, 1991).

5. Consider the "scarcity paradox." In an environment of increased economic growth and a rising standard of living, a new, generalized feeling of scarcity is permeating Western society. Though average incomes are substantially higher than they were 25 years ago, the belief in society that we do not have all that we need has become markedly more intense. Moreover, one can no longer ignore reports in the press stating that businesses, nonprofit organizations, and governments have had to slash essential expenditures and services. These reports appear much more frequently now than they did 25 years ago when the average income was half of what it is today. See the study by Hans Achterhuis, *Het rijk*

van de schaarste: Van Thomas Hobbes tot Michel Foucault (The Realm of Scarcity: From Thomas Hobbes to Michel Foucault) (Baarn: Ambo, 1988), pointing out that in previous centuries the word "scarcity" was never used in a general sense; cited from Bob Goudzwaard and Harry de Lange, *Beyond Poverty and Affluence: Towards a Canadian Economy of Care*, trans. and ed. Mark Vander Vennen, with foreword by Maurice F. Strong (Toronto: University of Toronto Press, 1994), 4, 96.

6. Manuel Castells, *The Rise of the Network Society* (London: Blackwell Science, 2000).

7. For more on this theme, see Goudzwaard and de Lange, *Beyond Poverty and Affluence*, 57–61, who state: "We may identify a grim by-product of Western society's increasing inability to meet care needs. As we saw with the poverty paradox, certain forms of poverty have reappeared and will reappear in the midst of affluent societies such as Canada. As is well known, what is relevant for the emergence of poverty is not just the amount of social assistance monies available but also the cost of living and the level of unemployment, both of which tend to rise as the costs of care rise. The 'fixed' living costs of every household are critical here. Higher costs for medical care and education directly affect the level of poverty of poor families. And the more that the costs of care increase in relation to the drop in price of industrial products, the more people on the poor side of society will become squeezed" (60–61).

8. Elmar Altvater, *Das Ende des Kapitalismus wie wir ihn kennen* [*The End of Capitalism As We Know It*] (Münster: Verlag Westfälisches Dampfboot, 2005), 112.

9. Adam Smith, *An Inquiry into the Nature and the Causes of the Wealth of Nations*, 5 books in 2 vols. (London: W. Strahan & T. Cadell, 1776), book 5, chap. 1.

10. Bob Goudzwaard, *Capitalism and Progress: A Diagnosis of Western Society*, trans. and ed. Josina Van Nuis Zylstra (Grand Rapids: Eerdmans), 55–117 (part 2).

11. Janice Gross Stein, *The Cult of Efficiency* (Toronto: House of Anansi, 2002).

12. George Soros, *The Crisis of Global Capitalism: Open Society Endangered* (New York: PublicAffairs, 1998), xx.

13. Helmut Tietmeyer, quoted in *Le Monde diplomatique*, March 1996.

14. Andrew Carnegie, *The Gospel of Wealth and Other Timely Essays*, ed. Edward C. Kirkland (Cambridge, MA: Belknap Press of Harvard University Press, 1962), 16–17.

15. Ibid., 29.

16. Nobel Prize–winning economist Jan Tinbergen has shown that in a market economy long-term scarcities have no influence on today's prices. Markets have a "time horizon" of no longer than eight to ten years. See Goudzwaard and Lange, *Beyond Poverty and Affluence*, 83.

6. Guaranteed Security

1. Edy Korthals Altes, *Heart and Soul for Europe: An Essay on Spiritual Renewal* (Assen: Van Gorcum, 1999), 139; John Stott, *Human Rights and Human Wrongs: Major Issues for a New Century* (Grand Rapids: Baker Books, 1999), 101.

2. In "The Evolving Battlefield," John S. Foster and Larry D. Welch state: "In the Vietnam conflict, the US dropped almost 3 times as much explosive tonnage as we used in World War II, killing an estimated 365,000 Vietnamese civilians"; in *Physics Today* 53 (December 2000): 31, http://www.physicstoday.org/pt/vol-53/iss-12/p31.html. The authors are citing statistics from S. I. Kulter, ed., *Encyclopedia of the Vietnam War* (New York: Scribners, 1996), 283.

3. Altes, *Heart and Soul for Europe*, 140.

4. United Nations Centre for Disarmament, *The Relationship between Disarmament and Development: Report of the Secretary-General*, Study Series 5 (New York: United Nations, 1982), chart II.2:18.

5. Ibid. The report (90–107) contains a calculation by the American economist Wassily Leontief that traces both an accelerated arming of the world and a "disarmament scenario" in which military expenditures drop to 75 percent and ultimately to 60 percent of their current relative volume. In the first case, by the year 2000 national incomes per capita of the population would have dropped 33 percent; in the second case, they would have risen more than 160 percent. The corresponding figures for the poor Asian countries were 2 percent and 47 percent.

Perhaps the situation of the state of New Mexico provides a microcosm for the relationship between military spending and human development. For more than two decades, New Mexico has received more net US federal spending per capita than any other state. Most of that spending is military (New Mexico is home to three nuclear weapons facilities and two nuclear waste-disposal sites). For every dollar New Mexicans spend in federal tax, they receive $2.37 back from the federal government. However, according to a Fordham University study ranking each of the 50 states in overall social health (not unlike the annual United Nations Development Program [UNDP] country-by-country comparisons), New Mexico ranks dead last. It has the second highest rate of poverty and child poverty in the nation. By 1997 it had the third highest gap between rich and poor in the country; as reported by the Los Alamos Study Group, *A Little Primer on Plutonium and Poverty in New Mexico* (2005?), 1–2.

6. Former Canadian senator and ambassador for disarmament to the UN Douglas Roche calculates that as of 2005 there were at least 30,741 nuclear weapons in existence, of which at least 16,741 were operational strategic and tactical weapons (Douglas Roche, *Beyond Hiroshima* [Ottawa: Novalis, 2005], 34).

7. As reported by Stott, *Human Rights and Human Wrongs*, 102–3, despite the collapse of the Cold War, Great Britain in the 1990s ordered four Trident submarines, each of which carries a maximum of 96 independently targeted nuclear warheads. Each submarine therefore is capable of carrying 600–800 times more firepower than the Hiroshima bomb.

8. Roche, *Beyond Hiroshima*, 18.

9. Friends Committee on National Legislation, "A Glut of Military Spending," *Washington Newsletter*, no. 641 (March 2000): 1. The FCNL works tirelessly on Capitol Hill, interacting with legislators on various issues and using its own research as a resource. The FCNL's outstanding, careful research is taken largely from reports provided by the Congressional Research Office.

10. Jimmy Carter, "The Nobel Lecture Given by the Nobel Peace Prize Laureate 2002, Jimmy Carter," 3, http://www.nobel.no/eng_lect_2002b.html.

11. The FCNL estimates that in 2005 the US government spent $783 billion on past and present military activities; see Friends Committee on National Legislation, *Washington Newsletter*, no. 705 (March 2006): 5, which also reports:

> In total, we estimate the U.S. spent $783 billion in FY05 for past and present military activities. This included funding for the Defense Department, Energy Department nuclear weapons programs, military-related activities of other agencies, foreign military financing and training, the wars in Iraq and Afghanistan, mandatory spending for military retirement and health care, and the estimated portion on the national debt which can be attributed to past wars and military spending ($170 billion).

12. Friends Committee on National Legislation, "The False Promise of a Missile Shield," *Washington Newsletter*, no. 656 (June 2001): 6.

13. Michael Howard, *Clausewitz: A Very Short Introduction* (Oxford: Oxford University Press, 2002), 13.

14. Ibid.

15. F.-A. Aulard, ed., *Recueil de actes du Comité de salut public* (Record of the Acts of the Committee of Public Safety), 28 vols. (Paris: Imprimerie Nationale, 1899), 6:72.

16. Carl von Clausewitz, *On War*, trans. Michael Howard and Peter Paret (New York: Knopf, 1993), 734, 731.

17. As observed by Howard, *Clausewitz*, 51.

18. Harlan K. Ullman, James P. Wade, et al., *Shock and Awe: Achieving Rapid Dominance* (Washington, DC: Center for Advanced Concepts and Technology, National Defense University, December 1996), 20, http://www.dodccrp.org/publications/pdf/Ullman_Shock.pdf.

19. Quoted by Ira Chernus in "Shock and Awe: Is Baghdad the Next Hiroshima?" Common Dreams.org, January 27, 2003, http://www.commondreams.org/views03/0127-08.htm.

20. Nobel also built a number of luxurious resorts on the Mediterranean Sea, where in the midst of the overwhelming beauty of nature, people could commit suicide in peace.

21. UNICEF, Information: Impact of Armed Conflict on Children, "Patterns in Conflict: Civilians Are Now the Target," 1, http://www.unicef.org/graca/patterns.htm.

22. Henry Kissinger, *The White House Years* (Boston: Little, Brown, 1979).

23. Ibid., 217.

24. Chancellor Helmut Schmidt was a leading advocate for deploying US nuclear weapons on European soil.

25. On this theme, see also John Ralston Saul, *Voltaire's Bastards: The Dictatorship of Reason in the West* (New York: Vintage Books, 1993).

26. According to the Olaf Palme report *Common Security*, the estimated value of net weapons exports of the developed countries to the rest of the world rose (in 1978 prices) from $6.3 billion in 1970 to $16.1 billion per year in 1977–79 (The Independent Commission on Disarmament and Security Issues, *Common Security: A Blueprint for Survival* [New York: Simon & Schuster, 1982], 94).

27. *Time*, April 18, 1983, 21.

28. Quoted in Richard Barnet, *The Economy of Death* (New York: Atheneum, 1969), 9.

29. René Girard, *Things Hidden Since the Foundation of the World*, trans. Stephen Bann and Michael Metteer (Stanford, CA: Stanford University Press, 1978), 255.

30. Quoted in John Weldon and Clifford Wilson, *Approaching the Decade of Shock* (San Diego: Master Books, 1978).

31. See, for example, George F. Kennan, *The Nuclear Delusion: Soviet-American Relations in the Atomic Age* (New York: Pantheon Books, 1983).

32. The term comes from former UN Secretary-General Perez de Cuellar; cited in Stott, *Human Rights and Human Wrongs*, 101.

33. Brigadier General David A. Deptula (United States Air Force), one of the key architects of the air campaign of Desert Shield/Desert Storm, observes: "The Gulf War began with more targets in one day's attack plan than the total number of targets hit by the entire Eighth Air Force in all of 1942 and 1943—more separate target air attacks in 24 hours than ever before in the history of warfare"; see his *Effects-Based Operations: Change in the Nature of Warfare*, Aerospace Foundation, Defense and Airpower Series (Arlington, VA: Aerospace Education Foundation, 2001), 2, http://www.aef.org/pub/ps book.pdf. Some 220,000 bombs were dropped (ibid., 9). According to Paul F. Walker and Eric Stambler, 109,876 aircraft sorties, or an average of 2,500 sorties per day, dropped a total tonnage estimated at 88,500. Desert Storm's 59,000 tons per month outstripped the Vietnam monthly average of 34,000 tons. A common misperception is that the accuracy of bombing reached remarkable new heights in Desert Storm; in fact, only 7.4 percent of the bombs dropped were precision-guided (". . . And the Dirty Little Weapons," *Bulletin of the Atomic Scientists*, 47, no. 4 [May 1991]: 20–24, http://www.thebulletin.org/article .php?art_ofn=may91walker).

34. See, for example, the work of Economists for Peace and Security (formerly ECAAR), whose trustees include 10 Nobel Prize–winning economists (http://www.epsusa.org).

35. World Resources Institute, *The 1993 Information Please Environmental Almanac* (New York: Houghton Mifflin, 1993), 79.

36. As reported in Bread for the World, *Hunger 1992: Second Annual Report on the State of World Hunger* (Washington, DC, 1991), 116, 119, the Economic Commission for Africa estimated that in 1990 the increase in African oil import costs caused by the Gulf crisis totaled $2.7 billion; India estimated that it lost $5.8 billion as a result of the crisis, and Pakistan, $2.1 billion.

37. Friends Committee on National Legislation, "Economic Sanctions and Iraq," *Washington Newsletter*, no. 667 (June 2002): 3. A family living on US$20 per month was considered "fortunate," reports Richard McCutcheon, *The Iraq War as Globalized War*, Project Ploughshares Working Papers (Waterloo, ON: Project Ploughshares, 2002), 6, http://www.ploughshares .ca/libraries/WorkingPapers/wp023.pdf. Safe water and sanitation were huge problems. In 2002 UNICEF estimated that 500,000 tons of raw sewage was discharged directly into fresh water bodies every day, with 300,000 tons in Baghdad alone. It was therefore not surprising that each child under 5 years of age suffered an average of 14 diarrheal episodes per year (these figures come from UNICEF, "The Situation of Children in Iraq: An Assessment Based on the United Nations Convention on the Rights of the Child, reprinted March 2003, http://www.humanitarianinfo.org/sanctions/handbook/docs_handbook/UNICEF - Children inIraq.pdf, 23, 21; and UNICEF Press Release, "Overview: Children and Women in Iraq, http://www.unicef.org/media/media_9779.html, 1). Unemployment was at least 50 percent, according to the French Ministry of Foreign Affairs, "IRC [International Committee of the Red Cross] Special Report—Iraq: A Decade of Sanctions," *Gulf Investigations* (December 1999), http://www.gulfinvestigations.net/document79.html.

38. Friends Committee on National Legislation, "Economic Sanctions and Iraq," 3. The estimate was made by Denis Halliday, former UN assistant secretary-general and humanitarian coordinator in Iraq for 1990–98. See also Joy Gordon, "Starving Iraq: 1990–2002," *Harper's Magazine*, November 2002.

39. Madeleine Albright stated this in responding to a question posed to her on the program *60 Minutes* on May 11, 1996.

40. In congressional testimony, General Tommy Franks said that the purpose of the zones was to demonstrate "a continued and significant troop presence to enhance deterrence and show the U.S.'s commitment to force Saddam to comply with sanctions and WMD inspections. They . . . ensure [that] the ingress and egress routes . . . necessary to prosecute an expanded war against Iraq [would] remain sufficiently clear of sophisticated surface-to-air missile systems." Franks's statement had nothing to do with establishing no-fly zones for humanitarian purposes. Congressional testimony given by General Tommy Franks in 2001, quoted in Jeremy Scahill, "No-Fly Zones: Washington's Undeclared War on 'Saddam's Victims,'" *IraqJournal.org*, December 2, 2002, 3, http://www.iraqjournal .org/journals/021202.html.

41. John Pilger, "The Secret War: Iraq War Already Underway," *Mirror*, December 20, 2002.

42. The Colorado Campaign for Middle East Peace documented news reports of each bombing that was reported, http://www.ccmep.org/us_bombing_watch.html.

43. The calculation was made by Hans von Sponeck based on personally verified and double-checked stories. In 1999 alone, according to "Air Strike Reports" that von Sponeck began compiling that year, there were 132 bombings that caused civilian casualties. Von Sponeck stated, "The number of people killed were 120, the number of people hurt, 442. That's only in the year 1999" (cited in Scahill, "No Fly Zones," 3–4). In "The Iraq War as Globalized War," written in 2001, Richard McCutcheon cites an internal UN document

which "analyzes 46 of 143 bombing runs conducted during 1999. It records 110 civilian casualties, 350 serious injuries, over 60 houses destroyed, and over 400 livestock killed—livestock, of course, are a significant source of food and income," 5, http://www.ploughshares.ca/libraries/WorkingPapers/WPlist.html.

Von Sponeck resigned his position in protest in 2000, calling the economic sanctions against Iraq "a tragedy." He had replaced Denis Halliday, who resigned the same position for the same reasons in 1998. Shortly after von Sponeck resigned, Jutta Burghardt, head of the World Food Program in Iraq, followed suit, for the same reasons (as reported in Friends Committee on National Legislation, "Economic Sanctions and Iraq," 1).

44. Quoted in Scahill, "No-Fly Zones," 3.

45. Ibid.

46. Quoted in Friends Committee on National Legislation, "Economic Sanctions and Iraq," 1. Mairead Corrigan Maquire won the prize for her peace and reconciliation work in Ireland. She is the cofounder of the Northern Ireland Peace Movement (later renamed the Community of Peace People).

47. During a Doctors without Borders visit to Iraq just before the 2003 invasion, a frustrated Iraqi woman, referring to the devastation caused by the sanctions imposed by the United Nations, told a Canadian medical doctor, "Show me the difference between democracy and Saddam!" (a story told by Calgary medical doctor Dr. David Swann at the conference "Speaking of War and Peace" on April 12, 2003, in Edmonton, Alberta). Shortly before the invasion, 500 Shiite Muslim clerics called on everyone to fight against the United States.

48. In a September 27, 1993, speech at the United Nations, as reported by Noam Chomsky in *Hegemony or Survival* (New York: Henry Holt, 2003), 15.

49. Perhaps that explains why, in the 2004 election, so much serious electoral attention was paid to the characteristics of the candidates' wives and the president's daughters, for example, or to the past military pursuits of John Kerry and George W. Bush.

50. Rev. Dr. Martin Luther King Jr. once said that he could not confront the racism around him without first confronting the racism within his own heart. Even now, if we are to make a genuine contribution to peacebuilding, one that helps to reverse the spirals of ideology, we cannot do so without first confronting our own capacity for revenge.

51. As reported in the *Toronto Star*, May 2, 2001, A1, A16.

52. It is likely that September 11, 2001, actually interfered with the decision to implement a Ballistic Missile Shield, which the administration had wanted to announce as soon as it possibly could.

53. Friends Committee on National Legislation, "Addressing the Threat of Biological Weapons," *Washington Newsletter*, no. 666 (May 2002): 8.

54. Quoted in Federation of American Scientists, "Original U.S. Interpretation of the BWC [Biological Weapons Convention]," http://www.fas.org./bwc/usinterpretation.htm. See also William M. Arkin, "'Sci-Fi' Weapons Going to War," *LATimes.com*, December 8, 2002, for a chilling description of the newest weapons being developed by the United States that are designed to "incapacitate."

55. See, for example, an Associated Press report, "Russia Warns against Weapons in Space," *Toronto Star*, June 3, 2005, A11.

56. Friends Committee on National Legislation, "Fuzzy Logic on Missile Defense," *Washington Newsletter*, no. 656 (June 2001): 2, reporting that "South Africa, Ukraine, Kazakhstan, Belarus, Argentina and Brazil have abandoned their nuclear programs and joined the Non-Proliferation Treaty as non-nuclear weapon states."

57. As quoted by Chomsky in *Hegemony or Survival*, 229.

58. Quoted by Project Ploughshares in "Opposing Weapons in Space," *Ploughshares Monitor* 23, no. 3 (Autumn 2002), http://www.ploughshares.ca/libraries/monitor/mons02a.html.

59. Friends Committee on National Legislation Bulletin, "Stop New Nuclear Weapons," February 2005, http://www.fcnl.org/pdfs/nuclear/BunkerBuster.pdf. See also Friends Committee on National Legislation, "President Seeks More for New Nuclear Weapons," *Washington Newsletter*, no. 685 (March 2004): 7–8.

60. Friends Committee on National Legislation Bulletin, "Administration Seeks Funds to Make U.S. Nuclear Weapons More 'Reliable,'" *Washington Newsletter*, no. 705 (March 2006): 6.

61. See, for example, Roche, *Beyond Hiroshima*, 17.

62. These quotations are from *The National Security Strategy of the United States of America* (September 2002, http://www.whitehouse.gov/nsc/nss.pdf) and several presidential addresses: June 6, 2002, announcing the formation of the Department of Homeland Security; June 23, 2003, New York City; January 20, 2004, "State of the Union Address"; March 19, 2004, "President Bush Reaffirms Resolve to War on Terror, Iraq, and Afghanistan: Remarks by the President on Operation Iraqi Freedom and Operation Enduring Freedom"; April 13, 2004, "Press Conference of the President." The documents cited make clear that spreading freedom internationally is inseparably bound up with America's own interests: "By helping to secure a free Iraq, Americans serving in that country are protecting their fellow citizens." Similarly, Bush declared: "We must stay the course, because the end result is in our nation's interest." "The U.S. national security strategy will . . . reflect the union of our values and our national interests."

63. White House Press Release, "President Sworn-In to Second Term," January 20, 2005, http://www.whitehouse.gov/news/releases/2005/01/20050120-1.html. The words "freedom," "free," and "liberty" appear no less than 49 times in the address.

64. James Skillen of the Center for Public Justice in Washington (DC) observes that the National Security Strategy "presents freedom as a transcendent mission, a supranational standard, a universal eschatological goal and a world-historical spirit, to which the United States and other countries simply must subordinate themselves." Skillen calls this "freedom-idealism at its grandest. . . . The language of idealism makes the American pretension seem humble. The United States is merely a humble servant of the world-historical spirit of freedom, which is the higher subject of history now ushering in the final order of the ages. . . . Freedom is lord, and America is its prophet." He describes this view as an outgrowth of "Wilsonian exceptionalism." He quotes Tod Lindberg as saying that the White House is "firmly aligning itself with Francis Fukuyama's universalist 'end of history' vision," and as observing that President Bush's June 2002 West Point speech "is nothing less than the founding document of a new international order, with American power at its center and the spread of freedom as its aim." "Lindberg even goes so far as to say that what President Bush 'is now promoting with this liberty doctrine is not [just] a model. It is the answer and it is final.'" See James W. Skillen, *With or against the World? America's Role among the Nations* (New York: Rowan & Littlefield, 2005), 102–3.

65. In a kind of diabolical dance, a macabre twisting of the gospel is also playing directly into the hands of the ideology of guaranteed freedom today. "Rapture" theology is focused on a specific understanding of the geographical State of Israel that often finds itself opposed to solutions of reconciliation with Israel's Arab neighbors on "theological" grounds. That perspective has experienced a powerful resurgence in the United States, and it is exceedingly dangerous to underestimate its impact at the most senior levels of the present US administration. See, for example, Donald W. Musser, D. Dixon Sutherland, and Daniel A. Puchalla, "Dangerous Faith: Religion and Foreign Policy in the Administration of George W. Bush," in *War or Words? Interreligious Dialogue as an Instrument of Peace*, ed. Donald W. Musser and D. Dixon Sutherland (Cleveland: Pilgrim, 2005), 75–104. See also George Monbiot, "Religious Fundamentalists Are Driving Bush's Middle East

Policy," *The Guardian*, April 20, 2004. Finally, see Grace Halsell, *Prophecy and Politics: Militant Evangelists on the Road to Nuclear War* (Westport, CT: Lawrence Hill, 1986), and the study by David E. Holwerda, *Jesus and Israel: One Covenant or Two?* (Grand Rapids: Eerdmans, 1995).

66. For more on this theme, see Wendell Berry, *Citizenship Papers* (Washington, DC: Shoemaker & Hoard, 2003), 2.

67. *The National Security Strategy* (2002), 1.

68. See, for example, Perez Hoodbhoy's "Afghanistan and the Genesis of Global Jihad," in *Peace Research* 37, no. 1 (May 2005): 15–30. Hoodbhoy quotes an interview with Zbigniew Brzezinski, former national security adviser during the Carter administration, in which he defended the policy: "What is most important to the history of the world? The Taliban or the collapse of the Soviet Empire? Some stirred-up Muslims or the liberation of Central Europe and the end of the Cold War?" (29).

69. As reported by Steven M. Kosiak, "FY 2007 Request: DOD Budget Continues to Grow, Modest Program Cuts," *Update*, Center for Strategic and Budgetary Assessments, February 6, 2006, 1, http://www.csbaonline.org/4Publications/Archive/U.20060206.FY07 Request/U.20060206.FY07Request.pdf#; as well as Friends Committee on National Legislation, "The Runaway Military Budget: An Analysis," *Washington Newsletter*, no. 705 (March 2006): 3. The 2007 Defense Department expenditure request totals $439.3 billion; the balance is largely Department of Energy costs for nuclear weapons activities. These expenses are not earmarked for specific conflicts. According to the House Budget Committee's Democratic staff, from September 11, 2001, through 2006, the United States will have spent over $445 billion outside of this budget process on the wars in Afghanistan and Iraq (FCNL, "The Runaway Military Budget," 4).

70. When the costs of Afghanistan and Iraq are included, the US military budget at least equals that of the rest of the world.

71. The 2000 figure (including Department of Energy nuclear weapons costs) was $323 billion, or a difference of $140 billion (not adjusted for inflation). The 2000 figure comes from FCNL, "The Runaway Military Budget," 3.

72. Ibid., 5. The 2005 interest payments on debt for past wars totaled $170 billion (of a total of $352 billion in interest payments). Federal funds outlays do not include trust funds, such as Social Security and Medicare, whose revenue comes from dedicated payroll taxes.

73. The 2006 debt projections appear in ibid., 5, based on data from the White House Office of Management and Budget. The 2005 interest payments on debt for past military expenditures totaled $170 billion (out of $352 billion in total interest payments) (ibid., 5).

74. Friends Committee on National Legislation, *Washington Newsletter*, no. 695 (March 2005): 10.

75. Friends Committee on National Legislation, "The President's War Budget: Too Much for the Wrong Priorities," *Washington Newsletter*, no. 685 (March 2004): 4. The United States gives 0.12 percent of its GDP toward official development assistance.

76. Scholars of Guillaume Groen van Prinsterer, a nineteenth-century Dutch statesman who reflected a great deal on the French Revolution, particularly in his book *Lectures on Unbelief and Revolution* (1847; 2nd ed., 1868), ought to take note. Groen was a forerunner of Christian statesman Abraham Kuyper.

77. Approximately 300 metric tons of depleted uranium were used in the first Gulf War, largely in desert areas. According to a Veterans Affairs report dated September 10, 2002, of the slightly under 700,000 soldiers deployed in that war, 221,000 of them have been awarded disability. These are mostly people now in their mid-thirties, who entered the war in excellent health. There is no demonstrated link between the so-called Gulf War Syndrome and depleted uranium. But the anecdotal evidence, also from doctors in Iraq,

Afghanistan, and Bosnia, cries out for a moratorium on its use until the effects have been thoroughly studied.

78. The first justification was Hussein's alleged link to al-Qaeda, then his alleged weapons of mass destruction, and finally, much later, came an appeal to invade on humanitarian grounds. The first two were seemingly based partly on skewed intelligence processes and were reinforced by an uncritical, powerful mass media.

Conspicuously absent by their silence in this series of three were two additional rationales. The first is the "vital interests" motive for the invasion. Iraq has 112 billion barrels of proven oil reserves, with the potential of 200 billion more. According to the US Department of Energy, it also has 110 trillion cubic feet of natural gas. By contrast, the US has 22 billion barrels of proven reserves (as noted in Jeremy Scahill, "Oil is Our Damnation," *The Progressive*, December 2002, 3, http://www.progressive.org/node/1411). Further, if you control Iraq oil, according to the former director general for planning at the Iraqi Oil Ministry, "you are halfway there to controlling the world oil. And with your substantial hold on the Saudi fields, then you are in complete control of oil supplies for a long time to come" (ibid., 3). "Diplomacy" as a means toward removing Saddam Hussein from power could not address the issue of who controls Iraq's oil.

Secondly, prior to 9/11 a strategic rationale for invasion was articulated in a report prepared by the Project for the New American Century—a think tank established in 1997 by Donald Rumsfeld, Dick Cheney, Paul Wolfowitz, Jeb Bush, and others (as reported in *The Independent*, according to David Crane, "Scepticism Growing in Britain over War in Iraq," *Toronto Star*, business section, C2, January 22, 2003; and "Jumping the Gun on Iraq," *MoveOn Peace Bulletin*, September 25, 2002, 3). It states: "The United States has for decades sought to play a more permanent role in Gulf regional security. While the unresolved conflict with Iraq provides the immediate justification, *the need for a substantial American force presence in the Gulf transcends the issue of the regime of Saddam Hussein*" ("Rebuilding America's Defenses: Strategy, Forces and Resources for a New Century," A Report of the Project of the New American Century, September, 2000, http://www.newamerican century.org/RebuildingAmericasDefenses.pdf, 14, emphasis added). This position may well have reflected the viewpoint of some within the US administration. And it may account for widespread reports that well over two years after the invasion the United States had developed plans to build fourteen permanent military bases in Iraq. The military authorization bill (HR 5122), signed on October 17, 2006, prohibits the expenditure of any monies on these bases for the 2007 fiscal year (see Friends Committee on National Legislation, "Congressional Action on Iraq: Updates," http://www.fcnl.org/issues/item .php?item_id=1919&issue_id=35).

79. Quoted in *The National Security Strategy of the United States* (2002), 11.

80. As René Girard has shown in his trenchant analyses of the "scapegoat" mechanism, in response to real violence and threat, a group sometimes chooses to "sacrifice" or expel certain elements that the community once prized in order to preserve the unity of the group. He calls this process "sacralized" violence. In an unconscious manner, the community may see such "controlled" acts of violence as a way of preventing the chaos of rampant, uncontrolled violence. Though regrettable, these sacrifices are seen as necessary for the survival and cohesion of the people.

In this light, it is striking how often President Bush has appealed to and praised the "unity" of the American people in the aftermath of 9/11. In a speech to a joint House and Senate discussion of the emerging National Homeland Security strategy on July 16, 2002, the president stated: "In the war on terror, the American people are showing tremendous strength and great resolve. Our unity is a great weapon in this fight."

81. As reported by Haroon Siddiqui, "U.S. Envoy Connects Dots between Iraq, Israel," *Toronto Star*, April 25, 2004.

82. Juan Cole, a professor of modern Middle Eastern history at the University of Michigan, stated that "many of the voters came out to cast their ballots in the belief that it was the only way to regain enough sovereignty to get American troops back out of their country" (as reported by Linda McQuaig in "Linda McQuaig Says Iraqis Voted Because They Want U.S. Troops Out," *Toronto Star*, February 5, 2005).

83. Antonia Juhasz, "The Hand-Over That Wasn't: Illegal Orders Give the U.S. a Lock on Iraq's Economy," *Los Angeles Times*, August 5, 2004. The *Economist* quote comes from Naomi Klein, "Bring Halliburton Home," *The Nation*, November 24, 2003.

84. Juhasz, "The Hand-Over That Wasn't."

85. The apostle Paul wrote, "It is for freedom that Christ has set us free. Stand firm, then, and do not let yourselves be burdened again by a yoke of slavery" (Gal. 5:1). We have been set free for freedom, not for the yoke of control and slavery.

86. René Girard, *Things Hidden Since the Foundation of the World*, 255.

87. At that time tracked online: http://www.citiesforpeace.org.

88. Further, in mid-December 2003, the *Los Angeles Times* conducted a random national poll, which found that 72 percent of Americans believed that the president had not produced sufficient evidence for starting a war. Only 22 percent said that omissions in Iraq's declaration would justify war. Only 20 percent said that Bush's advisers were giving him a balanced view. Only 26 percent would support unilateral military action in Iraq. And 67 percent said that war would increase the likelihood of terrorist attacks. See Maura Reynolds, "Most Unconvinced on Iraq War," http://www.latimes.com, December 17, 2002.

Segue 2. Two Paths before Us

1. "Torah" means "law/instruction." In our Western view of things, every use of the word "law" has the connotation of a restriction of freedom, an imposition of rules that takes away our liberty. But for Jewish, Muslim, and Christian people, the torah means first and foremost a path to walk on, a "direction," a route secure from harm. It is the path along which blessing comes. This is the meaning we have in mind here.

7. Colliding Ideologies

1. "Spoils of War: California's Economy Could Grab Back Old Defense Jobs in a New Surge of Military Spending," *Los Angeles Times*, August 8, 2004.

2. Benjamin Barber, *Jihad vs. McWorld: How Globalism and Tribalism Are Reshaping the World* (New York: Random House, Times Books, 1995).

3. Accordingly, in 1999, when the United Nations was affirming a resolution on "Prevention of an Arms Race in Outer Space" to support the Outer Space Treaty of 1967, the United States, together with Israel and Micronesia (!), abstained, while 163 other countries voted in favor.

4. US Space Command, *Vision for 2020* (Peterson AFB, CO: US Space Command, 1996), 32, http://www.fas.org/spp/military/docops/usspac/visbook.pdf.

5. "Report of the Commission to Assess United States National Security Space Management and Organization," Washington, DC, January 11, 2001, 17, http://www.space .gov/docs/fullreport.pdf.

6. Henri Tincq, interview with René Girard, trans. Jim Williams, "What Is Occurring Today Is a Mimetic Rivalry on a Planetary Scale," *Le Monde*, November 6, 2001, 2, http:// theol.uibk.ac.at/cover/girard_le_monde_interview.html.

7. The first figure comes from the US Census Bureau's Foreign Trade Statistics "Annual Trade Highlights: 2005 Highlights," 1, http://www.census.gov/foreign-trade/statis tics/highlights/annual.html. It is also reported in the Economic Policy Institute's "Trade Picture" (February 10, 2006), 1, http://www.epinet.org/content.cfm/webfeatures_econin

dicators_tradepict20060210. The second figure comes from "The Budget for Fiscal Year 2007, Historical Tables," Table 15.6, 316, http://www.whitehouse.gov/omb/budget/fy2007/pdf/hist.pdf.

8. The Tao Teh King (Liber 157), *The Equinox*, vol. 3, no. 8, trans. by Ko Yuen (Aleister Crowley), chap. 61. The English has been modernized here.

8. Globalization

1. Such as the study by John Gray, *False Dawn: The Delusions of Global Capitalism* (New York: Free Press, 1999); and Manuel Castells's trilogy, *The Information Age: Economy, Society and Culture* (Oxford: Blackwell, 1996–98): vol. 1, *The Rise of the Network Society* (1996; rev. ed., 2000); vol. 2, *The Power of Identity* (1997; 2nd ed., 2004); vol. 3, *End of Millennium* (1998; rev. ed., 2000). See also the sources cited in note 5, below.

2. *Time*, February 3, 1997.

3. Analysis from Johannes Witteveen's excellent essay, "Economic Globalisation in a Broader, Long-Term Perspective: Some Serious Concerns," in *The Policy Challenges of Global Financial Integration*, ed. Jan Joost Teunissen (The Hague: Fondad, 1998). Witteveen comments, "The growing importance of private capital flows to developing countries creates a serious risk of cyclical disturbances to the development process. These capital flows, and especially portfolio investment, can be highly volatile" (21).

4. Ibid.

5. In their book *Global Dreams* (New York: Simon & Schuster, 1994), Richard J. Barnet and John Cavanaugh speak of four dimensions in the process of globalization: the emergence of "Global Information and Images," the "Global Shopping Mall" (including the Arms Bazaar), "Global Working Places," and "Global Financial Markets." For the prestigious Group of Lisbon in its report *Limits to Competition* (Cambridge, MA: Massachusetts Institute of Technology, 1995), globalization is related primarily to the rise of mega-infrastructures for world production and services and to the emergence of a global civil society. They also include the rise of global styles of governance and of new global styles of perception and consciousness. In this respect their report bears some resemblance to the analysis of Roland Robertson in his book *Globalization: Social Theory and Global Culture* (Thousand Oaks, CA: Sage Publications, 1992).

In her challenging book *Building a Win-Win World: Life beyond Economic Warfare* (San Francisco, CA: Barrett-Koehler, 1996), Hazel Henderson interprets globalization as a combination of six processes that are mutually interactive. They therefore accelerate the rise of global interdependence. They are the growth of (1) worldwide forms and types of industrialism and technology; (2) work and migration; (3) finance; (4) the human effects on the biosphere; (5) militarism and arms trafficking; and (6) communications and planetary culture.

6. See, among others, especially Hans Achterhuis, *Het rijk van de schaarste* (The Realm of Scarcity) (Baarn: Ambo, 1988); Stephen Toulmin, *Cosmopolis: Hidden Agenda of Modern Times* (Chicago: University of Chicago Press, 1992); and Paul Hazard, *The European Mind: The Critical Years, 1680–1715*, 3 vols. (New York: Fordham University Press, 1990).

7. See especially Ninan Koshy, ed., *Globalization: The Imperial Thrust of Modernity* (Bombay: Vikan Adhyayan Kendra, 2002), which on 1–32 includes the essay "Globalization and Modernity," by Bob Goudzwaard and Julio de Santa Ana.

8. For a careful analysis of this, see Ulrich Duchrow and Franz J. Hinkelammert, *Property for People, Not for Profit* (New York: Zed Books, 2004).

9. This section closely follows the explanation found in the essay mentioned above (see note 7), "Globalization and Modernity," by Bob Goudzwaard and Julio de Santa Ana.

10. John Locke used that expression to defend colonialism and the settling of America. In his limited perception, the Indian men were hunters and so did not cultivate the soil.

He therefore saw the establishment of property rights on American soil by the white invaders as entirely legitimate.

11. The Group of Lisbon, *Limits to Competition*, 62.

12. Ibid.

13. See, for example, Immanuel Wallerstein, *The Capitalist World-Economy* (Cambridge: Cambridge University Press, 1979), 19; and Giovanni Arrighi, *The Long Twentieth Century: Money, Power, and the Origins of Our Times* (New York: Verso, 1995).

14. See note 1 of chap. 5.

15. For more on the relationship between these sectors of the economy, on the distinction between "directly productive" and "transductive" labor, and on the historical roots of the view of economic life that has led to this paradox, see Bob Goudzwaard and Harry de Lange, *Beyond Poverty and Affluence: Towards a Canadian Economy of Care*, trans. and ed. Mark Vander Vennen, with foreword by Maurice F. Strong (Toronto: University of Toronto Press, 1994), chap. 2.

16. For further discussion on this topic, see Bob Goudzwaard, "Who Cares? Poverty and the Dynamics of Responsibility: An Outsider's Contribution to the American Debate on Poverty and Welfare," in *Welfare in America: Christian Perspectives on a Policy in Crisis*, ed. Stanley W. Carlson-Thies and James W. Skillen (Grand Rapids: Eerdmans, 1996).

17. UNDP, *Human Development Report 1992*, 11, http://hdr.undp.org/reports/global/1992/en/.

18. United Nations Development Programme, *Human Development Report 2002* (New York: Oxford University Press, 2002), 31, http://hdr.undp.org/reports/global/2000/en/.

19. As observed by Goudzwaard and de Lange, *Beyond Poverty and Affluence*, 85, this advantage, known as seigniorage, consists of the difference between the actual costs of making the money and the value that the money possesses on the international exchange (just as earlier in history the value of a coin rose when a lord, a seignior [or seigneur], validated it and permitted his image to be engraved on it). The United States, as holder of the most important key currency, has profited the most from seigniorage. Already in the 1960s, the United States was able to invest enormous sums in Latin America and Europe, not to mention the Vietnam War, though in doing so it also had to sustain substantial losses in gold. In 1971, however, the Nixon administration eliminated the practice of exchanging dollars for gold. The advantage of seigniorage then became crystal clear. Severing the tie between dollars and gold permitted the United States to maintain and increase its already high level of consumption by means of an almost permanent deficit in its balance of payments. At the same time, countries not permitted to generate their own international liquidities, particularly those in the third world, found it increasingly difficult to hold their heads above water.

20. In their "A Synopsis, Limits to Growth: The 30-Year Update," Donella Meadows, Jorgen Randers, and Dennis Meadows present ten different scenarios for the future. The report notes that "under the 'business as usual scenario,' world society proceeds in a traditional manner without major deviation from the policies pursued during most of the 20th century. In this scenario, society proceeds as long as possible without major policy change. . . . But a few decades into the 21st century, growth of the economy stops and reverses abruptly" (14). Available at http://sustainer.org/tools_resources/books.html#books. As calculated by, among others, Herman Daly. Based on current projections alone, The World Wildlife Fund's "Living Planet Report 2006" notes that by 2050 humanity as a whole will need at least two planets' worth of natural resources to support current standards of living (the report is available at http://www.panda.org/news_facts/publica tions/key_pub lications/living_planet_report/index.cfm).

21. Sir Nicholas Stern, "The Stern Review on the Economics of Climate Change," Executive Summary, ii, available at http://www.hm-treasury.gov.uk/independent_reviews/stern_review_economics_climate_change/sternreview_summary.cfm.

22. Samuel P. Huntington, *The Clash of Civilizations and the Remaking of World Order* (New York: Touchstone, 1996). In contrast to Huntington's view, our approach is that ethnic differences will lead to a clash only if some ideology is at work. The cause is therefore ideology, not ethnic and religious differences themselves. In our view, the danger of Huntington's approach is that, in principle, it can even lead to unnecessary tensions between peoples and religions.

Segue 3. The Rise of Social Paradoxes and Structural Violence

1. The word "sacralized" here refers to the process of demonizing, scapegoating, and eliminating the other, as described, for example, by René Girard in his examination of the roots of violence.

2. See, for example, René Girard, *Violence and the Sacred*, trans. Patrick Gregory (Baltimore: Johns Hopkins University Press, 1977); *The Scapegoat*, trans. Yvonne Freccero (Baltimore: Johns Hopkins University Press, 1989); *Things Hidden since the Foundation of the World*, trans. Stephen Bann and Michael Metteer (Stanford, CA: Stanford University Press, 1978); and *I Saw Satan Fall Like Lightning*, trans. and foreword by James G. Williams (Maryknoll, NY: Orbis Books, 2001).

3. Michael Hardt and Antonio Negri, *Empire* (Cambridge, MA: Harvard University Press, 2001).

4. Susan Sell, "Multinational Corporations as Agents of Change: The Globalization of Intellectual Property Rights," in *Private Authority and International Affairs*, ed. A. Claire Cutler, Virginia Haufler, and Tony Porter (Albany: State University of New York Press, 1999), 188, 172.

5. Julian Saurin, "The Private Capture of Public Goods," in *Environmental Politics* 10 (2001): 79.

6. See, for example, Sheldon Rampton and John Stauber, *Weapons of Mass Deception: The Uses of Propaganda in Bush's War on Iraq* (New York: Penguin, 2003).

7. See Michel Foucault, *Discipline and Punish: The Birth of the Prison*, trans. Alan Sheridan (New York: Vintage Books, 1995), 185.

8. There certainly are nonviolent, positive inclusions that occur in the struggle against violence, such as the positive inclusion of countries in the United Nations' regime of human rights, international laws, and international agreements for the protection of life and the environment (the Convention on Biodiversity serves as one example). Regrettably, however, implementation is usually meager.

9. Widening Ways of Economy, Justice, and Peace

1. See, for example, Hannah Arendt, *The Human Condition* (Chicago: University of Chicago Press, 1958). For more on how her analysis engages economic life, see Bob Goudzwaard and Harry de Lange, *Beyond Poverty and Affluence: Towards a Canadian Economy of Care*, trans. and ed. Mark Vander Vennen, with foreword by Maurice F. Strong (Toronto: University of Toronto Press, 1994), 99–100.

2. Regrettably, in our view, all too often the ideologically driven polarization of today's debate, combined with a modernist urge to suppress all "religious" viewpoints from the public square, undermines the dialogue of healing and hope that today's world so desperately needs.

3. Thayer and Smith, "Greek Lexicon entry for Beelzeboul," in "The NAS New Testament Greek Lexicon," 1999, http://www.biblestudytools.net/Lexicons/Greek/grk.cgi?number=954&version=nas.

4. With reference to Baal, the Catholic Encyclopedia (New York: The Encyclopedia Press, Inc., 1914), for example, notes that "Baal is the genius-lord of the place and of all

the elements that cause its fecundity; . . . he is the male principle of life and reproduction in nature, and such is sometimes honoured by acts of the foulest sensuality," http://www.newadvent.org/cathen/02175a.htm. The iconography of Baal is steeped in images of male agricultural fertility. Hosea 2:5, referring to Baal, among others, says "'I will go after my lovers, who give me my food and my water, my wool and my linen, my oil and my drink.'"

5. See notes 1 and 2 for "Segue 3. The Rise of Social Paradoxes and Structural Violence."

6. René Girard, *The Scapegoat*, trans. Yvonne Freccero (Baltimore: Johns Hopkins University Press, 1989).

7. Ibid., 207, emphasis original.

8. Much has been written about South Africa's Truth and Reconciliation Commission. See, for example, Nobel Prize–winning Commission Chair Desmond Tutu's article "The Struggle for Social Justice in Post-Apartheid South Africa," in *Peace Research* 37, no. 11 (May 2005): 109–12, where Tutu describes how the Truth and Reconciliation Commission

> rejected the twin options of a type of Nuremburg trial and the general amnesia of blanket amnesty [109]. [Instead of] an orgy of retribution and revenge, . . . the world was awed by the spectacle of the Truth and Reconciliation process when victims of frequently gruesome atrocities revealed a mind-boggling nobility and generosity of spirit in the magnanimous willingness to forgive the perpetrator. . . . We resolved to look the beast in the eye, to let victims tell their story, to risk opening wounds which had seemed to have healed when they were in reality festering, we opened those wounds, cleansed them and poured on them the balm of acknowledgement, of giving voice to hurt, of rehabilitating the dignity of those who for so long were anonymous, faceless victims. Perpetrators were given the chance to come to terms with what they had done, to make a full disclosure and then to obtain amnesty in an example of restorative justice which was more about healing than about punishment, more about forgiveness and reconciliation than about retribution and revenge. . . . The Truth and Reconciliation Commission (TRC) was a way of hope, of faith that . . . even the worst perpetrator still remained a child of God with the capacity to change, that each of us has the capacity to become a saint.
>
> Forgiveness and reconciliation have been shown not to be nebulous namby-pamby things. No, they are the stuff of *real politik*. The alternative, the way of revenge, of retribution, leads to a ghastly *cul-de-sac*—the spiral of reprisal provoking counter reprisal ad infinitum ending with no security, no peace but a toll in human lives and property that is inexorable and exorbitant. (109–10)

9. G. K. Chesterton, *Orthodoxy* (Garden City, NY: Image Books, 1959).

10. Ibid., 28–29.

11. Mammon is the biblical name for the idol of money, Molech for the idol of military power, and Baal for the idol of national survival and fertility.

12. Friedrich Weinreb, *Ik die verborgen ben* (The Hague: Servire, 1967; repr., 1974).

13. Esther 4:14.

14. Weinreb, *Ik die verborgen ben*, 89.

15. Lesslie Newbigin describes the role of God's faithful followers as that of patient revolutionaries, those who both anticipate the new heavens and the new earth, as well as participate in God's redemptive works here and now.

16. Stanley Hauerwas, *The Peaceable Kingdom: A Primer in Christian Ethics* (Notre Dame, IN: University of Notre Dame Press, 1983), 105.

17. John Ralston Saul, *Voltaire's Bastards: The Dictatorship of Reason in the West* (New York: Vintage Books, 1993), 82.

18. The United States and other countries also vigorously pursued weapons exports in the 1970s (and beyond), with clear spiraling effects. Bob Goudzwaard, *Idols of Our Time*

(Downers Grove, IL: InterVarsity, 1984; repr., Sioux Center, IA: Dordt Press, 1989), 87–89, traces this development:

> Remember that in 1969 the United States recommitted itself to a strategic arms race, breaking through its own ceiling of military sufficiency. But the beginning of the seventies is of particular economic interest. Then another ceiling was broken: the volume of money created in the world. The United States severed the official tie between gold and the dollar, thereby giving itself and other countries a free hand to make dollars and other key currencies in enormous quantities. According to the calculations of Robert Triffin, a renowned monetary expert, the quantity of international currencies (dollars, yens, marks, francs and so on) available in the world grew more in a three-year period (1969 to 1972) than in the whole history of the world from Adam and Eve to 1969 (Robert Triffin, "Gold and the Dollar Crisis: Yesterday and Tomorrow," *Essays in International Finance* 132 [December 1978]: 4).
>
> What explains such a staggering explosion of money in the world? To make a long story short: every dollar made in the United States costs no more than its production costs. In the international exchange, however, it receives the full value of the dollar. When the United States created large quantities of dollars, the outgoing stream of dollars became a powerful mechanism allowing its economy to invest in other countries, to buy foreign companies, and to channel military expenditures to foreign countries when necessary (as in Vietnam) at minimal expense. Prior to 1970 the tie to gold held the volume of money in check. But severing the tie—a strategy of the powerful expansion interests of the Western world—eliminated the restriction on international money creation. Money supply is an instrument necessary to the ideology of prosperity. . . .
>
> This fundamental step had consequences. When the flood of money poured over the world, naturally the value of the dollar and its related currencies dwindled. One could buy less with a dollar than before. Third-world countries in particular were affected by this larceny—they received progressively less valuable dollars for the resources they exported to the West. To the third-world countries which could still muster their strength, this was the signal to react strongly. A few formed the OPEC bloc, and its participating countries raised their oil prices. The first energy crisis was real. It was provoked by the Western countries themselves, which in their greed had no patience for limiting money supply and energy consumption. . . . Western nations had to pay billions of dollars more for their oil, and their balance of payments (that is, the relation between receivables and foreign debts) was lost. How did they respond to this imbalance? . . .
>
> First, they made new money! The money explosion increased instead of decreased. In the next three years, from 1972 to 1975, world money reserves doubled (Robert Triffin, "Gold and the Dollar Crisis," 4). Second, they borrowed from the oil countries, which had become instantly rich. Enormous international credit was exchanged between states, making the burden of debt of many countries skyrocket. Third, they increased exports. These exports came mainly from the most technologically advanced sector of the Western economies: weapons production. In one year, from 1973 to 1974, the weapons exports of the United States doubled from four billion to eight billion dollars, due to the application of Nixon's new "arm our allies" doctrine.
>
> What was the combined effect of these reactions? Making new money meant a new depreciation of the dollar. The price of the dollar tumbled. This drop meant again a lower return on exports to the oil countries. The expansion of weapons exports meanwhile raised the weapons ceiling in the world as a whole. The Arab countries saw the military arsenal of Israel grow, and at the same time they received less and

less for their oil. . . . They felt they had no choice but to raise their oil prices again. That increase occurred in 1978, and the second energy crisis became a reality.

19. Richard F. Grimmett, "CRS Report for Congress: Conventional Arms Transfers to Developing Nations, 1997–2004," August 29, 2005, Congressional Research Service, Library of Congress, 82.

20. Ibid.

21. In 2004, the United States accounted for 53.4 percent of all arms deliveries worldwide (ibid., 4). In 1976 Jimmy Carter stated: "We cannot have it both ways. We can't be both the world's leading champion of peace and the world's leading supplier of arms." Quoted in the Committee on Administration, US House of Representatives, *The Presidential Campaign, 1976*, part 1, *Jimmy Carter* (Washington, DC: US Government Printing Office, 1978), 266–75.

22. See Federation of American Scientists, "Fast Facts," 1, http://fas.org/asmp/fast_facts .htm#WorldMilitaryExpenditures; as well as the Federation's "Eliminating Taxpayer Subsidies for Arms Sales" (2002?), http://fas.org/asmp/campaigns/subsidy.html. Arms trade is typically exempt from free trade agreements.

In its report "Arms Trade Insider," The Council for a Livable World identified a process whereby arms procurement and arms exports are driving each other upward—a process whereby the United States is in an arms race with itself. The report states that after, and occasionally even before, new weapons roll off the assembly line, they are offered to foreign customers. Each overseas sale of top-of-the-line US combat equipment represents an incremental decrease in US military superiority. The gradual decline in military strength spurs politicians, the military, and the defense industry to press for higher military spending to procure increasingly sophisticated equipment superior to weapons shipped overseas. This latest technology is again offered to foreign customers, and the cycle begins anew (#51, August 9, 2001, as observed in Anup Shah, "The Arms Trade Is Big Business," http://www.globalissues.org/Geopolitics/ArmsTrade/BigBusiness .asp#GeopoliticalandEconomicAgendas).

23. Frida Berrigan and William D. Hartung, with Leslie Heffel, World Policy Institute, "U.S. Weapons at War 2005: Promoting Freedom or Fueling Conflict?" June 2005, 2, http://www.worldpolicy.org/projects/arms/reports/wawjune2005.html.

24. Federation of American Scientists, "Fast Facts," 1. In 2003 the United States supplied arms to 72 percent of the world's conflicts (Berrigan and Hartung, "U.S. Weapons at War 2005," 2). In "Globalized Weaponry," Tamar Gabelnick and Anna Rich observe that "profit motives in the military industry have resulted in arms export decisions that contravene such U.S policy goals as preserving stability and promoting human rights and democracy (*Foreign Policy in Focus* 5, no. 16 [June 2000]: 3), http://www.fpif.org/briefs/ vol5/v5n16arms.html.

The practice of "arming the enemy" has intensified after the events of September 11, 2001. Arms trade export barriers have been relaxed in order to help arm countries in the fight against terrorism. Arms trade restrictions were lifted with both Pakistan and India, for example, both of which possess nuclear weapons, and each of whom has careened perilously close to war with the other. The US ambassador to India was positively gushing over the new markets open to American arms manufacturers as a result of this relaxation. As another example, after September 11, 2001, Congress permitted arms sales to Azerbaijan despite the fact that it was at war with Armenia. To "balance" this, it also sold military equipment to Armenia.

25. As stated in a report by Control Arms, "The Arms Industry" (2005?), 1, http://www .controlarms.org/the_issues/arms_industry.htm.

26. The treaty is a joint initiative launched by Oxfam International, Amnesty International, and the International Action Network on Small Arms (IANSA), under the "Control Arms" campaign.

27. The oldest name applied to Christians, according to the book of Acts, was those who "belonged to the Way" (Acts 9:2). Jesus said of himself, "I am the way and the truth and the life" (John 14:6). Even all non-Christian religions have as a trademark being oriented to a way. Islam means literally "obedience, submission" to the commandments. Buddhism teaches the sevenfold path; Taoism refers in its name (Tao means "way") to going on a way.

28. In Jacques Ellul, *The Subversion of Christianity*, trans. Geoffrey W. Bromiley (Grand Rapids: Eerdmans, 1986).

29. James Wolfenson, former president of the World Bank, declares that "it is inconsistent to preach the benefits of free trade and then maintain the highest subsidies and barriers for precisely those goods in which poor countries have a comparative advantage." Quoted in Susan Brown, "The Road to Peacebuilding: You Can't Get There From Here," presented to the United Nations Department of Economic and Social Affairs, New York, November 15, 2004, 18, http://www.un.org/esa/peacebuilding/Action/DesaTaskForce/papers_egm20041115/TheRoadtoPeacebuilding_Brown.pdf.

30. Such as Project Ploughshares (http://www.ploughshares.ca).

31. "Economy" is a word that at first glance has no normative significance, or it would mean to have as few costs and as much earnings as possible. But it is a word with a deep and almost completely abandoned background. *Oikos* means housekeeping, and *nomos* refers to administering a household with care. Jesus used the word on a number of occasions, especially when he spoke of evil stewards—literally, "economists"—whose land had not borne sufficient fruit, and who had not given their coworkers food on time (Luke 12:42; 16:1–12). Economy is therefore primarily taking care of people and nature. But most ideologies throw precisely that element to the wind when the issue is about the economy or economic growth.

32. As advocated, for example, by the international ATTAC movement (http://www.attac .org).

33. For more on this theme, see Brad Breems (Trinity Christian College, Palos Heights, IL), "Bad Fences Make Bad Neighbors" (unpublished paper delivered at the Institute for Christian Studies, Toronto, March 18, 2004; see the report of Breems' address available at http://www.icscanada.edu/perspective/issues/perspective_2004-04.pdf.

34. This comes from a speech that President Bush delivered in September 2002 (as noted in Juan Stam, "Bush's Religious Language," *The Nation*, December 22, 2003, http://www.thenation.com/doc/20031222/stam). President Bush has used this expression in numerous speeches, including in his speech to the UN on November 10, 2001 (http://www .september11news.com/PresidentBushUN.htm).

35. The organization "Peaceful Tomorrows"—the phrase comes from Martin Luther King Jr.—has been adamant with President Bush and the White House in the demand that the United States and the world community not use the deaths of their family members as justification for war. Some of their members have traveled to Afghanistan to meet victims of the bombing that took place there, and they have documented their findings in a gripping document called "Afghan Portraits of Grief: The Civilian/Innocent Victims of U.S. Bombing in Afghanistan." See http://www.peacefultomorrows.org.

A poignant story comes from one response in the horrific aftermath of the Twin Towers' devastation. A man was searching through the rubble in New York. His wife had been killed in the tragedy, and he was looking for some remnant, something of her. A television news channel interviewed him, the interview was finished, and he started walking away. But then he turned and called the interviewers back and insisted that the cameras roll again. They did, and he said, "If even one person dies as a result of what has happened here today, then my wife's death will have been in vain." That grieving man knew, in a profound and deep way, the heart of the minesweeper guideline.

36. John Maynard Keynes, "Economic Possibilities for Our Grandchildren" (1930), in *Essays in Persuasion* (New York: Norton, 1963), 358.

37. For a more complete exposition on the difference between postcare and precare economies and on the feasibility of having a precare economy, see Goudzwaard and de Lange, *Beyond Poverty and Affluence*.

38. The World Alliance of Reformed Churches has adopted this as a better and far more inspiring vision for the world economy than the uniformity of the tunnel economy: "The material wealth of the wealthy has grown enough. Their trees are now mature and should leave space for new trees to develop and blossom. Our alternative is an orchard of blossoming economies, each bearing its own kind of fruit. The time has come for radical change if total catastrophe is to be prevented and all creation is to enjoy fullness of life" ("WARC Taskforce Report 2004," written for its General Council meeting in Accra, 2004).

39. On conversion to a genuinely sustainable economy, see especially Goudzwaard and de Lange, *Beyond Poverty and Affluence*; as well as the work of Herman E. Daly. Daly's works include, among others, *Ecological Economics*, with Joshua Farley and Jon D. Erickson (Washington, DC: Island Press, 2005), *For the Common Good: Redirecting the Economy toward Community, the Environment, and a Sustainable Future*, with John B. Cobb Jr., revised and expanded edition (Boston: Beacon Press, 1994), *Beyond Growth: The Economics of Sustainable Development* (Boston: Beacon Press, 1997), *Steady-State Economics* (2nd edition with new essays) (Washington, DC: Island Press, 1991), and *Ecological Economics and the Ecology of Economics: Essays in Criticism* (Northhampton, MA: Edward Elgar Publishing, 2000). Daly is a former senior economist, Environment Department, The World Bank.

Beyond Poverty and Affluence, 105–6, reports a European example. In 1983 the Netherlands Scientific Council for Government Policy, a research arm of the national government, published *A Policy-Oriented Survey of the Future*. The council tried to trace the country's future over a ten-year period, assuming adoption of one of three scenarios: further expansion of the market economy ("export-led growth"), extension of the welfare state ("consumption-oriented growth"), or implementation of the economics of enough ("stewardship," "a sustainable society," "the economics of care," or "the economics of voluntary austerity"). With the help of a Leontief-type input/output model and after adding a "quality of work" category because of the requirements of the "sustainable society" perspective, a research group of the council projected the likely outcomes of each of the three scenarios.

In its accompanying research study, *The Limits and Possibilities of the Economic System in Holland*, the research group concluded that the economics of enough would have a more favorable impact than either the market-economy or the welfare-state scenarios on employment levels, quality of work, the environment, energy saving, capital transfer to the third world, and government deficits. This would be true if the Dutch people were willing simply to maintain average income and consumption levels at their present plane (in no year was there a decrease in income and consumption of more than 3 percent) and if they agreed to cooperate in orienting society, as a whole and in its parts, to these broader ends. The latter study also explored in detail what each scenario would achieve in terms of specific policy objectives. With respect to minimizing unemployment, the researchers found that the economics of enough would decrease unemployment substantially more than either of the other two scenarios (by approximately twice as much), if the Dutch people were willing to accept, in exchange for a higher quantity and quality of work, a maximum reduction of 5 percent in their level of consumption. The study observes, "Thanks to the relatively painless goal restrictions, very favorable values are found for the goal variables, with exceptional optimization" (105). The 1983 reports, together with an extensive English summary, were published by the council (Plein 1813, nr. 2, 2514 JN, The Hague).

40. J. Richard Middleton and Brian J. Walsh, *Truth Is Stranger Than It Used to Be* (Downers Grove, IL: InterVarsity, 1995), 192.

41. As observed by Economists Allied for Arms Reduction (ECAAR), "Military vs. Social Spending: Warfare or Human Welfare" (2004), 1, http://www.epsusa.org/publica tions/fact sheets/milexMDG.pdf. The copyrighted article contains the following graph and text (slightly adapted here):

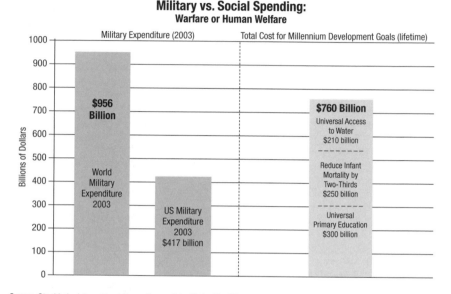

Source: Stockholm International Peace Research Institute, http://first.sipri.org/non_first/result_milex.php and *The Costs of Attaining the Millennium Development Goals*, World Bank, http://www.worldbank.org/html/extdr/mdgassessment.pdf.

The article goes on to say, "in 2003, the world spent more than $900 billion on its militaries, with the US contributing nearly 50% of the total. World military expenditure in one year is greater than would be required to fulfill the Millennium Development Goals in 11 years. If 10% of world military expenditure, or 20% of US military expenditure, were diverted yearly, the MDG could be fully funded."

42. Brown, "The Road to Peacebuilding," 4. Her sources are the UNDP's *Human Development Index 2002*; and Paul Collier, *Breaking the Conflict Trap: Civil War and Development Policy* (Washington, DC: World Bank, 2003).

Kofi Annan has written:

> In fact, to many people in the world today, especially in poor countries, the risk of being attacked by terrorists or with weapons of mass destruction, or even of falling prey to genocide, must seem relatively remote compared to the so-called "soft" threats—the ever-present dangers of extreme poverty and hunger, unsafe drinking water, environmental degradation and endemic or infectious disease. Let's not imagine that these things are unconnected with peace and security, or that we can afford to ignore them until the "hard threats" have been sorted out. We should have learned by now that a world of glaring inequality—between countries and within them—where

many millions of people endure brutal oppression and extreme misery is never going to be a fully safe world, even for its most privileged inhabitants (quoted by Friends Committee on National Legislation [FCNL], "Foreign Aid—Global Development Vs. War on Terror?" *Washington Newsletter*, no. 685 [March 2004], 7).

43. The term "virtual war" comes from Michael Ignatieff, *Virtual War* (Toronto: Penguin Canada, 2000), a new style of conflict that, he argues, began with the Kosovo conflict and was made possible by technological advances.

44. Parallel internal discussions about the inadequacy of the just-war/pacifist dilemma and the need for a new paradigm are taking place simultaneously within the Christian, Jewish, and Islamic communities. See Bob De Vries, "Making Peace in Palestine" (unpublished draft, 2002). See also Eknath Easwaran, *Nonviolent Soldier of Islam: Badsha Khan, A Man to Match His Mountains* (Tomales, CA: Blue Mountain Center of Meditation, 1999); Mohammed Abu-Nimer, *Nonviolence and Peace Building in Islam: Theory and Practice* (Gainesville: University Press of Florida, 2003). On the discussion within Judaism, see articles by Naomi Goodman and E. Gendler in *War and Its Discontents: Pacifism and Quietism in the Abrahamic Traditions*, ed. James Patout Burns (Washington, DC: Georgetown University Press, 1996); and within Christianity, see Glenn Stassen, *Just Peacemaking: Transforming Initiative for Justice and Peace* (Louisville: Westminster John Knox, 1992).

45. Repeatedly in Scripture, God recites a refrain similar to this one, which appears after a book of entirely nonmilitary laws and immediately after the Jubilee legislation: "If you follow my decrees and are careful to obey my commands, . . . I will grant peace in the land . . . and the sword will not pass through your country" (Lev. 26:3, 6). God makes a direct connection between obedience to nonmilitary laws, such as "There should be no poor among you" (Deut. 15:4), and military security.

46. There were no chariots in Israel until David, who kept 100 of them (2 Sam. 8:4)—rejecting the dictum God gave to Joshua in Josh. 11:1–9 to burn chariots and hamstring horses (that prohibition is the context of Deut. 20:1). Solomon then acquired thousands of horses and chariots and traded them with the surrounding nations (1 Kings 10:26–29). Micah called the militarization of God's people by means of the horse and chariot "the beginning of sin to the Daughter of Zion" (Mic. 1:13). The Hebrew word for "beginning" here means "chief," "cardinal," "paramount," "preeminent," "of the highest rank." And the prophets rail against Israel's horses and chariots: "There is no end to their . . . horses . . . [and] chariots" (Isa. 2:7). The horse and chariot is the biblical symbol of military might (Ps. 20:7). But Yahweh's horses and chariots are victorious, not any of the nations' (see the story of Elisha in 2 Kings 6:15–17).

47. As Jesus enters Jerusalem (which means "City of Peace"), he weeps over it, saying, "If you, even you, had only known on this day what would bring you peace—but . . . the days will come upon you when your enemies will . . . encircle you and hem you in on every side . . . [and] dash you to the ground" (Luke 19:41–44).

48. These comments merely scratch the surface of the remarkable, startling material about war and peace in the Bible—material that much of the Christian community has missed almost entirely due to its fixated adherence to the just-war/pacifist lens and the resulting hermeneutical errors.

49. We are not advocating a kind of "biblicism," in which Bible texts are lifted out of context and simply applied as proof texts to today's world. The misuse of Rom. 13 today is a clear example of biblicism. Commentators and pundits have routinely lifted Rom. 13 out of its context within the rest of Scripture, particularly God's clear expectations of justice and peace throughout the Old and New Testaments, and simply applied it as a "proof text" to contemporary conflict situations. The result has been the sanctioning of even horrific government military actions—the precise opposite of what Paul intended.

50. For an incisive analysis of the collision between NATO's doctrine and the Nuclear Non-Proliferation Treaty, see Ernie Regehr, "Rebuilding Confidence in the NPT [Nuclear Non-Proliferation Treaty]," *Ploughshares Monitor* 26, no. 1 (Spring 2005): 2, http://www .ploughshares.ca/libraries/monitor/monm05a.htm.

51. See John Paul Lederach, *Building Peace: Sustainable Reconciliation in Divided Societies* (Washington, DC: United States Institute of Peace Press, 1997), 39.

52. See note 7 for chap. 4.

53. In addition to John Paul Lederach, *Building Peace*, see his *The Journey Toward Reconciliation* (Scottdale, PA: Herald Press, 1999); and *Moral Imagination: The Art and Soul of Social Change* (New York: University of Oxford Press, 2004); as well as Jarem Sawatsky, "Extending the Peacebuilding Timeframe: Revising Lederach's Integrative Framework," *Peace Research* 37, no. 11 (May 2005): 123–30. See also Mary B. Anderson, *Do No Harm: How Aid Can Support Peace—or War* (Boulder, CO: Lynne Rienner, 1999).

54. Center for Defense Information and Foreign Policy in Focus, *A Unified Defense Budget for the United States* (Washington, DC: Center for Defense Information; Foreign Policy in Focus, March 2004), 4, http://www.cdi.org/news/mrp/Unified-Budget.pdf. The report removes $51 billion that would fund legacy military systems and other systems of significantly suspect defense value and puts the equivalent amount into nonproliferation programs, development aid, peacekeeping operations (also through the UN), and homeland security programs.

55. Report of the International Commission on Intervention and State Sovereignty, *The Responsibility to Protect* (Ottawa: International Development Research Centre, December 2001), http://www.iciss.ca/pdf/Commission-Report.pdf.

56. Ibid., xi. See too the later Report of the UN Secretary-General to the General Assembly, moving toward operationalizing the concept of human security: "In Larger Freedom: Towards Development, Security and Human Rights for All" (March 21, 2005), http://www .un.org/largerfreedom. The report itemizes action strategies under the headings "Freedom from Want," "Freedom from Fear," and "Freedom to Live in Dignity."

The *Responsibility to Protect* report declares that core elements of the "Responsibility to Protect" concept are "not just the responsibility to *react* to an actual or apprehended human catastrophe, but [also] the responsibility to *prevent* it, and the responsibility to *rebuild* after the event (17, with original emphasis)." Prevention involves addressing the cause of conflicts that put populations at risk. Reaction addresses situations of compelling human need with nonmilitary measures and, in extreme cases, with military intervention. And rebuilding involves assisting with reconciliation and reconstruction that addresses the causes of the harm the intervention was designed to halt. The report further explains:

> The fundamental components of human security—the security of people against threats to life, health, livelihood, personal safety and human dignity—can be put at risk by external aggression, but also by factors within a country, including "security" forces. Being wedded still to too narrow a concept of "national security" may be one reason why many governments spend more to protect their citizens against undefined external military attack than to guard them against the omnipresent enemies of good health and other real threats to human security on a daily basis. . . .
>
> The traditional, narrow perception of security leaves out the most elementary and legitimate concerns of ordinary people regarding security in their daily lives. It also diverts enormous amounts of national wealth and human resources into armaments and armed forces, while countries fail to protect their citizens from chronic insecurities of hunger, disease, inadequate shelter, crime, unemployment, social conflict and environmental hazard. When rape is used as an instrument of war and ethnic cleansing, when thousands are killed by floods resulting from a ravaged countryside and when citizens are killed by their own security forces, then it is just

insufficient to think of security in terms of national or territorial security alone. The concept of human security can and does embrace such diverse circumstances. (15)

The promise of this approach is that it has the potential to provide an alternative to *autarcheia*, the Greco-Roman legal doctrine of the "self-sufficiency" of states, which largely governs the just-war paradigm.

57. United Nations Press Release, "United Nations General Assembly Establishes Peace-building Commission" (December 20, 2005), http://www.un.org/ga/president/60/summit followup/pbcpr051220.pdf. General Assembly President Jan Eliasson stated, "This reso-lution would, for the first time in the history of the United Nations, create a mechanism which ensures that for countries emerging from conflict, post-conflict does not mean post-engagement of the international community." Regrettably, however, the Peacebuilding Fund designed to support the commission relies entirely on voluntary contributions.

58. Ernie Regehr and Peter Whelan, "Reshaping the Security Envelope," Project Ploughshares Working Papers (Waterloo, ON: Project Ploughshares, November 2004), http://ploughshares.ca/libraries/WorkingPapers/wp044.pdf.

59. David Suzuki and Holly Dressel, *Good News for a Change: Hope for a Troubled Planet* (Toronto: Stoddart, 2002).

60. For more information on Oikocredit, see http://www.oikocredit.org. For a further description, see also Leo Andringa and Bob Goudzwaard, *Globalization and Christian Hope: Economy in the Service of Life*, trans. Mark Vander Vennen (Toronto: Public Justice Resource Centre, 2003), 18–19.

61. See the Nobel Foundation's press release, http://nobelprize.org/nobel_prizes/peace/laureates/2006/press.html.

62. Stephen Berk, *A Time to Heal: John Perkins, Community Development, and Racial Reconciliation* (Grand Rapids: Baker Books, 1997).

63. For more information, see the John M. Perkins Center for Reconciliation and Development, http://www.jmpf.org.

64. Isa. 2:4. Many such detailed conversion plans have been developed; for example, see George McRobie, *Small Is Possible* (San Francisco: Harper & Row, 1981).

65. It is in knowing the meaning of enough that we receive a sense of abundance, for abundance is the awareness of having more than enough. Yet it is precisely a sense of abundance that is being lost today, even though we live in a society of unprecedented wealth. Beyond a level of enough, distortions therefore enter the picture. Just as under-development brings about damage to people, so too does overdevelopment. The English language acknowledges this reality. It is striking, for example, to note that our English word "luxury" comes from the Latin word *luxatio*, which means "dislocation," as in the dislocation of an arm or joint.

ACKNOWLEDGMENTS

Every book, like every life, has its own story, with veins of care, attention, exuberance, and frustration supporting it like roots running up from under the earth. The story of this book begins in the early 1980s, when one of us, Bob Goudzwaard, wrote a relatively slim volume entitled *Idols of Our Time*. *Idols* was translated from Dutch into English by a second one of us, Mark Vander Vennen, which marks the beginning of a longstanding, magnificent collaboration. *Idols* was written in response to the international and national tensions of the early 1980s. It was an attempt to show that faith, especially authentic Christian faith, can help to illuminate highly complex political, social, and economic problems, because within them lies a spiritual dimension filled with worldviews, ideologies, and even forms of contemporary idolatry.

Idols proved to be a success and until very recently was assigned in college courses, including political science classes taught by a third one of us, David Van Heemst. Noticing that *Idols* was becoming dated, David approached Bob with the idea of writing a new edition, and he had some fresh ideas. So began the beautiful community of three that produced *Hope in Troubled Times*.

In our community of three, each of us contributed substantial original material. Bob provided leadership and the bulk of the content, Mark acted as the overall editor, and David served as a crucial sounding board.

Beyond us, however, many people helped in the birthing of this book. Our own intensive back-and-forth dialogue resulted in a continual refinement and improvement of the text. But the text was significantly enhanced by frank and critical feedback from a number of readers. Still other people provided essential practical help and support. Without the generosity of this larger community of interest, this book would not have materialized, at least in its present form. We are honored to thank them here. Of course, gratefully acknowledging them does not necessarily imply that they agree with the content of the book or that they are responsible in any way for its shortcomings, which lie entirely with us.

For their assistance, we wish to publicly express our heartfelt gratitude to Peter Vander Meulen, Rabbi Dow Marmur, John Witte, Javed Akbar, Edy Korthals Altes, Lambert Zuidervaart, Brian Walsh, William Van Geest, Kathy Vander Grift, Michael Goheen, Nicholas Wolterstorff, Robert Vander Vennen, Harry Schat, William F. Ryan, SJ, Petrus Simons, Harry Kits, Citizens for Public Justice, Jonathan Chaplin, the Institute for Christian Studies, Byron Borger of Hearts and Minds Bookstore, Archbishop Njongonkulu Ndungane, Marian Culverwell, Gregory Baum, Lavinia Browne, Duane Shank, Walter Ross, and Martin Robra. We are also deeply grateful to all who participated in a symposium on an early draft of the book held at the Institute for Christian Studies, Toronto, on March 18, 2005.

Special thanks go to all those who have generously and publicly endorsed the book and to our outstanding agent, Lee Davis Creal, whose passion for the themes in this book led her to come out of "retirement" in order to represent it. We are immensely grateful to the team at Baker Publishing Group, whose patient work has been nothing short of superb, particularly Robert Hosack, Jeremy Cunningham, Jeremy Wells, Paula Gibson, Caitlin Mackenzie, and Karen Steele. And we especially thank our families, who have graciously realigned themselves to create space for this unusual new addition to their lives.

Gerald Vandezande has championed this book since its inception. His enthusiasm and encouragement have been unflagging and essential, and his own life is a resounding witness to the themes of this book; our thanks are expressed in the book's dedication to him. During the making of the book, David Van Heemst's young daughter Ellie was stricken with severe viral encephalitis; to our community of three, her journey of illness and recovery, and the exquisite care and attention given by her twin sister Maggie, became a living metaphor of the vulnerability and resilience of life in God's world that occupies us throughout the book.

Finally, words cannot begin to express our deep appreciation to Archbishop Desmond Tutu—a towering giant of a man, a true Esther in our time—for the gift of his compelling foreword. His life is an uncompromising, eloquent expression of *ubuntu*, in which a person is a person through other persons, and where the humanity of one is inextricably bound up in the humanity of another.

One concluding note. As events unfolded around the globe, we became even more persuaded that the systematic elimination of the spiritual or religious dimension from most contemporary economic and social research, not to mention from public debate, is a serious, perhaps even fatal, obstacle to finding genuine practical solutions to social, economic, and environmental problems. That led us to broaden our audience beyond people of our own faith to people of other faiths, and beyond academicians to decision-makers, leaders, and politicians. In addition, Bob Goudzwaard has had the privilege of traveling extensively in the South and the East. At the request of the World Alliance of Reformed Churches and the World Council of Churches, he has consulted with church movements and citizens seeking a better understanding of the dynamics of our time, particularly globalization. Throughout such consultations it became increasingly clear that it is difficult for people of non-Western cultures to enter the current debate about the future of the world, because the debate assumes a modernist, Western way of reasoning. It is as if well-educated citizens of the South or the East need to study at a Western university (or one of its affiliates) in order to be taken seriously. That reality, along with our study of the present conflicts in the Middle East, made us increasingly aware of the immense, yawning communication gaps in our time. These gaps originate at least partly in Western intellectual arrogance. Our prayer is that this book might contribute in some small way, at a deeper level than that offered by Western modernity, to genuine intercultural and interreligious dialogue and understanding.

Bob Goudzwaard
Mark Vander Vennen
David Van Heemst
January 2007

INDEX